PLANT BASED DIET COOKBOOK FOR BEGINNERS #2020

500 Quick & Easy, Affordable Recipes that Novice and Busy People Can Do | 2 Weeks Meal Plan to Reset and Energize Your Body

By

Wilda Buckley

TABLE OF CONTENTS

DESCRIPTION

Cravings? Unhealthy foods? Preservatives? All of it, we know that it's not good to our body but we have no choice because we don't even know what to do! We don't have any idea on how to stop those three unhealthy eating. That is why I am here, bringing this book and hoping you will start your journey on doing a diet.

Plant-based Diet. As the name suggests, it's a diet high in fruits, vegetables, nuts, seeds and wholegrains, although it includes everything from a semi-vegetarian diet through a vegan diet and even towards a raw vegan diet if you really want (although please be aware that we haven't included many raw vegan recipes in this book).

Depending on your philosophical approach, you may choose to limit or even eliminate foods like meat, dairy, eggs, honey and even their derivatives such as gelatin.

It really comes down to you- you can shape your plant-based diet to be however you want.

Go 100% plant-based, opt for a vegetarian diet or even just fill your diet with tons of plants and eat small amounts of animal foods. The choice is yours! By now you know that you do not need to cut meat out completely from your diet if considering a plant-based diet, you are just required to make savvier choices when standing in the meat aisle and, of course, if purchasing animal products. I am sure there are many people breathing a sigh of relief regarding the above.

Meat is not bad for you, meat products are rich in vitamins, iron, and protein. However, processed meats such as hams are high in sodium, whereas red meats may be filled with saturated fats. When it comes to your health, both of these should be avoided. Rather, opt for white meats such as fish and chicken. These lower your risk remarkably in reference to chronic disease.

Apart from making more mindful decisions, choosing a plant-based diet will greatly improve your overall health. Filled with plenty of fresh fruits, vegetables, legumes, seeds, and nuts, one will always be left feeling satisfied after a meal.

The reason for considering a plant-based diet is the nutritional benefits it carries. Fresh foods are vital for overall health and provide us with much-needed vitamins, minerals, and fiber.

Consumption of foods that are higher in plant fibers can help improve health. Although it may be difficult to transition, it is not impossible to do so as long as you have the right guide. Let this book serve as your guide so that you will become successful in your transition to the plant-based diet.

This book cover

- Plant-Based Basic Guidelines
- What to Eat and What to Avoid
- Benefits
- Tips to Start
- 2-Week Meal Plan

And much MORE!

Still thinking? I gave you the headlines but still undecided? All you have to do is think for yourself or even for your family. Give this book to them and let them do the plant based diet to become healthier! Get up! Go click the buy button now!

INTRODUCTION

What Does A Plant-Based Diet Mean?

Natural, non-GMO, nearby, plant-based. It appears to be each day there's new nourishment and diet marks to learn on the off chance that you need to comprehend where your food is coming from or how it impacts your wellbeing.

Plant-put together diets all depend concerning the degree to which an individual incorporates creature items in their standard dietary patterns. Before you start tossing everything out of your icebox, how about we separate the nuts and bolts of eating a plant-based eating regimen.

The key to extraordinary wellbeing is straightforward. It doesn't mean going through hours enduring at the rec center. It doesn't mean allowing up young ladies' evenings or get-togethers. It doesn't mean squeezing for 30 days or attempting another eating regimen at regular intervals. It doesn't come in pill structure.

It implies eating a plant-based eating routine

A plant-based diet regimen doesn't mean being a veggie lover (even though it can), it just implies that most of each supper originates from the beginning, entire, and natural. It's tied in with investigating and finding the delights of entire nourishments in their natural state and utilizing them to raise your wellbeing higher than ever.

Incredible wellbeing implies awakening very much refreshed, experiencing the day free of diverting longings, having a solid insusceptible framework, feeling invigorated to do things that are beneficial for you like working out, taking a yoga class or two and afterward having the option to appreciate quality time with loved ones. A plant-based eating routine backings and upgrades the entirety of this.

For what reason should most of what we eat originate from the beginning?

Eating more plants is the first nourishing convention known to man to counteract and even turn around the ceaseless diseases that assault our general public. Plants and vegetables are brimming with large scale and micronutrients that give our bodies all that we require for a sound and productive life. By eating, at any rate, two suppers stuffed with veggies consistently, and nibbling on foods grown from the ground in the middle of, the nature of your wellbeing and at last your life will improve.

The most widely recognized wellbeing worries that individuals have can be reduced by this one straightforward advance. Things like weight, inadequate rest, awful skin, quickened maturing, irritation, physical torment, and absence of vitality would all be able to be decidedly influenced by expanding the admission of plants and characteristic nourishments. As a general public, we've come to acknowledge that usual inconveniences like cerebral pains, consistent weariness, PMS, and a throbbing painfulness are simply part of life. We protest through them and perhaps go to the drug store for help, however, what we wind up doing is quieting the message our bodies are attempting to send to us. A decent lion's share of the time these are indications of a supplement inadequacy.

Also, when we increment the utilization of plant nourishments, we lessen our admission of prepared nourishments that obstruct our bodies' capacity to work at its most noteworthy potential. This empowers better waste end, flushes poisons, and upgrades supplement assimilation.

Naturally, we over figure how we ought to eat

Would it be advisable for me to add creature protein increasingly to every supper? What does solid fat even mean? Do I attempt these new enhancements and super-nourishments? Each time I pivot somebody has an inquiry concerning what to eat for a specific sickness or issue they have. Even though I talk explicitly to every individual's worries, it generally comes down to a similar center message: what level of your eating regimen is comprised of leafy foods?

Not exclusively does a plant-based eating routine do ponders for your body, it expands your empathy, lessens your carbon impression, and causes space for you to turn into an increasingly valid variant of yourself by furnishing your body with the most flawless fuel it to can get.

Get Health with a Plant-Based Diet

Consider the possibility that one fundamental change could put you on the way to better wellbeing. What's more, imagine a scenario in which changes could even spare you from corpulence, coronary illness, and disease.

The less meat and dairy you eat the less fat you take in. This goes far with regards to keeping up solid weight and cholesterol levels.

In case you're wondering whether you should evaluate a plant-based diet, consider the main five advantages recorded beneath.

What Is a Whole Food Plant-Based Diet?

Numerous individuals who pursue a plant-based diet for wellbeing reasons attempt to adhere to a whole nourishments plant-based (WFPB) diet, which spotlights on eating nourishments in their entire structure, as they show up in nature. Somebody eating a WFPB food may likewise restrain their utilization of prepared or refined nourishments, for example, oil, refined sugar, white flour, and bundled snacks made with synthetics.

What Is Veganism?

Veganism is a way of life that looks to bar the utilization of creatures, however much as could reasonably be expected. Going vegan is generally a choice one makes dependent on moral reasons, in the wake of finding out about the creature farming industry's poor treatment of animals, just as the business's high ecological effect.

Does Plant-Based Mean Vegan?

The terms vegan and plant-based are frequently utilized reciprocally — and keeping in mind that the two times are fundamentally the same as there are a couple of contrasts.

A vegan eats a plant-based diet — yet that is just a single some portion of veganism. Notwithstanding nourishments like dairy, meat, fish, eggs, and nectar, vegans additionally maintain a strategic distance from creature determined added substances like gelatin and lanolin. Furthermore, vegans expand their conviction that animals ought not to be utilized by people past what's on their plates, running from beautifying agents to family cleaning items to dress to furniture.

Alternately, somebody who eats a plant-based eating routine isn't a vegan. The inspiration driving veganism is the creatures and regularly the Earth, while the inspiration driving a plant-based eating routine is generally wellbeing or weight loss (however, that is not an immovable standard). Hence, individuals following a plant-based eating routine may treat it like only that — an eating regimen — and in this way every so often eat creature items; they may eat nourishments made with creature determined added substances; they may likewise still purchase dress, furnishings or different things produced using creature materials, for example, cowhide, fleece, and hide; and they may purchase individual cleanliness items that were tried on creatures.

All things considered, eating a plant-based diet with wellbeing as your inspiration is as yet an extraordinary thing. Not exclusively can eating, for the most part, plants help forestall and invert sickness, help in weight loss, and streamline wellbeing. Yet, you'll additionally appreciate the positive reactions of helping your ecological impression, and you'll hurt fewer creatures.

Plant-Based Vs. Vegan & Vegetarian

In some major ways, vegetable-based diets are different from vegan or vegetarian diets. Vegans and vegetarians that eat foods that are refined packaged, and may not even end up eating a healthy diet.

Someone who follows a plant-based diet can choose to eat vegan or vegetarian and may or may not use animal products. Some people who follow a generally plant-based diet can consume some products of animal origin, but they include a very small portion of their diet.

PLANT-BASED BASIC GUIDELINES

When people see the word plant-based, they often feel as though they are going to live off of salad for the rest of their lives. Yes, salad is always an excellent choice and can be very delicious when made the proper way; this is not going to be your only food source; you are not a rabbit!

A plant-based diet is based around eating whole plant foods. This means you will be cutting out all of the high refined foods like oil, refined sugar, and bleached flour. On top of cutting these foods out, you will also begin to minimize or exclude how much egg, dairy products, and meat you eat! Instead, you will be able to enjoy whole grains, vegetables, fruits, tubers, and all types of legumes.

The key to a successful plant-based diet is to gift yourself a variety in your diet. Leafy-vegetables are going to be important, but those alone simply do not add up to enough calories! When you think about it, you would have to consume pounds upon pounds of kale to even reach your calorie goals. Calories are important because, without enough of them, you will end up feeling deprived and exhausted. For that reason, the plant-based diet is filled with delicious foods for you to try for yourself!

Benefits of a Plant-Based Diet

When people begin a diet, it is typically because they want to change something, and their current diet just isn't doing the trick. If this sounds like you, you are not alone! Whether your goal includes losing weight, improving your energy, or helping out a health issue you have, the plant-based diet may be able to benefit you.

Weight Loss

One of the major reasons men and women alike begin a plant-based diet is for the weight loss benefits! Unfortunately, around 69% of adults in the United States fall under the overweight and obese category. Fortunately, all of that can change by making the proper lifestyle and diet changes!

As you begin to adopt a plant-based diet, you will begin to eat foods that are naturally lower in calories and higher in fiber. This means that you will be eating less, getting full quicker, and staying full for a longer period of time. The fewer calories you take in, the more weight you are going to lose!

Diabetes

As you begin to eat whole foods, this will automatically provide you with the proper vitamins and minerals to boost your health. There was a study completed on 200,000 individuals where it was found that individuals who followed a plant-based diet have a 34% lowered risk of developing type 2 diabetes compared to individuals who followed a standard American diet. This could be due to the fact that a plant-based diet has the ability to improve blood sugar control.

Cognitive Power

Some whole foods you will be enjoying on a plant-based diet will have a higher number of antioxidants. Studies have found that these plant compounds and antioxidants may be the key to slowing down the progression of Alzheimer's Disease and other cognitive issues. In fact, there was another study performed on 31,000 individuals who follow a plant-based lifestyle, and they had a reduced risk of 20% for developing cognitive impairment in the first place!

Heart Disease

One of the top qualities a plant-based diet is known for is being very heart-healthy. These studies about the plant-based diet rotate directly around the types of food that are being consumed, along with the quality of the food. It was found that whole foods such as legumes, nuts, whole-grains, vegetables, and fruits are all key to lowering one's risk of developing heart disease. This study was compared to those who ate refined foods like refined grains, fruit juices, and sugary drinks, which are all associated with increasing the risk of heart disease. When you eat the right foods, you get the best results!

Of course, there are many other incredible benefits that a plant-based diet can offer you, but the four above are some of the more popular reasons that people begin the diet in the first place!

Guide to Meal Planning

While meal planning can seem complicated, the key to success is making it as simple as possible! Especially if you are just starting out, there is no need to overwhelm yourself! The only way you are going to experience the benefits of a plant-based diet is if you stick to your diet!

As you begin, I don't want you to feel like you are torturing yourself! A new diet is meant to give you a new lease on life. You will be eating better foods, trying new things, and getting healthier along the way! For this reason, try not to put too much stress on yourself!

Believe it or not, you are going to goof up a lot! Welcome to being human! We are creatures of habit, so we like to eat the same foods we have been eating our whole life. Luckily, through hard work and dedication, you can change these habits and help yourself become healthier! Let's face it, when it comes down to it, you are most likely the only one putting food in your mouth! Your results are completely in your hands.

Step One:

Write it down! With the internet, there are plenty of online resources. You will want to take a few moments to find a planning sheet. Often times, when we keep something or plan something in our head, it is easy to get buried with the million other responsibilities you have that day. Instead, take the time to write your meal plan down; that way, it is right in front of you when you need it!

Step Two:

We all have busy schedules, but this doesn't mean that you shouldn't take some of that precious time for yourself! When you are making your plan, you will want to look for events the week before. Is there a work meeting or party that could get in the way of a meal? That is perfectly okay; all you have to do is plan for it!

When people first begin a plant-based diet, they are fearful of going out and being social. The good news is that in the modern age, a number of different restaurants are becoming more plant-based friendly. If you do have a social event, try to make a plan! You can go on their website to check out their menu ahead of time or simply ask a few questions before you order. As long as the meal is as little processed as possible, you will stay on the right track!

Step Three:

If you are just starting out, I suggest only planning for one meal. Whether that be breakfast, lunch, or dinner, choose something that will typically take you the most time. When you plan ahead, this will help save you time in the long run! For this reason, I typically choose dinner. For breakfast and lunch, you can keep it extremely simple. Lunch is especially easy to plan for because you can either have a salad or the dinner leftovers!

Step Four:

Once you have your meal picked out, plan it out for the week! As a beginner, you may only want to plan for one or two days the first week. As you become more comfortable with your diet, you can plan for more! All you will have to do is select two recipes from this book, choose the two days you want to make these meals, and you are on your way to becoming a meal planning expert!

Step Five:

Once you have your recipes selected and your meal plan set, take the time to write up a shopping list before you even hit the store. This will assure you stick to your list instead of grabbing random ingredients that will just go bad at the end of the week because you didn't use it! Meal planning has the ability to save you time and money when you work on doing it properly!

Shopping List

If you are looking for a place to start, below you will find a shopping list that contains some good staples to keep in your fridge and cabinets. Keep in mind that most of these foods are going to be perishable. While this may seem like a pitfall, fresh produce is going to be much healthier for you compared to the foods that have additives to keep their shelf life. With that in mind, meal planning is going to be important to keep you from wasting food and money!

Fruit

- Melon
- Bananas
- Apples
- Lemons

- Limes
- Oranges
- Grapes
- Mixed Berries

Vegetables

- Asparagus
- Avocado
- Tomatoes
- Onions
- Sweet Potatoes
- Regular Potatoes
- Cauliflower

- Broccoli
- Mushrooms
- Lettuce
- Kale
- Carrots
- Squash

Cooking Items

- Nutritional Yeast

- Plant-based Milk

- Seasonings

- Maple Syrup

- Stevia

Pantry Items

- Black Beans
- Chickpeas
- Whole Grain Pasta
- Risotto
- Whole Grain Pasta

- Oats
- Kidney Beans
- Nuts
- Seeds

With all of this in mind, it is now time to get to the best part of the plant-based diet; the recipes! Whether you are looking for a meal, snack, or dessert, this book has got you covered! As you flip through the recipes, jot down some of your favorites! The hardest part is getting started, but once you begin, there will be no stopping you or the incredible results that come with the diet. When you are ready, let's take a look.

How Does It Work

Reasons To Follow A Plant-Based Diet

1. Improve Your Health Status

Over the past 5 years, scientific articles that show the benefits of increasing the consumption of plant-based foods have not ceased to be published, articles that indicate that following a more plant-based diet helps prevent and even reverse some of the diseases that they cause more incidences of deaths in the western world, being in many situations more effective than medication or surgical interventions.

This type of plant-based diet is the only one that has been shown to reverse the number 1 cause of deaths - heart attacks. Doctors such as Dean Ornish and Caldwell Esselstyn proved with their studies that they follow a low-saturated vegetable diet, rich in complex carbohydrates and basically vegetable-based protein, and changing some lifestyle habits (moving the body at least 30 min/day) cardiovascular diseases can be reversed.

A vegetable-based diet also helps prevent certain types of cancer, reduces the incidence of heart disease and diabetes, cholesterolemia, hypertension, Alzheimer's, Parkinson's disease, rheumatoid arthritis, ulcers, and vaginal infections.

A plant-centered diet has a positive effect on the prevention of accumulation of abdominal fat, the appearance of acne, aging, allergies, asthma, body odor, cellulite, eczema, metabolic syndrome, and body weight control.

With just increasing the consumption of fruits and vegetables, we increase the chances of extending our life expectancy, but a life with a higher quality of health. On the contrary, the consumption of meat and other foods of animal origin, such as dairy products, have shown that possibly due to its high content of saturated fats, arachidonic acid, and Hemo iron, life is shortened.

The consumption of meat, fish, dairy, and eggs also increases exposure to antibiotics, mercury, and other heavy metals and xenoestrogens in fish and carcinogenic substances in meat that are formed when cooked at high temperatures.

Contrary to popular belief, most vegans get enough protein in their diet, consume more nutrients than the average of omnivores, and usually maintain an adequate weight. There are only two vitamins that we cannot find in plant foods, these are vitamin D, which we get from sun exposure, and vitamin B12, produced by micro bacteria that live on earth, and from which one should be supplemented.

2. Maintain Your Proper Weight

The evil of many is the accumulation of weight that one adds up over the years, from the age of 22, the only thing that can grow is a belly or a tumor. So to prevent the birth of both follows, a vegetable diet will be our ally.

The reality is that if we consume many vegetables in our dishes, the caloric intake of these will decrease since, on average, a cup of vegetables gives us between 10-50 kcal. And if above, we are replacing with these ingredients other fatty, sweet, and processed foods, you will undoubtedly be reducing the calories consumed at the end of the day, and you will even feel fuller since you will consume more fiber.

3. Eat Healthy And Economical

Many people believe that eating healthy or plant-based foods is expensive, and they turn to processed food or junk, "fast food" because they believe it is the most economical. Certainly, this is not reality.

Visiting a fast-food restaurant such as Burger King and/or Mc Donalds to buy hamburgers, fries, and sodas will not be cheaper than buying 1 package of lentils, 1 package of rice, 1 onion and a bag of frozen spinach with what you can prepare a delicious and complete stew for the whole family.

The only thing you save by consuming these junk food restaurants is time, cooking time. But believe me that once you get into the kitchen, you can prepare twice as many servings, freeze them, and you have them for other days of the week. It's just about being practical and sometimes a little creative, playing with different spices, seasonal vegetables, and different cereal or legumes.

Lentils, beans, and peas are some of the most economical and high nutritional value foods you can find in the supermarket. When we talk about fruits and vegetables, we should always go for the options that are in season, and even buy extra when they are on sale and freeze them for when it is not their time. So I do with blueberries and other fruits of the forest, to have a proper reserve of local production in winter.

WHAT TO EAT AND WHAT TO AVOID

Food to Consume on a Plant-Based Diet

When it comes to a plant-based diet, a person can never run of options. There is a wide range of food items that are all sourced from the plants. All you need is a basic understanding of plant-based food, and it will eventually become easier to cook healthy plant-based food. Following are the list of items that you can freely consume on the plant-based diet.

Fruits

There is simply no restriction on the consumption of fruits; in fact, the more, the better! As we know that fruits are our largest source of fibers, carbs, and vitamins, they can ensure good health and active metabolism. Commonly consumed fruits include:

- Apples
- Citrus fruits
- Berries
- Bananas
- Grapes
- Melons
- Avocados

Vegetables

A person can survive just fine without animal meat, but he cannot live a healthy life without the use of vegetables in his life. It is said that a person's platter should be filled with colorful veggies to ensure good health. The following are common vegetables to use on a plant-based diet:

- Cauliflower
- Broccoli
- Kale
- Beetroot
- Asparagus
- Carrots
- Tomatoes
- Peppers
- Zucchini
- Potatoes
- Beets
- Sweet potatoes
- Butternut squash

Legumes

Legumes form another group of a plant-sourced item which should be added to the diet to increase protein content. Moreover, they are a rich source of carbs and vital minerals:

- Black beans
- Chickpeas
- Lentils

- Peas

- Kidney beans

Seeds and Nuts

Seeds and nuts are little bombs of energy and nutrients; their constant use in food greatly increases the nutritional value of your diet:

- Pumpkin seeds
- Chia seeds
- Hemp seeds
- Flax seeds
- Almonds

- Pecans
- Brazil nuts
- Cashews
- Macadamias
- Pistachios

Healthy Fats

Since animal fats cannot be consumed on a plant-based diet, a person is only left with healthy choices of vegetable oils to choose from. Olive oil is commonly used for cooking purposes, and others can be used occasionally for salad dressing, etc.:

- Avocado oil
- Walnut oil
- Chia seed oil
- Hemp seed oil

- Sesame oil
- Flaxseed oil
- Olive oil
- Canola oil

Whole Grains

Whole grains also form another essential group of food for the plant-based diet since they are the primary source of energy. Commonly used grains are as follows:

- Brown rice
- Oats
- Spelt
- Buckwheat

- Quinoa
- Whole grain bread
- Rye
- Barley

Like grains, all the products extracted from them are completely permissible on this diet, such as wheat-based flours, chickpea or rice flour, etc.

Plant-Based Milk

Animal milk cannot be consumed on the plant-based diet, so people are only left with plant-based milk to use in recipes. Fortunately, there are now many options of plant-based milk available on the market, or you can also prepare them at home if needed. Following are commonly used plant-based milk:

- Almond milk

- Coconut milk

- Soy milk

- Rice milk

- Oat milk

- Hemp milk

Foods to Avoid

The plant-based diet draws quite a clear line between food to eat and food to avoid. Everything non-sourced from plants is considered inappropriate for this diet, which may include all of the following food items:

- Butter, ghee, and other solid animal fats

- Animal meat: poultry, seafood, pork, lamb, and beef

- Dairy products

- Sugary foods: biscuits, cakes, and pastries

- All refined white carbohydrates

- Excessive salt

- All processed food products

- Processed vegan and vegetarian alternatives (which may contain salt or sugar)

- Deep-fried food

Avoid these Foods:

Meat: red meat, processed meat, fish, poultry, seafood.

Dairy products: yogurt, milk, cheese, butter, half and half, cream, whey.

Eggs: chicken, duck, quail, ostrich.

Plant fragments (often include plant-based replacement foods): added fats, oils *, margarine.

The oil, even the best olive oil, is 100% fatty, dense in calories and poor in nutrients.

Refined sugar: white sugar, beet sugar, barley malt, brown sugar, icing sugar, fructose, cane juice crystals, cane sugar, brown rice syrup, corn syrup,

Refined grains: white rice, white flour, quick-cooking oatmeal

Protein isolates: I am isolated from pea protein, from proteins, seitan.

Drinks: soft drinks, fruit juices, isolated from pea, sports drinks.

Common Food-Based Mistakes

Settling in with a new diet plan is always a confusing experience, but with time and understanding, anyone can avoid repeating the same mistakes over and over again. The following are a few common mistakes people make on the plant-based diet:

More Focus on Carbohydrates:

Plants do not only contain carbohydrates; there is a range of nutrients that can be consumed by ingesting a variety of plant-based food. People end up consuming more carbohydrates, and it simply adds to their obesity, which is not healthy. Limit yourself to carbohydrate intake as per your actual needs.

Compromising on Proteins

People falsely believe that proteins can only be sourced from animal products, and that plants cannot provide proteins—which is far from the truth! Plant-based food, like most beans and lentils, contain a high amount of proteins, do don't compromise on protein intake.

Processed Meal

Remember, the plant-based diet does not mean you should avoid only animal-based food, but it mainly prevents you from eating anything not sourced from plants, and that includes processed meals. Avoiding such items is necessary in order to harness the true benefits of the diet.

Refined Carbs

Like saturated fats, refined carbs are also not healthy, as they simply raise blood sugar levels and are obtained by processing complex carbs. Their intake should be limited to the plant-based diet.

Omega 3

Fish and seafood are not the only sources of omega 3; people on a plant-based diet often forget this fact and do not care to find better Omega 3 substitutes. Seeds and nuts are also a good source of omega 3, and they can be eaten frequently on this diet to meet needs.

BENEFITS

There are many benefits to follow this diet mainly overall increase in wellness and being less sick. The concept has been around for a long time that increasing consumption of plant-derived foods makes the person more active and healthier. These people also seem to be happier and less irritated which makes life easier and far more relaxing. There are other advantages which comes with the diet. Some of them are listed below:

There's no need to count calories in this diet. It can be a tedious and time-wasting task that a busy person cannot afford. This diet simply allows some food and restricts the rest. A calorie doesn't tell much about the food, what nutrients are in it or is it healthy or not.

It is a good way to lose weight. A recent 2018 control experiment showed that people that follow a vegan diet rather than those who eat meat, were more likely to lose weight. The study followed obese participants following normal diets and some following vegan diets and the result was that dieters almost lost 15 pounds in 4 months.

Plant-based foods are full of carbs and fiber which fills up the stomach quickly making you feel less hungry. You will consume less of the foods that will be no good for you like sodas or candies. Cravings will not hit you as hard as if you were hungry.

There is a higher quantity of water in plant-based food which increases body metabolism and reduces appetite. Water has many benefits, being hydrated makes you have better hair, skin and makes you look fresh.

Eating mostly plant-based foods increases mortality by preventing life long diseases. A recent 2019 done by the American Heart Association showed that plant-eaters were less likely to develop heart diseases. It is also linked with lowering the chances of stroke, diabetes type 2, hypertension, and obesity.

It also has shown to increase insulin sensitivity in diabetic patients. In the 2009 study, over tens of thousands of participants were approached and the percentage of vegans developing diabetes was found to be 2.9% less than others. A review published in 2018 stated that diabetes is improved when following any diet that increases plant content.

By following this diet, you will not only help yourself in becoming better but also push the environment to progress in the right direction. A lot of pollutants come from Barnes and poultry farms. Making meat puts high stress on our planet and by consuming less of it, you are leaving less of a carbon footprint. Also, by this diet, you are discouraging the use of meat as well.

It doesn't require any sort of investment and a person can begin it as soon as they decide to. Plant-based products are everywhere and even in a normal diet, take a big portion of it. Some dieting programs and fads take a lot of money from people giving only temporary results but this diet has shown to reduce the most amount of weight.

For some people starting this diet can be hard but if you want to reach your weight loss goals or become generally more fit than this diet is suited for you.

Top Five Benefits of a Plant-Based Diet

1.) Lower Cholesterol

Becoming environmentally friendly can significantly bring down the measure of LDL cholesterol in your blood - the awful kind that can prompt coronary illness and stroke. Maintain a strategic distance from margarine, cut out greasy meats, and settle on plant-based nourishments. Dairy and creature items are stacked with fat and have no fiber. Plant-based diets contain no cholesterol at all. That implies veggie lover sustenance is vastly improved for your heart and your wellbeing. It's even been demonstrated by an ongoing report out of St. Michael's Hospital in Toronto, which found that a low-fat plant-based diet can bring down LDL cholesterol by 28 percent.

2.) Lower Blood Pressure

At the point when you eat greasy meats and dairy items, the consistency of your blood increments, setting more weight on the veins. A plant-based diet tops you off with veggies and natural products, which are high in potassium. The higher intake of potassium balances blood thickness. This is the reason veggie lovers and vegetarians will, in general, have lower paces of hypertension, "the quiet executioner," as per observational examinations distributed in the Nutrition Review.

3.) Prevent Cancer

High-fat weight control plans have been connected to higher paces of malignant growth. Truth be told, the Physicians Committee for Responsible Medicine's Cancer Project demonstrated veggie lovers to be 40 percent less inclined to create cancerous growth than meat-eaters. The meat will, in general, be high in saturated fat and low in fiber. Fiber assumes an essential job in keeping your stomach related framework spotless and solid, expelling disease-causing mixes before they can make hurt. A veggie lover diet and vegetarian diet are high in fiber, low in soaked and trans-fats and regularly incorporate a more organic product, vegetables and other malignancy averting phytochemicals.

4.) Avoid Heart Disease

The American Heart Association says 83 million Americans have some cardiovascular infection, and a large number of the hazard factors, for example, corpulence, are at unequaled highs. Be that as it may, you lessen your hazard. Research has discovered that a regular, low-fat, plant-based diet can help diminish cholesterol, add to weight reduction and lower pulse. All of which lead to heart issues.

5.) Maintain Healthy Weight and Fitness

The individuals who pursue a plant-based, veggie lover or vegan diet, for the most part, devour fewer calories and have lower body loads than the individuals who don't, as indicated by the Mayo Clinic. A plant-based diet doesn't ensure weight reduction. You'll need to keep your admission of desserts and greasy nourishments low, pick entire grains, eat an assortment of foods grown from the ground, and pick without fat and low-fat dairy items. Additionally, recall that cooking strategy tallies. Steam, bubble, flame broil or meal as opposed to singing. Your new diet will even give you restored vitality for physical exercise.

Step by step instructions to Transition to a Plant-Based Diet

Aside from merely maintaining a strategic distance from meat, there are approaches to facilitate the change to a principally plant-based diet. Increment the measure of grains, products of the soil on your plate bit by bit until the meat is the littlest bit of your supper. An online vegetarian conveyance administration can make the procedure basic.

TIPS TO START

How do You Start a Plant-Based Diet?

There are a few lifestyle changes one needs to do to start a plant-based diet. Going in too strongly will cause tension to build up only to be blown when a craving hit. Some may find it very difficult to follow but you only need to keep a few points in mind to achieve success.

Increase greens in your diet. A variety of vegetables are present for choosing to offer different flavors and textures for soothing your tongue. Pick vegetables regularly for meal bases and a replacement for unhealthy snacks. The crunchiness and flavors of some veggies might decrease the likelihood of eating junk food.

Most healthy diets don't just forbid the consumption of fats but instead tells you to replace bad fats which are derived from animals with good ones derived from plants. Seeds and olive oil are a good source of healthy fats which do not increase the body cholesterol levels.

Cut down meat, especially red meat as much as you can. You can still consume it if you are following a more lenient diet but it is discouraged. Replace your meat with seafood or tofu which can be a good substitute for it.

Rather than putting desserts on the table, you should place fruits or fruit dishes. They are a healthier option with the same hints of sugar to satisfy the sweet tooth. Some people crave sugar more, they can slowly cut off sugar from their diet by switching it for sweet fruits instead.

Replace everyday cow's milk for plant-derived milk such as soy, almond, rice or coconut. Milk is an important part of a diet that is impractical to fully remove from the diet.

Stay away from foods that have a lot of sugar like a Pepsi or are high in fat like french fries. Also, do not buy processed food because they are riddled with salt and sugar, which are enemies to your body. Be aware that not every nutrient is being provided fully and arrange a replacement for that. Vit B12 is present in some cereal and in nutritional yeast. Iron is also less consumed so eat a healthy dose of cabbage, spinach or kidney beans to make up for it.

Shopping List

Here are a few things that you should be including in your shopping cart:

- Any kind of fresh produce — both fruits and veggies. Go for dark, leafy greens. You can avoid avocados if you have a heart condition.

- Go for dried lentils and beans. If you opt for the canned version, it is best to shop for low-salt or low-sodium items. Rinse the beans well if they include salt.

- Look for raw nuts with no extra oil. Nut butters are also good, but they are high in calories, so use them cautiously. Go for flax and chia seeds along with sunflower, sesame, and pumpkin seeds.

- Shop for dried fruits, but use them cautiously, as they are high in calories.

- 100% whole grain bread. Do not fall for wheat flour, enriched wheat flour, organic wheat flour, unbleached wheat flour.

- Any type of whole grain like farro, quinoa, bulgur, rice, hull-less barley, polenta, millet, coarse cornmeal, and oatmeal.

- Rolled oats

- Grape nuts

- Original cheerios

- Shredded wheat

- Bran flakes

- Any unsweetened non-dairy beverage

- Sauce with no animal products

- Salad dressings with no oil

- Citrus juice or zest

- Vinegars like apple cider, white, balsamic, unseasoned rice vinegar, and white wine vinegar

- Hot sauces

- Mustards

- Herbs and spices

Understanding Plant Micronutrients

Plants are rich in micronutrients that come from the soil they grow in, the basics of life they need to grow, the phytochemicals they use to protect themselves, attract insects and adapt to the changes around them. As plants are unable to move as animals do, they have a uniquely full tool chest of macro and micro-nutrients that enable them to adapt to the changing environment around them. These micronutrients are just as valuable to humans as they are to the plants but in different ways.

Below is a breakdown of the basic micronutrients found in fruits, vegetables, nuts, seeds, and legumes.

Vitamins

Vibrant vegetables and fruits are a dense source of vitamins that are essential to overall health and wellness.

Vitamin A: Also known as beta-carotene is a carotenoid found in yellow, orange and dark green fruits and veg, most notably carrots, spinach, and broccoli. It protects against infections and is essential for eye and skin health.

Vitamin Bs: This group of vitamins is responsible for maintaining the nervous system and cognitive function, DNA and blood cell production.

- **1** is responsible for nervous system health and aids in the breakdown and absorption of food. Found in peas, whole grains, and most fruits and vegetables.

- **2** is responsible for energy production and healthy skin and eyes and found in asparagus, spinach, and broccoli.

- **3** is great for healthy skin and energy production and is found in peanuts, avocados, peas, and mushrooms.

- **6** is also essential for energy production and is found in chickpeas, potatoes, banana, squash, and nuts.

- **9** is also known as folate and is essential for fetal development and growth and healthy cell division. It is found in legumes, asparagus, spinach, arugula, kale, and beets.

- **12** is predominantly sourced from animal products but you can find it in some organic soy products but most notably nutritional yeast.

Vitamin C: An essential vitamin important for cell growth and energy production as well as tissue repair and wound healing. It is one of the most powerful antioxidants and is found in strawberries, spinach, Brussel sprouts, sweet potatoes, and tomatoes.

Vitamin E: A powerful antioxidant that protects the body from free radical damage including premature aging. It's of great support to the immune system, protecting it against external pathogens. It is found in sunflower seeds, almonds, hazelnuts, spinach, and broccoli.

Vitamin K: This vitamin plays a major role in the clotting cascade and also in bone health. It is found in all green leafy veg as well as cruciferous veg and green tea.

Minerals

Macro-minerals: we need these in large quantities from our diet.

Calcium: This essential mineral plays roles in bone, heart, muscle and nerve health. Foods high in calcium are spinach, collard greens, seeds, almonds, soybeans, and butter beans.

Chloride: This mineral plays a part in body fluid balance including digestive juices. It is found in sea salt, tomatoes, lettuce, celery, and rye bread.

Magnesium: This mineral regulates blood sugar and assists in energy production. It also helps your muscles, kidneys, bones and heart function effectively. It is found in spinach, quinoa, dark chocolate, almonds, avocado, and black beans.

Phosphorous: This mineral is found in bones and works with calcium in maintaining healthy mineral balance within the body. It is found in pumpkin, sunflower seeds, lentils, chickpeas, oatmeal, and quinoa.

Sodium: The current population gets excess sodium from all pre-packaged foods and restaurant meals, so there is no need to go looking for extra sodium in the diet.

Potassium: This mineral is essential in blood pressure balance, muscle health, and nerve function. It is found in avocado, bananas, apricots, grapefruit, potatoes, mushrooms, cucumbers and zucchini.

Trace Minerals: We just need tiny amounts of these from our foods.

Copper: Essential in the formation of red blood cells and iron absorption. It is found in whole grains, beans, potatoes, cocoa, black pepper, and dark leafy greens.

Cobalt: This trace mineral works closely with B12 in the formation of hemoglobin. It is found in nuts, broccoli, oats, and spinach.

Manganese: Plays many roles in enzyme activity and cellular level antioxidants. It is found in pineapple, peanuts, brown rice, spinach, sweet potato, pecans, and green tea.

Iodine: Essential for thyroid function, you can find it in seaweed, lima beans, and prunes.

Iron: Used to make hemoglobin and as a carrier for essential nutrients in the blood. In plant form, it is found in cashews, spinach, whole grains, tofu, potatoes, and lentils.

Selenium: A trace mineral essential in the role of reproduction, DNA production, and antioxidant function. It is found in brazil nuts, lentils, cashew nuts, and potatoes.

Zinc: As your body doesn't store zinc, it needs to be consumed daily because it plays important roles in nutrient metabolism, immune system maintenance, and enzyme function. It is found in legumes, nuts, seeds, potatoes, kale and green beans.

Colors

The colors in fruits and vegetables point to what kinds of nutrients they contain.

White foods: Contain sulfur and can have anti-cancer properties. Found in cauliflower, garlic, leeks, and onions.

Green foods: Contain lutein and vitamin K. Found in dark leafy greens, broccoli, avocado.

Purple foods: Contain anthocyanins, which are powerful antioxidants. Found in blueberries, eggplant, red cabbage, and blackberries.

Red foods: Contain lycopene and has therapeutic properties for the heart. Found in strawberries, watermelon, tomatoes, and red bell peppers.

Vegan Super Foods

To be clear, most superfoods are already vegan, but there are some that are particularly high in nutrient content. The following are the top vegan superfoods available today. These should be incorporated into your diet every chance you get. The following are twelve of the best superfoods that you will find at your local grocery store.

Dark Leafy Greens

Kale, swiss chard, spinach, and collard greens are all classed as dark leafy greens and these superfoods should be incorporated into your daily meal plan. Not only are they a great digestive aid due to their high fiber content, but they're also dense sources of vitamins C and K, zinc, calcium, magnesium, iron and folate. They have a high antioxidant profile that assists the body in removing harmful free radicals which in turn reduces the risk of cancer, heart disease, and stroke.

Berries

Natures little antioxidants are also the most delicious and delicate fruits we know. Berries host an array of benefits to the body and each one has its own special powers:

Strawberries contain more vitamin C than oranges! They are antioxidant rich and provide us with fiber, potassium, anthocyanins, and folate. Strawberries reduce the risk of cancer, are supportive in the control of diabetes, and are great anti-inflammatories.

Blueberries are one of the most antioxidant-rich foods out there. They contain manganese and vitamins C and K, are supportive of cognitive function and mental health.

Raspberries are rich in vitamin C, selenium and phosphorus. Research shows they are beneficial in controlling blood sugar in diabetics. They are a great source of quercetin that is known to slow the onset and growth of cancer cells.

Blackberries are incredibly high in antioxidants and fiber and are loaded with phytochemicals that fight cancer. They are also packed with vitamin C and K.

Nuts and Seeds

Nuts and seeds are a vegan's best friend when it comes to texture, variety, healthy fats, and proteins. They are incredibly nutrient dense and contain excellent levels of fats, protein, complex carbs, fiber. They are loaded with vitamins and minerals that are easily absorbed and fun to eat, while at the same time helping to protect our bodies against disease. Every nut and seed have their own special traits:

Pine nuts have an excess amount of manganese.

Brazil nuts are the leading source of selenium.

Pistachios are well known for their lutein content that supports eye health Almonds and sunflower seeds are great sources of vitamin E.

Cashews have more iron than any other food in this category.

Pumpkin seeds are one of the best possible sources of zinc.

Olive Oil

A staple of the Mediterranean diet for a reason, this oil is rich in antioxidants and monounsaturated fats that support cardiovascular health, prevent strokes and feed your hair and skin like nothing else. Despite being fat, it actually supports healthy weight maintenance.

Mushrooms

The best vegan meat source there is but they're low in calories while being high in protein and fiber. They're a great source of B vitamins, vitamin D, potassium and selenium. They are high in antioxidants, support healthy gut bacteria and are beneficial in weight loss.

Seaweed

Used in medicine for centuries, seaweed has antiviral properties and has recently tested positively in killing certain cancer cells. Seaweed benefits cholesterol levels and is rich in antioxidants that are proven to lower the instance of heart disease. Seaweed is incredibly rich in vitamin A, C, D, E and K, and also B vitamins. It's brimming with iron and iodine which is essential for thyroid function, as well as having decent amounts of calcium, copper, potassium, and magnesium.

Garlic

Garlic is a powerful medicinal ally to have on hand. It is rich in vitamins B6 and C, but most importantly, it boosts immune function, lowers blood pressure, improves cholesterol levels and supports cardiovascular health. Fresh garlic is brimming with antioxidants that have a potent effect on overall health.

Avocado

Avocado is a great source of MUFAs (Mono-Unsaturated Fatty Acids) which is a huge factor in cardiovascular function. They support vitamin and mineral absorption, healthy skin, hair, and eyes, improved digestive function and also contains twenty vitamins and minerals. Avocados provide anti-inflammatory activity and are loaded with soluble fiber.

Turmeric

Highly anti-inflammatory and has potent anti-cancer properties. It has been shown to provide pain relief in arthritic conditions and supports liver health due to its high antioxidant levels. Turmeric can be hard to absorb however so taking it with black pepper improves its absorptivity.

Chia Seeds

These tiny seeds are packed full of omega 3 fatty acids, in fact, they are one of the best vegan sources out there. They are also antioxidant rich and packed with protein, calcium, iron and soluble fiber. Due to this, they are recommended to reduce the occurrence of cardiovascular disease, diabetes, and obesity. They are healing to the digestive tract, contribute to feelings of fullness so support weight loss, they can help lower cholesterol and best of all, when mixed with water, they make a great egg substitute.

Legumes

A study was conducted that investigated what the longest living people and cultures in the world had in common. The only dietary thing they shared was that legumes were a huge part of their diet, in fact, the longest living people in the world at these every day. Legumes are rich in protein, fiber, and complex carbohydrates but also contain potassium, magnesium, folate, iron, B vitamins, zinc, copper, manganese, and phosphorus. These little guys are highly nutritious and loaded with soluble fiber that benefits colon health, feed healthy bacteria and reduce the risk of colon cancer.

Spirulina

Spirulina is a blue-green alga that is brimming with vitamins, minerals, and antioxidants. Algae is the greens of the sea and pack the same benefits as vegetables of the land in terms of being nutrient dense, but something about growing under the sea makes them like the Superman of vegetables. They are a great supplemental form of protein but also contain potassium, magnesium, calcium, iron, phosphorous, vitamins A and C. They benefit the cardiovascular system by lowering the risk of cholesterol and high blood pressure. They also play a role in mental health by supporting serotonin production while working simultaneously to help eliminate heavy metals and toxins from the body.

2-WEEK MEAL PLAN

Days	Breakfast	Lunch	Dinner	Snacks
1	Grilled Cauliflower Wedges	Coconut Curry Noodle	Tomato Gazpacho	Hummus without Oil
2	Roasted Pumpkin & Brussels sprouts	Collard Green Pasta	Tomato Pumpkin Soup	Quick Peanut Butter Bars
3	Black Bean-Tomato Chili	Jalapeno Rice Noodles	Cauliflower Spinach Soup	Healthy Cauliflower Popcorn
4	Roasted Balsamic Red Potatoes	Rainbow Soba Noodles	Avocado Mint Soup	Crisp Balls Made with Peanut Butter
5	Easy Homemade Chunky Applesauce	Spicy Pad Thai Pasta	Creamy Squash Soup	Tempting Quinoa Tabbouleh
6	Avocado Fruit Salad with Tangerine Vinaigrette	Spinach Pasta	Zucchini Soup	Hummus Made with Sweet Potato
7	General Tso's Cauliflower	Linguine with Wine Sauce	Creamy Celery Soup	Healthy Protein Bars
8	Roasted Curried Chickpeas and Cauliflower	Cheesy Macaroni with Broccoli	Avocado Cucumber Soup	Chocolate Avocado Mousse
9	Chickpea Mint Tabbouleh	Soba Noodles with Tofu	Creamy Garlic Onion Soup	Fudge
10	Smoky Cauliflower	Pasta with Roasted Red Pepper Sauce	Avocado Broccoli Soup	Chocolate Chip Cookies
11	Spice Trade Beans and Bulgur	Pasta with White Beans and Olives	Green Spinach Kale Soup	Oatmeal & Peanut Butter Bar
12	Frankenstein Avocado Toast	Plant Based Keto Lo Mein	Cauliflower Asparagus Soup	Chocolate Chip Banana Pancake
13	The Quick And Easy Bowl Of Oatmeal For Breakfast	Vegetarian Chowmein	African Pineapple Peanut Stew	Mixed Seed Crackers
14	Almond Butter Toast With Sweet Potatoes And Blueberries	Veggie Noodles	Cabbage & Beet Stew	Crispy Squash Chips

BREAKFAST & SMOOTHIES

01. Grilled Cauliflower Wedges

Preparation time: 22 min
Cooking time: 40 min
Servings: 4

Ingredients:

- 1 huge head cauliflower
- 1 teaspoon ground turmeric
- 1/2 teaspoon squashed red pepper chips
- 2 tablespoons olive oil
- Lemon juice, extra olive oil, & pomegranate seeds, discretionary

Directions:

1. Remove leaves and trim originate from cauliflower. Cut cauliflower into eight wedges. Blend turmeric and pepper pieces. Brush wedges with oil; sprinkle with turmeric blend.

2. Grill, secured, over medium-high warmth or cook 4 in. from heat until cauliflower is delicate, 9 minutes on each side. Whenever wanted, shower with lemon juice and extra oil and present with pomegranate seeds.

02. Roasted Pumpkin & Brussels sprouts

Preparation time: 15 min
Cooking time: 35 min
Servings: 8

Ingredients:

- 1 medium pie pumpkin (around 3 pounds), stripped and cut into 3/4-inch 3D shapes
- 1 pound new Brussels grows, cut and split the long way
- 4 garlic cloves, meagerly cut
- 1/3 cup olive oil
- 2 tablespoons balsamic vinegar
- 1 teaspoon ocean salt
- 1/2 teaspoon coarsely ground pepper
- 2 tablespoons minced crisp parsley

Directions:

1. Preheat broiler to 400°. In an enormous bowl, consolidate pumpkin, Brussels sprouts, and garlic. In a little bowl, whisk oil, vinegar, salt, and pepper; shower over vegetables and hurl to cover.

2. Move to a lubed 15x10x1-in. Preparing container. Cook 35-40 minutes or until delicate, blending once. Sprinkle with parsley.

03. Black Bean-Tomato Chili

Preparation time: 10 minutes
Cooking time: 35 minutes
Servings: 6

Ingredients:

- 2 tablespoons olive oil
- 1 huge onion, cleaved
- 1 medium green pepper, cleaved
- 3 garlic cloves, minced
- 1 teaspoon ground cinnamon
- 1 teaspoon ground cumin
- 1 teaspoon bean stew powder
- 1/4 teaspoon pepper
- 3 jars (14-1/2 ounces each) diced tomatoes, undrained
- 2 jars (15 ounces each) dark beans,

washed and depleted

- 1 cup squeezed orange or juice from 3 medium oranges

Directions:

1. In a Dutch broiler, heat oil over medium-high warmth. Include onion and green pepper; cook and mix 8-10 minutes or until delicate. Include garlic and seasonings; cook brief longer.

2. Mix in extra fixings; heat to the point of boiling. Lessen heat; stew, secured, 20-25 minutes to enable flavors to mix, blending incidentally.

04.Roasted Balsamic Red Potatoes

Preparation time: 10 minutes
Cooking time: 30 minutes
Servings: 6

Ingredients:

- 2 pounds little red potatoes, cut into wedges

- 2 tablespoons olive oil

- 3/4 teaspoon garlic pepper mix

- 1/2 teaspoon Italian flavoring

- 1/4 teaspoon salt

- 1/4 cup balsamic vinegar

Directions:

1. Preheat stove to 425°. Hurl potatoes with oil and seasonings; spread in a 15x10x1-in. skillet.

2. Broil 25 minutes, blending midway. Sprinkle with vinegar; cook until potatoes are delicate, 5-10 minutes.

05.Easy Homemade Chunky Applesauce

Preparation time: 5 minutes

Cooking time: 20 minutes
Servings: 5

Ingredients:

- 7 medium McIntosh, Empire or different apples (around 3 pounds)

- 1/2 cup sugar

- 1/2 cup water

- 1 tablespoon lemon juice

- 1/4 teaspoon almond or vanilla concentrate

- Fueled by Chicory

Directions

1. Strip, center and cut every apple into 8 wedges. Cut each wedge across down the middle, place in a huge pan. Include remaining fixings.

2. Heat to the point of boiling. Diminish excitement; stew, secured until wanted consistency is come to, 15-20 minutes, mixing once in a while.

06.Avocado Fruit Salad with Tangerine Vinaigrette

Preparation time: 10 minutes
Cooking time: 15 minutes
Servings: 8

Ingredients:

- 3 medium ready avocados, stripped and meagerly cut

- 3 medium mangoes, stripped and meagerly cut

- 1 cup crisp raspberries

- 1 cup crisp blackberries

- 1/4 cup minced crisp mint

- 1/4 cup cut almonds, toasted

Dressing:

- 1/2 cup olive oil

- 1 teaspoon ground tangerine or orange strip

- 1/4 cup tangerine or squeezed orange

- 2 tablespoons balsamic vinegar

- 1/2 teaspoon salt

- 1/4 teaspoon naturally ground pepper

Directions:

1. Mastermind avocados and organic product on a serving plate; sprinkle with mint and almonds. In a little bowl, whisk dressing fixings until mixed; shower over a plate of mixed greens.

2. To toast nuts, prepare in a shallow container in a 350° stove for 5-10 minutes or cook in a skillet over low warmth until softly sautéed, mixing every so often.

07.General Tso's Cauliflower

Preparation time: 25 minutes
Cooking time: 20 minutes
Servings: 4

Ingredients:

- Oil for profound fat fricasseeing

- 1/2 cup generally useful flour

- 1/2 cup cornstarch

- 1 teaspoon salt

- 1 teaspoon preparing powder

- 3/4 cup club pop

- 1 medium head cauliflower, cut into 1-inch florets (around 6 cups)

- Sauce:

- 1/4 cup squeezed orange

- 3 tablespoons sugar

- 3 tablespoons soy sauce

- 3 tablespoons vegetable stock

- 2 tablespoons rice vinegar

- 2 teaspoons sesame oil

- 2 teaspoons cornstarch

- 2 tablespoons canola oil

- 2 to 6 dried pasilla or other hot chilies, cleaved

- 3 green onions, white part minced, green part daintily cut

- 3 garlic cloves, minced

- 1 teaspoon ground new gingerroot

- 1/2 teaspoon ground orange get-up-and-go

- 4 cups hot cooked rice

Directions:

1. In an electric skillet or profound fryer, heat oil to 375°. Consolidate flour, cornstarch, salt, and heating powder. Mix in club soft drink just until mixed (hitter will be slender). Plunge florets, a couple at once, into the player and fry until cauliflower is delicate and covering is light dark colored, 8-10 minutes. Channel on paper towels.

2. For the sauce, whisk together the initial six fixings; race in cornstarch until smooth.

3. In a huge pot, heat canola oil over medium-high warmth. Include chilies; cook and mix until fragrant, 2 minutes. Include a white piece of onions, garlic, ginger, and orange get-up-and-go; cook until fragrant, around 1 moment. Mix soy sauce blend; add to the pan. Heat to the point of boiling; cook and mix until thickened, 4 minutes.

4. Add cauliflower to sauce; hurl to cover. Present with rice; sprinkle with

daintily cut green onions.

08.Roasted Curried Chickpeas and Cauliflower

Preparation time: 15 minutes
Cooking time: 30 minutes
Servings: 4

Ingredients:

- 2 pounds potatoes (around 4 medium), stripped and cut into 1/2-inch solid shapes
- 1 little head cauliflower, broken into florets (around 3 cups)
- 1 can (15 ounces) chickpeas or garbanzo beans, flushed and depleted
- 3 tablespoons olive oil
- 2 teaspoons curry powder
- 3/4 teaspoon salt
- 1/4 teaspoon pepper
- 3 tablespoons minced crisp cilantro or parsley

Directions:

1. Preheat broiler to 400°. Spot initial 7 fixings in an enormous bowl; hurl to cover. Move to a 15x10x1-in. preparing containers covered with cooking shower.

2. Cook until vegetables are delicate, 30-35 minutes, blending every so often. Sprinkle with cilantro.

09.Chickpea Mint Tabbouleh

Preparation time: 15 minutes
Cooking time: 15 minutes
Servings: 4

Ingredients:

- 1 cup bulgur
- 2 cups of water

- 1 cup new or solidified peas (around 5 ounces), defrosted
- 1 can (15 ounces) chickpeas or garbanzo beans, washed and depleted
- 1/2 cup minced new parsley
- 1/4 cup minced new mint
- 1/4 cup olive oil
- 2 tablespoons julienned delicate sun-dried tomatoes (not stuffed in oil)
- 2 tablespoons lemon juice
- 1/2 teaspoon salt
- 1/4 teaspoon pepper

Directions:

1. In a huge pot, consolidate bulgur and water; heat to the point of boiling. Decrease heat; stew, secured, 10 minutes. Mix in crisp or solidified peas; cook, secured, until bulgur and peas are delicate, around 5 minutes.

2. Move to an enormous bowl. Mix in outstanding fixings. Serve warm, or refrigerate and serve cold.

10.Smoky Cauliflower

Preparation time: 15 minutes
Cooking time: 15 minutes
Servings: 8

Ingredients:

1. 1 huge head cauliflower, broken into 1-inch florets (around 9 cups)
2. 2 tablespoons olive oil
3. 1 teaspoon smoked paprika
4. 3/4 teaspoon salt
5. 2 garlic cloves, minced
6. 2 tablespoons minced new parsley

Directions:

1. Spot cauliflower in an enormous bowl. Consolidate the oil, paprika, and salt. Shower over cauliflower; hurl to cover. Move to a 15x10x1-in. Preparing container. Prepare, revealed, at 450° for 10 minutes.

2. Mix in garlic. Prepare 14 minutes longer or until cauliflower is delicate and daintily cooked, mixing every so often. Sprinkle with parsley.

11. Spice Trade Beans and Bulgur

Preparation time: 30 minutes
Cooking time: 2 hours
Servings: 10

Ingredients:

- 3 tablespoons canola oil, isolated
- 2 medium onions, slashed
- 1 medium sweet red pepper, slashed
- 5 garlic cloves, minced
- 1 tablespoon ground cumin
- 1 tablespoon paprika
- 2 teaspoons ground ginger
- 1 teaspoon pepper
- 1/2 teaspoon ground cinnamon
- 1/2 teaspoon cayenne pepper
- 1-1/2 cups bulgur
- 1 can (28 ounces) squashed tomatoes
- 1 can (14-1/2 ounces) diced tomatoes, undrained
- 1 container (32 ounces) vegetable juices
- 2 tablespoons darker sugar
- 2 tablespoons soy sauce
- 1 can (15 ounces) garbanzo beans or chickpeas, flushed and depleted
- 1/2 cup brilliant raisins

- Minced crisp cilantro, discretionary

Directions:

1. In a large skillet, heat 2 tablespoons oil over medium-high warmth. Include onions and pepper; cook and mix until delicate, 3-4 minutes. Include garlic and seasonings; cook brief longer. Move to a 5-qt. slow cooker.

2. In the same skillet, heat remaining oil over medium-high warmth. Include bulgur; cook and mix until daintily caramelized, 2-3 minutes or until softly sautéed.

3. Include bulgur, tomatoes, stock, darker sugar, and soy sauce to slow cooker. Cook, secured, on low 3-4 hours or until bulgur is delicate. Mix in beans and raisins; cook 30 minutes longer. Whenever wanted, sprinkle with cilantro.

12. Frankenstein Avocado Toast

Preparation time: 10 minutes
Cooking time: 5 minutes

Ingredients:

- 4 slices of whole wheat bread
- 1 avocado, cut in half and seeded
- 1 tablespoon lemon juice
- ½ teaspoon garlic powder
- A pinch of sea salt
- Decorative ingredients
- 1 nori leaf or a dark lettuce leaf
- Black beans
- Sliced red pepper
- Mexicrema dressing

Directions:

1. bread in a toaster or in a toaster oven.

2. While the bread is toasted, place the avocado in a bowl.

3. Add the lemon juice, garlic powder and salt, and pestle with a fork or potato masher.

4. Trim the nori leaf or dark lettuce to form the hair.

5. Decorate the Franken toast forming the hair with the nori or the lettuce, the eyes with the black beans, the mouth with the sliced pepper, and the frame of the face with the dressing.

13. The Quick And Easy Bowl Of Oatmeal For Breakfast

Preparation time: 5 minutes
Cooking time: 5 minutes

Ingredients:

- ½ cup of quick oatmeal
- ½ - ⅔ cup of hot or cold water
- ½ cup of vegetable milk
- 1 teaspoon of maqui berry powder or acai powder (optional)
- ½ cup of fresh grapes or berries
- banana (or a whole banana, if you prefer)
- Walnuts
- Seeds

Directions:

1. Combine oatmeal and water in a bowl, and let them soak for a few minutes.

2. Cut the banana and grapes or berries as you wish, and add them to the oatmeal.

3. Pour vegetable milk over oatmeal and fruits.

4. Cover with nuts, seeds, powdered maqui berry or acai powder. I use

walnuts and hemp seeds.

Almond Butter Toast With Sweet Potatoes And Blueberries

Preparation time: 5 minutes
Cooking time: 20 minutes

Ingredients:

- 1 sweet potato, sliced half a centimeter thick
- ¼ cup almond butter
- ½ cup blueberries

Directions:

1. Preheat the oven to 350-360 ° F (177 ° C).

2. Place the sweet potato slices on baking paper. Bake until soft, approximately 20 minutes

3. Serve hot, coat with peanut butter and cranberries. Store any leftover sweet potato slices, without dressings, in an airtight container inside the refrigerator for a week. Reheat them in a toaster or in a toaster oven and cover them as instructed.

14. Tropical Smoothie In A Bowl

Preparation time: 10 minutes
Cooking time: 0 minutes

Ingredients:

- 2 cups frozen mango pieces
- ½ cup frozen pineapple chunks
- 1 frozen banana
- ½ to 1 cup of vegetable milk
- 2 tablespoons chopped nuts of your choice
- ¼ cup chopped fruit of your choice
- Additional aderts

- 1 tablespoon flaxseed flour
- 1½ tablespoons coconut pieces

Directions:

1. Add the mango, pineapple, banana and vegetable milk (1 cup creates a thinner shake, and ½ cup makes it thicker) in a blender and mix everything until you get a smooth mixture.

2. Put the smoothie into a bowl and cover it with nuts and fruit.

15.Oatmeal Seasoned with Vegetables

Preparation time: 10 minutes
Cooking time: 7 minutes

Ingredients:

- 4 cups of water
- 2 cups of "cut" oatmeal (quick-cooking steel-cut oats)
- 1 teaspoon Italian spices
- ½ teaspoon Herbamare or sea salt
- 1 teaspoon garlic powder
- 1 teaspoon onion powder
- ½ cup nutritional yeast
- ¼ teaspoon turmeric powder
- 1½ cup kale or tender spinach
- ½ cup sliced mushrooms
- ¼ cup grated carrots
- ½ cup small chopped peppers

Directions:

1. Boil the water in a saucepan.

2. Add the oatmeal and spices and lower the temperature.

3. Cook over low heat without lid for 5 to 7 minutes.

4. Add the vegetables.

5. Cover and set aside for 2 minutes.

6. Serve immediately.

16.Pumpkin and Spice Oatmeal

Preparation time: 10 minutes
Cooking time: 0 minutes

Ingredients:

- 2 cups of vegetable milk
- 1 teaspoon pumpkin pie spice
- 4 seedless dates
- 2 tablespoons of raisins
- 2 cups pumpkin puree
- 2 cups of flaked oatmeal

Directions:

1. Mix the milk, dates, raisins, and spices in a blender.

2. Combine the milk mixture with the pumpkin puree and oatmeal in a medium container.

3. If the mixture is very thick, add a little more milk.

4. Cover and refrigerate for at least an hour or ideally overnight.

5. Enjoy the heat or the cold.

17.Millo and flaxseed pancakes

Preparation time: 10 minutes
Cooking time: 10 minutes

Ingredients:

- 3 cups oatmeal
- ½ cup of millet flour
- ½ cup ground flax seeds
- 1 teaspoon of sea salt
- 1½ teaspoon baking soda

- 2 teaspoons baking powder

- 4 cups vanilla almond milk

- 2 tablespoons rice vinegar

- 1 tablespoon maple honey or date paste

- 1 tablespoon pure vanilla extract

- 3 tablespoons unsweetened applesauce

Directions:

1. Mix the dry ingredients in a bowl.

2. In a different bowl, mix the liquid ingredients.

3. Pour the liquid ingredients over the dry ones and combine them well.

4. Process the mixture well in a blender until smooth and lump-free.

5. Heat a pan over medium-low heat.

6. Using a ladle, pour the desired amount of mixture into the pan.

7. Turn the pancake when bubbles appear on the top, and underneath it is firm for approximately 5 minutes.

18.Showy Avocado Toast

Preparation time: 10 minutes
Cooking time: 0 minutes

Ingredients:

- 2 slices of bread

- 1 avocado, sliced

- ½ lemon juice

- 2 tablespoons pumpkin seeds

- 1 pinch red pepper flakes

- 1 pinch smoked paprika

- 1 pinch of sesame seeds

- 1 pinch of salt

- 1 pinch of black pepper

Directions:

1. Toast the bread.

2. Place the avocado slices on the toast.

3. Sprinkle the lemon juice over the avocado.

4. Sprinkle pumpkin seeds, red pepper flakes, sesame seeds, salt and black pepper on top, to taste.

19.Millet And Buckwheat Muffins With Black Currants

Preparation time: 30 minutes
Cooking time:1 hour

Ingredients:

- ½ cup (90 g) of millet

- ½ cup (80 g) of unroasted buckwheat groats

- 4 chopped figs

- ¾ cup (160 ml) oatmeal or rice milk

- 1 tablespoon applesauce

- 1 heaped tablespoon (40 g) peanut butter

- 1 large ripe banana

- 1 pinch of sea salt

- 2 heaped teaspoons of baking powder

- ¾ cup (100 g) blackcurrants, fresh or frozen

Directions:

1. Dip millet and buckwheat overnight (or all day) in separate containers. Wash and drain (a filter can be used).

2. Soak the chopped figs in ¾ cup (160 ml) of oat milk for at least 30 minutes.

3. Heat the oven to 300-350 ° F (177 ° C).

4. Put the ingredients, except baking powder and blackcurrants, in a blender and mix them until a homogeneous lump is formed without lumps. Do not worry; It is supposed to be quite liquid since millet inflates considerably.

5. Now mix the baking powder. Unplug the blender and finally combine (DON'T LIQUID) the currants with a spoon.

6. Divide the dough into 9 muffin pans and bake for 33 to 35 minutes, until golden brown.

20.Apple And Pumpkin Pie

Preparation time: 30 minutes
Cooking time: 45 minutes

Ingredients:

- 1 spoon ground flax seeds + 2 ½ tablespoons water (flax egg)
- ½ cup all-purpose gluten-free flour (or oatmeal)
- 1 ½ cup quick-cooking oatmeal
- 1 tablespoon baking powder
- 1 teaspoon baking soda
- 2 tablespoons pumpkin pie spice
- 1 tablespoon cinnamon
- 4 medium granny smith apples
- ½ cup date pasta
- 1 cup pumpkin puree
- 1 teaspoon vanilla extract
- ¼ cup of water (optional)

Directions:

1. Preheat the oven to 350 degrees F.

2. Mix ground flaxseed (flax) seeds with water in a small bowl and set aside for 10 minutes.

3. Mix all dry ingredients in a large bowl.

4. Cut the apples into thin slices and place them in a container.

5. Add the pumpkin puree, vanilla extract, flaxseed with water, and date paste to apples and mix well.

6. merge the dry ingredients with the apples and mix well. Add water if the mixture seems to be too dry.

7. Place the mixture in an 8 x 11 (2 quarts) container suitable for baking and bake for 30-35 minutes.

21.Pumpkin And Oatmeal Bars

Preparation time: 10 minutes
Cooking time: 30 minutes

Ingredients:

- 3 cups thick oatmeal
- 1 cup seedless dates
- ½ cup of boiling water
- 2 teaspoons pumpkin pie spice
- 1 tablespoon ground flaxseed or chia seeds
- ¼ cup small sliced nuts (optional)
- ¼ cup of vegetable milk
- 1 cup mashed pumpkin

Directions:

1. Preheat the oven to 350 degrees Fahrenheit.

2. Cut the date into small pieces, put them in a bowl, and pour hot water. Rest for 10 minutes.

3. Add dry ingredients to the bowl and mix well.

4. Add dates to the dry ingredients along with water, pumpkins, and plant milk and mix well.

5. Cover the square bread with baking paper and push the mixture firmly into the bread.

6. Cook for 15-20 minutes.

7. Allow the mixture to cool completely in the container, then cut into 16 squares or 8 large bars.

8. Store in the refrigerator for up to 7 days.

22.Beginnings With Sweet Potato

Preparation time: 10 minutes
Cooking time: 10 minutes

Ingredients:

- 2 yams or baked sweet potatoes
- 2 peeled and sliced bananas
- 1 apple, without the heart and chopped
- ½ teaspoon ground cinnamon

Directions:

1. Peel and cut the yams or baked sweet potatoes.

2. Combine with bananas and apples.

3. Mix the cinnamon.

4. Briefly heat in a microwave oven. Serve hot.

23.Oatmeal Breakfast Muffins

Preparation time: 20 minutes
Cooking time: 45 minutes

Ingredients:

- 2½ cups of flaked oatmeal
- ½ cup oatmeal
- 1 teaspoon baking powder
- ½ teaspoon baking soda
- ½ teaspoon salt

- 1 tablespoon cinnamon
- ½ teaspoon ground nutmeg
- 4 ripe bananas, crushed
- 1 grated apple
- ½ cup non-dairy milk
- 2 teaspoons vanilla extract
- ½ cup raisins
- ½ cup chopped walnuts (optional)

Directions:

1. Preheat the oven to 300-350 ° F (177 ° C).

2. In a large bowl, combine and beat the dry ingredients.

3. In a small bowl, combine bananas, apple, non-dairy milk, vanilla, and stir until well combined.

4. mix the wet ingredients to the dry ones and combine them well. Add raisins and nuts, if you use them.

5. If you use a mold for 6 muffins, bake for 45 minutes. If you use a mold of 12 muffins bake for 35 minutes.

24.Blackberry And Lemon Muffins For Tea

Preparation time: 5 minutes
Cooking time: 45 minutes

Ingredients:

- 2 cups whole grain wheat flour for baking
- ½ cup of Sucanat (refined cane sugar)
- 1½ teaspoon baking powder
- 1 teaspoon grated lemon peel
- ½ cup natural soy yogurt
- 1 cup non-dairy milk
- 1 tablespoon lemon juice

- 2 egg substitutes (2 tablespoons ground flaxseed with 6 tablespoons water)
- 1 cup blackberries
- 2 tablespoons coconut with reduced-fat and sugar-free content (optional)

Directions:

1. Preheat to 350 ° F (177 ° C) in the oven.
2. Fill a paper-coated mold for 12 muffins (or use a non-stick skillet).
3. In a medium bowl, mix flour, sucanat sweetener, baking powder, and rubbed lemon peel.
4. In a separate bowl, mix soy yogurt, milk, lemon juice, and egg substitutes.
5. Pour into the dry mixture the wet mixture and stir until it is hot.
6. Carefully add blackberries.
7. In the prepared muffin pan, distribute the mixture evenly.
8. Sprinkle the coconut (optional) on top of the muffins.
9. Bake them for 45 minutes in the preheated oven or until one of them has a toothpick inserted in the middle. Until serving, let them cool slightly.

25.Cherry And Poppy Seed Muffins

Preparation time: 10 minutes
Cooking time: 30 minutes

Ingredients:

- Dry
- 1 cup (120 g) raw buckwheat flour
- 1 ¼ cup oatmeal (155 g) oatmeal
- 2 tablespoons poppy seeds
- 2 teaspoons cinnamon
- ½ teaspoon cardamom
- 2 teaspoons baking powder
- Wet
- 10 chopped figs
- A little more than 1 cup (260 ml) of vegetable milk, without sugar
- 2 ripe bananas
- 2 heaped tablespoons unsweetened applesauce
- 2 tablespoons peanut butter
- 1 pinch of sea salt (optional)
- ½ cup (50 g) dark chocolate (at least 70% cocoa), chopped
- 24 fresh or frozen cherries

Directions:

1. Preheat the oven to 180 ° C (355 ° F).
2. Cut the figs and soak them in vegetable milk for at least 30 minutes. If you want to dip it further, put it in the refrigerator.
3. While the figs are soaked, chop the chocolate and place it aside. Put all other dry ingredients in a bowl. Put the figs and milk into the mixer. Add all remaining wet ingredients and mix until smooth.
4. Pour the wet mixture over the dry ingredients and mix well. Make sure there are no lumps. Add chopped chocolate.
5. The mold is filled with 12 muffins (molded using silicon) with a lump and finally hits two cherries in each muffin.
6. Bake for 25-30 minutes. Allow it to cool a little before trying to remove it from the mold.

26.Cranberry Green Smoothie

Preparation time: 5 minutes
Cooking time: 1 minute
Serving: 4

Ingredients:

- 1/2 cup frozen cranberries
- 2 cups spinach
- 1/2 cup frozen chopped banana
- 1 tablespoon hemp seeds
- 3/4 cup almond milk, unsweetened
- 1/4 teaspoon cinnamon powder
- 3/4 cup water, cold

Directions:

1. Add all the ingredients in the order into a food processor and blender and then pulse for 1 to 2 minutes until blended.
2. Distribute the smoothie among glasses and then serve.

27.Strawberry and White Bean Smoothie

Preparation time: 5 minutes
Cooking time: 1 minute
Serving: 2

Ingredients:

- 1 cup cooked white beans
- 2 frozen bananas, chopped
- 1 cup strawberries, halved
- 1 tablespoon hemp seeds
- 1/2 teaspoon vanilla extract, unsweetened
- 3/4 cup of water

Directions:

1. Add all the ingredients in the order into a food processor and blender and then pulse for 1 to 2 minutes until blended.
2. Distribute the smoothie among glasses and then serve.

28.Peanut Butter Protein Smoothie

Preparation time: 5 minutes
Cooking time: 1 minute
Serving: 4

Ingredients:

- 2 cups kale
- 2 tablespoons hemp seeds
- 1 frozen banana
- 2 tablespoons cacao powder, unsweetened
- 1 tablespoon peanut butter
- 1 scoop vanilla protein powder
- 1 cup almond milk, unsweetened
- 2/3 cup water
- 2 cups of ice cubes

Directions:

1. Add all the ingredients in the order into a food processor and blender and then pulse for 1 to 2 minutes until blended.
2. Distribute the smoothie among glasses and then serve.

29.Cherry and Banana Smoothie

Preparation time: 5 minutes
Cooking time: 1 minute
Serving: 4

Ingredients:

- 1 cup cauliflower rice, frozen
- 2 tablespoons flesh of aloe vera
- 1 cup frozen sweet cherries
- 2 frozen bananas

- 1/2 cup almond milk, unsweetened

Directions:

1. Add all the ingredients in the order into a food processor and blender and then pulse for 1 to 2 minutes until blended.

2. Distribute the smoothie among glasses and then serve.

30. Turmeric Green Smoothie

Preparation time: 5 minutes
Cooking time: 1 minute
Serving: 4

Ingredients:

- 2 cups baby spinach leaves
- 1 frozen banana
- 2 oranges, peeled
- 2 tablespoon ginger, peeled, chopped
- 1/4 teaspoon ground black pepper
- 1 teaspoon ground turmeric
- 1/2 cup coconut milk, unsweetened
- 2 cups of water

Directions:

1. Add all the ingredients in the order into a food processor and blender and then pulse for 1 to 2 minutes until blended.

2. Distribute the smoothie among glasses and then serve.

31. Avocado Toast

Preparation time: 10 minutes
Cooking time: 15 minutes
Serving: 2

Ingredients:

- 2 slices of whole-wheat bread

- 1/4 of avocado, sliced
- 1 cup mixed salad greens
- 1/4 cup alfalfa sprouts
- 1/4 teaspoon ground black pepper
- 1/4 teaspoon salt
- 2 teaspoons sunflower seeds, unsalted
- 1 teaspoon apple cider vinegar
- 1 teaspoon olive oil
- 1/4 cup hummus

Directions:

1. Take a skillet pan, place it over medium heat and when hot, add bread slices and cook for 4 minutes until toasted on both sides.

2. Then take a medium bowl, add greens in it, season with black pepper and salt, add oil and vinegar and toss until mixed.

3. Spread hummus on one side of each toast, then top evenly with prepared green mixture, avocado, and sprouts and then sprinkle with sunflower seeds.

4. Serve straight away.

32. Chocolate and Banana Oatmeal

Preparation time: 5 minutes
Cooking time: 15 minutes
Serving: 2

Ingredients:

- 1 small banana, sliced
- 1 cup rolled oats, old-fashioned
- 1/4 teaspoon salt
- 2 tablespoons chocolate-hazelnut spread
- 2 cups of water

Directions:

1. Take a small saucepan, place it over medium-high heat, pour in water, stir in salt, and bring it to a boil.

2. Then add oats, stir until mixed, switch heat to medium level, and cook for 5 minutes or more until all the cooking liquid has been absorbed by the oats.

3. When done, remove the pan from heat, let oat stand for 3 minutes and then fluff with a fork.

4. Top oats with banana and chocolate-hazelnut spread and then serve.

33.French Toast with Berry Compote

Preparation time: 10 minutes
Cooking time: 30 minutes
Serving: 4

Ingredients:

- For French Toast:
- 4 bread slices, whole-grain, each about 3/4-inch thick
- 1/2 cup chickpea liquid or aquafaba
- 1/4 cup almond flour
- 1/4 teaspoon salt
- 1/8 teaspoon ground cinnamon
- 1/4 tablespoon orange zest
- 1 tablespoon maple syrup
- 3/4 cup almond milk, unsweetened
- For Berry Compote:
- 1/2 teaspoon maple syrup
- 1/2 cup frozen blueberries, thawed
- 1/4 cup applesauce

Directions:

1. Switch on the oven, then set it to 400 degrees F and let it preheat.

2. Meanwhile, take a medium bowl, add flour in it along with cinnamon, salt, maple syrup, and aquafaba and whisk until smooth.

3. Transfer this mixture to a shallow dish, then add orange zest and stir until mixed.

4. Take a skillet pan, place it over medium-low heat, and wait until it gets hot.

5. Then dip each slice of bread into the prepared mixture, let soak for a few seconds, then turn the slice and continue soaking for some more seconds.

6. Transfer bread slice into the heated skillet pan and then cook for 3 minutes per side until golden brown.

7. Transfer toast to a plate and repeat with the remaining bread slices.

8. Take a baking sheet, place a wire rack on it, then arrange prepared toast on it and bake for 10 minutes until crispy.

9. Meanwhile, prepare the berry compote and for this, place berries in a food processor, add maple syrup and apple sauce, and then pulse for 2 minutes until smooth.

10. When done, top the French toast with berry compote and then serve.

34.Chocolate Chip and Coconut Pancakes

Preparation time: 10 minutes
Cooking time: 20 minutes
Serving: 4

Ingredients:

- 2 bananas, sliced
- ¾ cup buckwheat flour
- 1 tablespoon coconut flakes,

- unsweetened
- 2 tablespoons rolled oats, old-fashioned
- 1/8 teaspoon sea salt
- 1/2 tablespoon baking powder
- 1/3 cup mini chocolate chips, grain-sweetened
- 1/4 cup maple syrup
- 1 teaspoon vanilla extract, unsweetened
- 1/2 tablespoon flaxseeds
- 1/4 cup of water
- 1/2 cup applesauce, unsweetened
- 1 cup almond milk, unsweetened

Directions:

1. Take a small saucepan, place it over medium heat, add flaxseeds, pour in water, stir until mixed and cook for 3 minutes or until sticky mixture comes together.

2. Then immediately strain the flaxseed mixture into a cup, discard the seeds, and set aside until required.

3. Take a large bowl, add oats and flour in it, stir in salt, baking powder, and coconut flakes and then whisk until combined.

4. Take another bowl, add flax seed reserve along with maple syrup, vanilla, applesauce, and milk and then whisk until combined.

5. Transfer this mixture into the oat-flour mixture, stir until combined, and then fold in chocolate chips until mixed.

6. Take a skillet pan, place it over medium-low heat, spray it with oil and when hot, pour in one-fourth of the batter, spread gently into a pancake shape, and cook for 5 minutes per side until golden brown on both sides.

7. Transfer pancake to a plate and repeat with the remaining batter.

8. Serve pancakes with sliced banana.

35.Chocolate Pancake

Preparation time: 15 minutes
Cooking time: 15 minutes
Serving: 6

Ingredients:

- 3/4 cup whole-grain flour
- 1 tablespoon ground flaxseed
- 2 tablespoons cocoa powder, unsweetened
- 1 tablespoon baking powder
- 1 tablespoon maple syrup
- 1/4 teaspoon of sea salt
- 1 tablespoon mini chocolate chips
- 1 teaspoon vanilla extract, unsweetened
- 1/4 cup applesauce, unsweetened
- 1 tablespoon apple cider vinegar
- 1 cup almond milk, unsweetened

Instructions:

1. Take a medium bowl, add flour and flaxseed in it, and then whisk in baking powder, cocoa powder, salt, and chocolate chips until well combined.

2. Take another bowl, add vanilla, maple syrup, vinegar and milk in it, whisk until mixed and then add this mixture into the flour.

3. Add apple sauce, whisk until smooth batter comes together, and let it stand for 10 minutes at room temperature

until thickened.

4. Then take a skillet pan, take a skillet pan, place it over medium heat, spray it with oil and when hot, pour in some of the prepared batter, spread gently into a pancake shape, and cook for 3 minutes per side until golden brown on both sides.

5. Transfer pancake to a plate and repeat with the remaining batter.

6. Serve straight away.

36.Chickpea Omelet

Preparation time: 10 minutes
Cooking time: 12 minutes
Serving: 2

Ingredients:

- 1 cup chickpea flour
- 4 ounces sautéed mushrooms
- 3 green onions, chopped
- 1/2 teaspoon garlic powder
- 1/2 teaspoon onion powder
- 1/2 teaspoon baking soda
- 1/3 cup nutritional yeast
- 1/4 teaspoon ground white pepper
- 1/4 teaspoon ground black pepper
- 1 cup of water

Directions:

1. Take a medium bowl, add chickpea flour in it, then add remaining ingredients except for onion and mushrooms and whisk until smooth batter comes together.

2. Take a frying pan, place it over medium heat, spray it with oil, and when hot, pour in half of the batter and spread it gently.

3. Top with half of mushroom and onion,

cook for 3 to 4 minutes until the bottom has turned nicely golden brown, then flip it and continue cooking for 2 minutes until cooked.

4. Transfer omelet to a plate and then repeat with the remaining batter.

5. Serve straight away.

37.Polenta with Pears and Cranberries

Preparation time: 10 minutes
Cooking time: 12 minutes
Serving: 4

Ingredients:

- 1 cup dried cranberries
- 1 teaspoon ground cinnamon
- 2 pears, peeled, cored, diced
- 1/4 cup brown rice syrup
- 2 cups of Polenta, warm

Directions:

1. Take a medium saucepan, place it over medium heat, add rice syrup, and cook for 2 minutes until hot.

2. Then add berries and pears, sprinkle with cinnamon, stir until mixed and cook for 10 minutes until tender.

3. Distribute polenta among bowls, top with cooked berries mixture, and then serve.

38.Fruit and Nut Oatmeal

Preparation time: 5 minutes
Cooking time: 10 minutes
Serving: 3

Ingredients:

- 2 tablespoons chopped apples
- 1/4 cup fresh berries

- 3/4 cup rolled oats
- 1/2 of banana, sliced
- 2 tablespoons apricot
- 2 tablespoons cranberries
- 1/4 teaspoon ground cinnamon
- 1/4 teaspoon of sea salt
- 2 tablespoons chopped walnuts
- 2 tablespoons raisins
- 2 tablespoons maple syrup
- 1 1/2 cup water

Directions:

1. Take a small saucepan, place it over high heat, add oats, pour in water, and bring it to a boil.
2. Switch heat to medium-low level, simmer for 5 minutes until oats have cooked, then remove the pan from heat and stir in salt and cinnamon.
3. Distribute oats evenly among bowls, top with remaining ingredients, drizzling with maple syrup in the end, and then serve.

39.Brown Rice Breakfast Pudding with Dates

Preparation time: 10 minutes
Cooking time: 12 minutes

Ingredients:

- 1 cup dates, pitted, chopped
- 3 cups cooked brown rice
- 1 apple, cored, chopped
- 1/4 teaspoon salt
- 1 cinnamon stick
- 1/4 cup raisins
- 1/4 teaspoon ground cloves

- 1/4 cup slivered almonds, toasted
- 2 cups almond milk, unsweetened

Directions:

1. Take a medium saucepan, place it over medium-low heat, add rice, stir in dates, cinnamon, and cloves, pour in milk, stir until mixed, and then cook for 12 minutes until thickened.
2. Then remove cinnamon stick from the pudding and remove the pan from heat.
3. Add apple and raisins into the pudding, season with salt, and stir until mixed.
4. Garnish pudding with almonds and then serve.

40.Overnight Oats with Chia

Preparation time: 8 hours and 5 minutes
Cooking time: 1 minute
Serving: 2

Ingredients:

- 2 bananas, peeled, sliced
- 1/2 cup mixed berries
- 1 1/2 cup rolled oats
- 2 tablespoons chia seeds
- 1/2 teaspoon cinnamon
- 2 tablespoons maple syrup
- 1 teaspoon vanilla extract, unsweetened
- 1/2 cup almond milk, unsweetened
- 1 cup of water

Directions:

1. Take two 16 ounces mason jars, add all the liquid ingredients in them evenly except for banana and berries, then shut the jars with lid and place

them in the refrigerator overnight.

2. When ready to eat, mix the oats, top with banana and berries and then serve.

41.Blueberry Smoothie Bowl

Preparation time: 5 minutes
Cooking time: 5 minutes
Servings: 2

Ingredients

- 1 tbsp. ground flaxseed
- 1 medium banana
- 4 ice cubes
- 1 cup blueberries
- ¾ cup unsweetened almond milk
- 1 tbsp. maple syrup
- ¼ cup nuts chopped

Directions

1. Blend all ingredients in high speed blender.
2. The mixture will be rather thick so make sure you have a good high-speed blender.
3. If you prefer a thinner consistency add more almond milk.
4. Garnish with chopped nuts and mint leaves.
5. Serve and enjoy!

NUTRITIONAL INFORMATION	
Amount per serving 252 g	
Total Calories	289 kcal
Fats	16.44 g
Protein	4.08 g
Total Carbs	36.72 g
Fiber	6.6 g
Starch	3.37 g

42.Chia Seeds Pudding With Fruits

Preparation time: 5 minutes
Cooking time: 5 minutes
Servings: 2

Ingredients

- 1 tbsp. Ground flaxseed
- ¼ tsp ground cinnamon
- ⅛ tsp ground nutmeg
- 1-2 tbsps. Pure maple syrup
- 1 tbsp. Chia seeds
- ½ cup almond milk

Topping

1. 1 banana, sliced
2. 1/2 cup fresh mango, cubes
3. 1 tbsp. Shredded coconut
4. Directions
5. In a bowl combine all ingredients and mix well.
6. Cover and place in the refrigerator overnight.
7. In the morning, stir the mixture and add in some almond milk or water.

8. For serving, set banana slice in serving jar.

9. Pour pudding in it.

10. Top with mango cubes and coconut.

11. Enjoy!

NUTRITIONAL INFORMATION	
Amount per serving 185 g	
Total Calories	156 kcal
Fats	1.71 g
Protein	1.67 g
Total Carbs	36.33 g
Fiber	3.1 g
Starch	3.17 g

43. Plant Based Strawberry Cream

Preparation time: 5 minutes
Cooking time: 0 minutes
Servings: 2

Ingredients

- 1 cup frozen strawberries
- 1/3 cup raw cashew butter
- 1/3 cup non-dairy plain yogurt
- 2 tsp. Fresh lemon juice
- 1/8 tsp. Salt

Directions

1. Add all of the ingredients to a food processor and process until it gets wet and chunky.

2. Scrape the sides and bottom well and process again for a couple of minutes or so until completely smooth and well mixed.

3. Pour mixture in container and chill for a couple of hours or overnight.

4. Spread it over whole grain bread.

5. Enjoy!

NUTRITIONAL INFORMATION	
Amount per serving 199 g	
Total Calories	322 kcal
Fats	16.11 g
Protein	2.66 g
Total Carbs	25.13 g
Fiber	3.6 g
Starch	0 g

44. Plant Based Rice Pudding

Preparation time: 5 minutes
Cooking time: 30 minutes
Servings: 4

Ingredients

- 1 can coconut milk
- 1/2 tsp ground cardamom
- 1/2 tsp cinnamon
- 2 tbsps. Maple syrup
- 1 1/2 cups cooked brown rice
- 2 tsp orange zest

Topping

1. Fresh berries
2. ¼ cup chopped almonds
3. Directions
4. Heat nonstick pot over medium heat, add milk and cardamom.

5. Cook it for one minute, then reduce heat to low and let simmer for 10 minutes.

6. Add the cinnamon and maple syrup and stir until combined.

7. Add rice in the same pan and simmer on medium-low heat for 10 minutes until the rice is mixed with milk and is creamy.

8. Stir in the orange zest.

9. Once cooked remove from heat.

10. Top rice pudding with fresh berries and nuts.

11. Enjoy!

NUTRITIONAL INFORMATION	
Amount per serving 146 g	
Total Calories	248 kcal
Fats	26.12 g
Protein	3.34 g
Total Carbs	27.57 g
Fiber	2.9 g
Starch	0 g

45.Quinoa With Berries

Preparation time: 5 minutes
Cooking time: 15 minutes
Servings: 4

Ingredients

- 2 cups almond milk
- 3/4 cups uncooked quinoa
- 1 tbsp. Almond butter
- 3 chopped walnuts

- 1 tbsp. Maple syrup
- 1 cup strawberries
- 1 oz. Sunflower seeds

Directions

1. Heat your nonstick pan over medium heat and pour milk into a saucepan.

2. Bring milk to a boil, add quinoa and reduce heat to medium.

3. Cover and simmer for 15 minutes or until the milk has been absorbed.

4. Remove from the heat, add some milk, almond butter, walnuts and maple syrup.

5. Stir and place the quinoa in a bowl.

6. Top with strawberries and sunflower seeds.

7. Serve and enjoy!

NUTRITIONAL INFORMATION	
Amount per serving 211 g	
Total Calories	314 kcal
Fats	14.05 g
Protein	8.9 g
Total Carbs	40.97 g
Fiber	5 g
Starch	0.17 g

46.Savory Zucchini Pancakes

Preparation time: 10 minutes
Cooking time: 10 minutes
Servings: 6

Ingredients

- 2 cup zucchini, grated

- 1 cup almond milk
- 1 cup chickpeas flour
- 1 tsp salt
- ¼ tsp freshly ground black pepper
- ½ red onion, chopped
- 1 handful cilantro leaves, chopped
- 1 green pepper, minced
- 1/2-inch ginger, grated
- Olive oil for frying

Directions

1. Add chickpeas flour, coconut milk and spices to a bowl and mix together
2. Add onion, zucchini, and cilantro and mix together.
3. Heat your skillet over low-medium heat, add oil.
4. Once oil is hot, add ¼ cup mixture and spread in pan.
5. Cook fritters for about 3-4 minutes per side.
6. Repeat with remaining batter.
7. Serve with garlic dip and enjoy!

NUTRITIONAL INFORMATION	
Amount per serving 69 g	
Total Calories	84 kcal
Fats	1.56 g
Protein	3.98 g
Total Carbs	13.52 g
Fiber	2 g
Starch	0 g

47. Pecan-Maple Granola

Preparation time: 10 minutes
Cooking time: 25 minutes
Servings: 4

Ingredients

- 1 teaspoon of vanilla extract
- ¼ cup of maple syrup
- ¼ cup of pecan pieces
- 1 ½ cups of rolled oats
- ½ a teaspoon of ground cinnamon
- Non-dairy milk of your choice

Directions

1. Prepare the oven by heating it to 300 degrees F.
2. Place parchment paper over a baking tray.
3. Combine the cinnamon, vanilla, maple syrup, pecan pieces and oats in a large bowl and stir to combine.
4. Transfer the mixture onto the baking tray and spread it over evenly.
5. Bake for 20 minutes, shift the granola around after 10 minutes.
6. Once cooked, take the granola out of the oven and leave it to cool down for 30 minutes.
7. Store in a container and serve with non-dairy milk.

48. Breakfast Scramble

Preparation time: 10 minutes
Cooking time: 20 minutes
Servings: 2

Ingredients

- 1 cup of fresh spinach
- 1/8 teaspoon of black pepper
- ½ a teaspoon of onion powder
- ½ teaspoon of garlic powder
- 1 tablespoon of vegetable broth
- 2 tablespoons of nutritional yeast
- ½ a diced bell pepper
- 4 ounces of sliced mushrooms

- 1 packet of extra firm tofu

Directions

1. Over medium temperature, heat a large frying pan.

2. Drain the tofu, place it in a bowl and mash it down with a fork.

3. Transfer the tofu into the frying pan and add the, pepper, garlic powder, onion powder, broth, nutritional yeast, bell pepper and mushrooms. Put a lid on the frying pan and leave it to cook for 10 minutes. Stir the ingredients after 5 minutes.

4. Add the spinach and cook for another 5 minutes, divide onto plates and serve.

49. Almond Waffles With Cranberries

Preparation time: 10 minutes
Cooking time: 10 minutes
Servings: 4

Ingredients

- 2 tbsp flax seed powder + 6 tbsp water

- 2/3 cup almond flour

- 2 ½ tsp baking powder

- A pinch salt

- 1 ½ cups almond milk

- 2 tbsp plant butter

- 1 cup fresh almond butter

- 2 tbsp pure maple syrup

- 1 tsp fresh lemon juice

Directions

1. In a medium bowl, mix the flax seed powder with water and allow soaking for 5 minutes.

2. Add the almond flour, baking powder, salt, and almond milk. Mix until well combined.

3. Preheat a waffle iron and brush with some plant butter. Pour in a quarter cup of the batter, close the iron and cook until the waffles are golden and crisp, 2 to 3 minutes.

4. Transfer the waffles to a plwwate and make more waffles using the same process and ingredient proportions.

5. Meanwhile, in a medium bowl, mix the almond butter with the maple syrup and lemon juice. Serve the waffles, spread the top with the almond-lemon mixture, and serve.

50. Chickpea Omelet With Spinach And Mushrooms

Preparation time: 10 minutes
Cooking time: 15 minutes
Servings: 4

Ingredients

- 1 cup chickpea flour

- ½ tsp onion powder

- ½ tsp garlic powder

- ¼ tsp white pepper

- ¼ tsp black pepper

- 1/3 cup nutritional yeast

- ½ tsp baking soda

- 1 small green bell pepper, deseeded and chopped

- 3 scallions, chopped

- 1 cup sautéed sliced white button mushrooms

- ½ cup chopped fresh spinach

- 1 cup halved cherry tomatoes for serving

- 1 tbsp fresh parsley leaves

Directions

1. In a medium bowl, mix the chickpea flour, onion powder, garlic powder, white pepper, black pepper, nutritional yeast, and baking soda until well combined.

2. Heat a medium skillet over medium heat and add a quarter of the batter. Swirl the pan to spread the batter across the pan. Scatter a quarter each of the bell pepper, scallions, mushrooms, and spinach on top, and cook until the bottom part of the omelet sets and is golden brown, 1 to 2 minutes. Carefully, flip the omelet and cook the other side until set and golden brown.

3. Transfer the omelet to a plate and make the remaining omelets using the remaining batter in the same proportions.

4. Serve the omelet with the tomatoes and garnish with the parsley leaves. Serve.

51. Sweet Coconut Raspberry Pancakes

Preparation time: 10 minutes
Cooking time: 15 minutes
Servings: 4

Ingredients

- 2 tbsp flax seed powder + 6 tbsp water
- ½ cup coconut milk
- ¼ cup fresh raspberries, mashed
- ½ cup oat flour
- 1 tsp baking soda
- A pinch salt
- 1 tbsp coconut sugar

- 2 tbsp pure date syrup
- ½ tsp cinnamon powder
- 2 tbsp unsweetened coconut flakes
- 2 tsp plant butter
- Fresh raspberries for garnishing

Directions

1. In medium bowl, mix the flax seed powder with the water and allow thickening for 5 minutes.

2. Mix in the coconut milk and raspberries.

3. Add the oat flour, baking soda, salt, coconut sugar, date syrup, and cinnamon powder. Fold in the coconut flakes until well combined.

4. Working in batches, melt a quarter of the butter in a non-stick skillet and add ¼ cup of the batter. Cook until set beneath and golden brown, 2 minutes. Flip the pancake and cook on the other side until set and golden brown, 2 minutes. Transfer to a plate and make the remaining pancakes using the rest of the ingredients in the same proportions.

5. Garnish the pancakes with some raspberries and serve warm!

52. Pumpkin-Pistachio Tea Cake

Preparation time: 30 minutes
Cooking time: 55 minutes
Servings: 4

Ingredients

- 2 tbsp flaxseed powder + 6 tbsp water
- 3 tbsp vegetable oil
- ¾ cup canned unsweetened pumpkin puree
- ½ cup pure corn syrup
- 3 tbsp pure date sugar

- 1 ½ cups whole-wheat flour
- ½ tsp cinnamon powder
- ½ tsp baking powder
- ¼ tsp cloves powder
- ½ tsp allspice powder
- ½ tsp nutmeg powder
- A pinch salt
- 2 tbsp chopped pistachios

Directions

1. Preheat the oven to 350 F and lightly coat an 8 x 4-inch loaf pan with cooking spray.In a medium bowl, mix the flax seed powder with water and allow thickening for 5 minutes to make the flax egg.

2. In a bowl, whisk the vegetable oil, pumpkin puree, corn syrup, date sugar, and flax egg. In another bowl, mix the flour, cinnamon powder, baking powder, cloves powder, allspice powder, nutmeg powder and salt. Add this mixture to the wet batter and mix until well combined.

3. Pour the batter into the loaf pan, sprinkle the pistachios on top, and gently press the nuts onto the batter to stick.

4. Bake in the oven for 50 to 55 minutes or until a toothpick inserted into the cake comes out clean. Remove the cake onto a wire rack, allow cooling, slice, and serve.

53.Creole Tofu Scramble

Preparation time: 10 minutes
Cooking time: 10 minutes
Servings: 4

Ingredients

- 2 tbsp plant butter, for frying

- 1 (14 oz) pack firm tofu, pressed and crumbled
- 1 medium red bell pepper, deseeded and chopped
- 1 medium green bell pepper, deseeded and chopped
- 1 tomato, finely chopped
- 2 tbsp chopped fresh green onions
- Salt and black pepper to taste
- 1 tsp turmeric powder
- 1 tsp Creole seasoning
- ½ cup chopped baby kale
- ¼ cup grated plant-based Parmesan cheese

Directions

1. Melt the plant butter in a large skillet over medium heat and add the tofu. Cook with occasional stirring until the tofu is light golden brown while making sure not to break the tofu into tiny bits but to have scrambled egg resemblance, 5 minutes.

2. Stir in the bell peppers, tomato, green onions, salt, black pepper, turmeric powder, and Creole seasoning. Sauté until the vegetables soften, 5 minutes.

3. Mix in the kale to wilt, 3 minutes and then, half of the plant-based Parmesan cheese. Allow melting for 1 to 2 minutes and then turn the heat off.

4. Dish the food, top with the remaining cheese, and serve warm.

54.Mushroom Avocado Panini

Preparation time: 15 minutes
Cooking time: 15 minutes
Servings: 4

Ingredients

- 1 tbsp olive oil

- 1 cup sliced white button mushrooms
- Salt and black pepper to taste
- 1 ripe avocado, pitted, peeled, and sliced
- 2 tbsp freshly squeezed lemon juice
- 1 tbsp chopped parsley
- ½ tsp pure maple syrup
- 8 slices whole-wheat ciabatta
- 4 oz sliced plant-based Parmesan cheese
- 1 tbsp olive oil

Directions

1. Heat the olive oil in a medium skillet over medium heat and sauté the mushrooms until softened, 5 minutes. Season with salt and black pepper. Turn the heat off.
2. Preheat a panini press to medium heat, 3 to 5 minutes.
3. Mash the avocado in a medium bowl and mix in the lemon juice, parsley, and maple syrup.
4. Spread the mixture on 4 bread slices, divide the mushrooms and plant-based Parmesan cheese on top.
5. Cover with the other bread slices and brush the top with olive oil.
6. Grill the sandwiches one after another in the heated press until golden brown and the cheese melted.
7. Serve warm.

55.Fruity Granola

Preparation time: 50 minutes
Cooking time: 30 minutes
Servings: 4

Ingredients

- 2 cups rolled oats
- ¾ cup whole-grain flour
- 1 tablespoon ground cinnamon
- 1 teaspoon ground ginger (optional)
- ½ cup sunflower seeds, or walnuts, chopped
- ½ cup almonds, chopped
- ½ cup pumpkin seeds
- ½ cup unsweetened shredded coconut
- 1¼ cups pure fruit juice (cranberry, apple, or something similar)
- ½ cup raisins, or dried cranberries
- ½ cup goji berries (optional)

Directions

1. Preparing the Ingredients.
2. Preheat the oven to 350°F.
3. Mix together the oats, flour, cinnamon, ginger, sunflower seeds, almonds, pumpkin seeds, and coconut in a large bowl.
4. Sprinkle the juice over the mixture, and stir until it's just moistened. You might need a bit more or a bit less liquid, depending on how much your

oats and flour absorb.

5. Spread the granola on a large baking sheet (the more spread out it is the better), and put it in the oven. After about 15 minutes, use a spatula to turn the granola so that the middle gets dried out. Let the granola bake until it's as crunchy as you want it, about 30 minutes more.

6. Take the granola out of the oven and stir in the raisins and goji berries (if using). Store leftovers in an airtight container for up to 2 weeks.

7. Serve with nondairy milk and fresh fruit, use as a topper for morning porridge or a smoothie bowl to add a bit of crunch, or make a granola parfait by layering with nondairy yogurt or puréed banana.

56. Pumpkin Steel-Cut Oats

Preparation time: 5 minutes
Cooking time: 30 minutes
Servings: 4

Ingredients

- 3 cups water
- 1 cup steel-cut oats
- ½ cup canned pumpkin purée
- ¼ cup pumpkin seeds (pepitas)
- 2 tablespoons maple syrup
- Pinch salt

Directions

1. Preparing the Ingredients.

2. In a large saucepan, bring the water to a boil.

3. Add the oats, stir, and reduce the heat to low. Simmer until the oats are soft, 20 to 30 minutes, continuing to stir occasionally.

4. Stir in the pumpkin purée and continue cooking on low for 3 to 5 minutes longer. Stir in the pumpkin seeds and maple syrup, and season with the salt.

5. Divide the oatmeal into 4 single-serving containers. Let cool before sealing the lids.

6. Place the containers in the refrigerator for up to 5 days.

57. Chocolate Quinoa Breakfast Bowl

Preparation time: 10 minutes
Cooking time: 30 minutes
Servings: 4
Ingredients

- 1 cup quinoa
- 1 teaspoon ground cinnamon
- 1 cup nondairy milk
- 1 cup water
- 1 large banana
- 2 to 3 tablespoons unsweetened cocoa powder, or carob
- 1 to 2 tablespoons almond butter, or

other nut or seed butter

- 1 tablespoon ground flaxseed, or chia or hemp seeds
- 2 tablespoons walnuts
- ¼ cup raspberries

Directions

1. Preparing the Ingredients.
2. Put the quinoa, cinnamon, milk, and water in a medium pot. Bring to a boil over high heat, then turn down low and simmer, covered, for 25 to 30 minutes.
3. While the quinoa is simmering, purée or mash the banana in a medium bowl and stir in the cocoa powder, almond butter, and flaxseed.
4. To serve, spoon 1 cup cooked quinoa into a bowl, top with half the pudding and half the walnuts and raspberries.

58. Savory Oatmeal Porridge

Preparation time: 10 minutes
Cooking time: 40 minutes
Servings: 4

Ingredients

- 2½ cups vegetable broth
- 2½ cups unsweetened almond milk or other plant-based milk
- ½ cup steel-cut oats
- 1 tablespoon farro
- ½ cup slivered almonds
- ¼ cup nutritional yeast
- 2 cups old-fashioned rolled oats
- ½ teaspoon salt (optional)

Directions

1. Preparing the Ingredients.

2. In a large saucepan or pot, bring the broth and almond milk to a boil. Add the oats, farro, almond slivers, and nutritional yeast. Cook over medium-high heat for 20 minutes, stirring occasionally.
3. Add the rolled oats and cook for another 5 minutes, until creamy. Stir in the salt (if using).
4. Divide into 4 single-serving containers.
5. Let cool before sealing the lids. Place the containers in the refrigerator for up to 5 days.

59. Muesli and Berries Bowl

Preparation time: 10 minutes
Cooking time: 50 minutes
Servings: 4

Ingredients

- For the muesli
- 1 cup rolled oats
- 1 cup spelt flakes, or quinoa flakes, or more rolled oats

- 2 cups puffed cereal
- ¼ cup sunflower seeds
- ¼ cup almonds
- ¼ cup raisins
- ¼ cup dried cranberries
- ¼ cup chopped dried figs

- ¼ cup unsweetened shredded coconut
- ¼ cup nondairy chocolate chips
- 1 to 3 teaspoons ground cinnamon
- For the bowl
- ½ cup nondairy milk, or unsweetened applesauce
- ¾ cup muesli
- ½ cup berries

Directions

1. Preparing the Ingredients.
2. Put the muesli ingredients in a container or bag and shake.
3. Combine the muesli and bowl ingredients in a bowl or to-go container.
4. Substitutions: Try chopped Brazil nuts, peanuts, dried cranberries, dried blueberries, dried mango, or whatever inspires you. Ginger and cardamom are interesting flavors if you want to branch out on spices.

60.Cinnamon And Spice Overnight Oats

Preparation time: 5 minutes
Cooking time: 30 minutes
Servings: 4

Ingredients

- 2½ cups old-fashioned rolled oats
- 5 tablespoons pumpkin seeds (pepitas)
- 5 tablespoons chopped pecans
- 5 cups unsweetened plant-based milk
- 2½ teaspoons maple syrup or agave syrup
- ½ to 1 teaspoon salt
- ½ to 1 teaspoon ground cinnamon
- ½ to 1 teaspoon ground ginger
- Fresh fruit (optional)

Directions

1. Preparing the Ingredients.
2. Line up 5 wide-mouth pint jars. In each jar, combine ½ cup of oats, 1 tablespoon of pumpkin seeds, 1 tablespoon of pecans, 1 cup of plant-based milk, ½ teaspoon of maple syrup, 1 pinch of salt, 1 pinch of cinnamon, and 1 pinch of ginger.
3. Stir the ingredients in each jar. Close the jars tightly with lids. To serve, top with fresh fruit (if using). Place the airtight jars in the refrigerator at least overnight before eating and for up to

5 days.

61.Baked Banana French Toast with Raspberry Syrup

Preparation time: 10 minutes
Cooking time: 35 minutes
Servings: 4

Ingredients

- For the french toast
- 1 banana

- 1 cup coconut milk
- 1 teaspoon pure vanilla extract
- ¼ teaspoon ground nutmeg
- ½ teaspoon ground cinnamon
- 1½ teaspoons arrowroot powder
- Pinch sea salt
- 8 slices whole-grain bread
- For the raspberry syrup
- 1 cup fresh or frozen raspberries, or other berries
- 2 tablespoons water, or pure fruit juice
- 1 to 2 tablespoons maple syrup, or coconut sugar (optional)

Directions

1. Preparing the Ingredients.
2. Preheat the oven to 350°F.
3. In a shallow bowl, purée or mash the banana well. Mix in the coconut milk, vanilla, nutmeg, cinnamon, arrowroot, and salt.
4. Dip the slices of bread in the banana mixture, and then lay them out in a 13-by-9-inch baking dish. They should cover the bottom of the dish and can overlap a bit but shouldn't be stacked on top of each other. Pour any leftover banana mixture over the bread, and put the dish in the oven.
5. Bake about 30 minutes, or until the tops are lightly browned.
6. Serve topped with raspberry syrup.
7. To Make the Raspberry Syrup
8. Heat the raspberries in a small pot with the water and the maple syrup (if using) on medium heat.
9. Leave to simmer, stirring occasionally and breaking up the berries, for 15 to 20 minutes, until the liquid has reduced.
10. Leftover raspberry syrup makes a great topping for simple oatmeal as a quick and delicious breakfast, or as a drizzle on top of whole-grain toast smeared with natural peanut butter.

62.Great Green Smoothie

Preparation time: 10 minutes
Cooking time: 0 minutes
Servings: 4

Ingredients

- 4 bananas, peeled
- 4 cups hulled strawberries
- 4 cups spinach
- 4 cups plant-based milk

Directions

1. Preparing the Ingredients.

2. Open 4 quart-size, freezer-safe bags. In each, layer in the following order: 1 banana (halved or sliced), 1 cup of strawberries, and 1 cup of spinach. Seal and place in the freezer.

3. To serve, take a frozen bag of Great Green Smoothie ingredients and transfer to a blender. Add 1 cup of plant-based milk, and blend until smooth. Place freezer bags in the freezer for up to 2 months.

63.Sunshine Muffins

Preparation time: 10 minutes
Cooking time: 30 minutes
Servings: 4

Ingredients

- 1 teaspoon coconut oil, for greasing muffin tins (optional)
- 2 tablespoons almond butter, or sunflower seed butter
- ¼ cup nondairy milk
- 1 orange, peeled
- 1 carrot, coarsely chopped
- 2 tablespoons chopped dried apricots, or other dried fruit
- 3 tablespoons molasses
- 2 tablespoons ground flaxseed
- 1 teaspoon apple cider vinegar
- 1 teaspoon pure vanilla extract
- ½ teaspoon ground cinnamon
- ½ teaspoon ground ginger (optional)
- ¼ teaspoon ground nutmeg (optional)
- ¼ teaspoon allspice (optional)
- ¾ cup rolled oats, or whole-grain flour
- 1 teaspoon baking powder
- ½ teaspoon baking soda
- Mix-ins (optional)
- ½ cup rolled oats
- 2 tablespoons raisins, or other chopped dried fruit
- 2 tablespoons sunflower seeds

Directions

1. Preparing the Ingredients.

2. Preheat the oven to 350°F.

3. Prepare a 6-cup muffin tin by rubbing the insides of the cups with coconut oil or using silicone or paper muffin cups.

4. Purée the nut butter, milk, orange, carrot, apricots, molasses, flaxseed, vinegar, vanilla, cinnamon, ginger, nutmeg, and allspice in a food processor or blender until somewhat smooth.

5. Grind the oats in a clean coffee grinder until they're the consistency of flour (or use whole-grain flour). In a large bowl, mix the oats with the baking powder and baking soda. Mix the wet ingredients into the dry ingredients until just combined. Fold in the mix-ins (if using). Spoon about ¼ cup batter into each muffin cup and bake for 30 minutes, or until a toothpick inserted into the center comes out clean.

6. The orange creates a very moist base, so the muffins may take longer than 30 minutes, depending on how heavy your muffin tin is. Store the muffins in the fridge or freezer, because they are so moist. If you plan to keep them frozen, you can easily double the batch for a full dozen.

64. Smoothie Breakfast Bowl

Preparation time: 10 minutes
Cooking time: 0 minutes
Servings: 4

Ingredients

- 4 bananas, peeled
- 1 cup dragon fruit or fruit of choice
- 1 cup Baked Granola
- 2 cups fresh berries
- ½ cup slivered almonds
- 4 cups plant-based milk

Directions

1. Preparing the Ingredients.

2. Open 4 quart-size, freezer-safe bags, and layer in the following order: 1 banana (halved or sliced) and ¼ cup dragon fruit. Into 4 small jelly jars, layer in the following order: ¼ cup granola, ½ cup berries, and 2 tablespoons slivered almonds.

3. To serve, take a frozen bag of bananas and dragon fruit and transfer to a blender. Add 1 cup of plant-based milk, and blend until smooth. Pour into a bowl. Add the contents of 1 jar of granola, berries, and almonds over the top of the smoothie, and serve with a spoon. Place the freezer bags in the freezer for up to 2 months. Store the jars of berries, granola, and nuts in the refrigerator for up to 1 week.

65. Pink Panther Smoothie

Preparation time: 10 minutes

Cooking time: 0 minutes
Servings: 4

Ingredients

- 1 cup strawberries
- 1 cup chopped melon (any kind)
- 1 cup cranberries, or raspberries
- 1 tablespoon chia seeds
- ½ cup coconut milk, or other nondairy milk
- 1 cup water
- (OPTIONAL)
- 1 teaspoon goji berries
- 2 tablespoons fresh mint, chopped

Directions

1. Preparing the Ingredients.
2. Purée everything in a blender until smooth, adding more water (or coconut milk) if needed.
3. Add bonus boosters, as desired. Purée until blended. If you don't have (or don't like) coconut, try using sunflower seeds for an immune boost of zinc and selenium.

66. Tortilla Breakfast Casserole

Preparation time: 10 minutes
Cooking time: 30 minutes
Servings: 4

Ingredients

- Nonstick cooking spray
- 1 recipe Tofu-Spinach Scramble
- 1 (14-ounce) can black beans, rinsed and drained
- ¼ cup nutritional yeast
- 2 teaspoons hot sauce
- 10 small corn tortillas
- ½ cup shredded vegan Cheddar or pepper Jack cheese, divided

Directions

1. Preparing the Ingredients.
2. Preheat the oven to 350ºF.
3. Coat a 9-by-9-inch baking pan with cooking spray.
4. In a large bowl, combine the tofu scramble with the black beans, nutritional yeast, and hot sauce. Set aside.
5. In the bottom of the baking pan, place 5 corn tortillas. Spread half of the tofu

and bean mixture over the tortillas. Spread ¼ cup of cheese over the top. Layer the remaining 5 tortillas over the top of the cheese. Spread the reminder of the tofu and bean mixture over the tortillas. Spread the remaining ¼ cup of cheese over the top.

6. Bake for 20 minutes. Divide evenly among 6 single-serving containers. Let cool before sealing the lids. Place the containers in the refrigerator for up to 5 days.

7. If you want to keep the casserole intact in the freezer, consider baking it in a disposable pan. Once cool, simply cover with foil and freeze.

67. Tofu-Spinach Scramble

Preparation time: 10 minutes
Cooking time: 40 minutes
Servings: 4

Ingredients

- 1 (14-ounce) package water-packed extra-firm tofu
- 1 teaspoon extra-virgin olive oil or ¼ cup vegetable broth
- 1 small yellow onion, diced
- 3 teaspoons minced garlic (about 3 cloves)
- 3 large celery stalks, chopped
- 2 large carrots, peeled (optional) and chopped

- 1 teaspoon chili powder
- ½ teaspoon ground cumin
- ½ teaspoon ground turmeric
- ½ teaspoon salt (optional)
- ¼ teaspoon freshly ground black pepper
- 5 cups loosely packed spinach

Directions

1. Preparing the Ingredients.

2. Press and drain the tofu by placing it, wrapped in a paper towel, on a plate in the sink. Place a cutting board over the tofu, then set a heavy pot, can, or cookbook on the cutting board. Remove after 10 minutes. (Alternatively, use a tofu press.)

3. In a medium bowl, crumble the tofu with your hands or a potato masher. Set aside.

4. In a large skillet over medium-high heat, heat the olive oil. Add the onion, garlic, celery, and carrots, and sauté for 5 minutes, until the onion is softened.

5. Add the crumbled tofu, chili powder, cumin, turmeric, salt (if using), and pepper, and continue cooking for 7 to 8 more minutes, stirring frequently, until the tofu begins to brown.

6. Add the spinach and mix well. Cover and reduce the heat to medium. Steam the spinach for 3 minutes.

7. Divide evenly among 5 single-serving containers. Let cool before sealing the lids.

8. Place the containers in the refrigerator for up to 5 days.

68. Mango Madness

Preparation time: 10 minutes

Cooking time: 30 minutes
Servings: 4

Ingredients

- 1 banana
- 1 cup chopped mango (frozen or fresh)
- 1 cup chopped peach (frozen or fresh)
- 1 cup strawberries
- 1 carrot, peeled and chopped (optional)
- 1 cup water

Directions

1. Preparing the Ingredients.
2. Purée everything in a blender until smooth, adding more water if needed.
3. If you can't find frozen peaches and fresh ones aren't in season, just use extra mango or strawberries, or try cantaloupe.

69.Savory Pancakes

Preparation time: 10 minutes
Cooking time: 30 minutes

Servings: 4

Ingredients

- 1 cup whole-wheat flour
- 1 teaspoon garlic salt
- 1 teaspoon onion powder
- ½ teaspoon baking soda
- ¼ teaspoon salt
- 1 cup lightly pressed, crumbled soft or firm tofu
- ⅓ cup unsweetened plant-based milk
- ¼ cup lemon juice (about 2 small lemons)
- 2 tablespoons extra-virgin olive oil
- ½ cup finely chopped mushrooms
- ½ cup finely chopped onion
- 2 cups tightly packed greens (arugula, spinach, or baby kale work great)
- Nonstick cooking spray

Directions

1. Preparing the Ingredients.
2. In a large bowl, combine the flour, garlic salt, onion powder, baking soda, and salt. Mix well. In a blender,

combine the tofu, plant-based milk, lemon juice, and olive oil. Purée on high speed for 30 seconds.

3. Pour the contents of the blender into the bowl of dry ingredients and whisk until combined well. Fold in the mushrooms, onion, and greens.

4. Spray a large skillet or griddle pan with nonstick cooking spray and set over medium-high heat. Reduce the heat to medium and add ½ cup of batter per pancake. Cook on both sides for about 3 minutes, or until set. After flipping, press down on the cooked side of the pancake with a spatula to flatten out the pancake. Repeat until the batter is gone.

5. Divide the cooked pancakes among 4 single-serving containers. Let cool before sealing the lids.

6. Place the airtight storage containers in the refrigerator for up to 4 days. To reheat, microwave for 1½ to 2 minutes. To freeze, place the pancakes on a parchment paper–lined baking sheet in a single layer. If there's more than one layer, place another piece of parchment paper over the pancakes and place the second layer on top. Place the baking sheet in the freezer for 2 to 4 hours. Transfer the frozen pancakes to a freezer-safe bag (cut the parchment paper and place a small piece between each pancake). To thaw, refrigerate overnight. Preheat an oven or toaster oven to 350ºF. Place the pancakes on a parchment paper–lined baking sheet and bake for 10 to 15 minutes, or stack the pancakes on a plate and microwave for 2 to 3 minutes.

SOUPS AND STEWS

70. Tomato Gazpacho

Preparation time: 30 minutes
Cooking time: 55 minutes
Servings: 6

Ingredients:

- 2 Tablespoons + 1 Teaspoon Red Wine Vinegar, Divided
- ½ Teaspoon Pepper
- 1 Teaspoon Sea Salt
- 1 Avocado,
- ¼ Cup Basil, Fresh & Chopped
- 3 Tablespoons + 2 Teaspoons Olive Oil, Divided
- 1 Clove Garlic, crushed
- 1 Red Bell Pepper, Sliced & Seeded
- 1 Cucumber, Chunked
- 2 ½ lbs. Large Tomatoes, Cored & Chopped

Directions:

1. Place half of your cucumber, bell pepper, and ¼ cup of each tomato in a bowl, covering. Set it in the fried.

2. Puree your remaining tomatoes, cucumber and bell pepper with garlic, three tablespoons oil, two tablespoons of vinegar, sea salt and black pepper into a blender, blending until smooth. Transfer it to a bowl, and chill for two hours.

3. Chop the avocado, adding it to your chopped vegetables, adding your remaining oil, vinegar, salt, pepper and basil.

4. Ladle your tomato puree mixture into bowls, and serve with chopped vegetables as a salad.

5. Interesting Facts:

6. Avocados themselves are ranked within the top five of the healthiest foods on the planet, so you know that the oil that is produced from them is too. It is loaded with healthy fats and essential fatty acids. Like race bran oil it is perfect to cook with as well! Bonus: Helps in the prevention of diabetes and lowers cholesterol levels.

71. Tomato Pumpkin Soup

Preparation time: 25 minutes
Cooking time: 25 minutes
Servings: 4

Ingredients:

- 2 cups pumpkin, diced
- 1/2 cup tomato, chopped
- 1/2 cup onion, chopped
- 1 1/2 tsp curry powder
- 1/2 tsp paprika
- 2 cups vegetable stock
- 1 tsp olive oil
- 1/2 tsp garlic, minced

Directions:

1. In a saucepan, add oil, garlic, and onion and sauté for 3 minutes over medium heat.

2. Add remaining ingredients into the saucepan and bring to boil.

3. Reduce heat and cover and simmer for 10 minutes.

4. Puree the soup using a blender until smooth.

5. Stir well and serve warm.

72. Cauliflower Spinach Soup

Preparation time: 45 minutes
Cooking time: 45 minutes
Servings: 5

Ingredients:

- 1/2 cup unsweetened coconut milk
- 5 oz fresh spinach, chopped
- 5 watercress, chopped
- 8 cups vegetable stock
- 1 lb cauliflower, chopped
- Salt

Directions:

1. Add stock and cauliflower in a large saucepan and bring to boil over medium heat for 15 minutes.
2. Add spinach and watercress and cook for another 10 minutes.
3. Remove from heat and puree the soup using a blender until smooth.
4. Add coconut milk and stir well. Season with salt.
5. Stir well and serve hot.

73. Avocado Mint Soup

Preparation time: 10 minutes
Cooking time: 10 minutes
Servings: 2

Ingredients:

- 1 medium avocado, peeled, pitted, and cut into pieces
- 1 cup coconut milk
- 2 romaine lettuce leaves
- 20 fresh mint leaves
- 1 tbsp fresh lime juice

- 1/8 tsp salt

Directions:

1. Add all ingredients into the blender and blend until smooth. Soup should be thick not as a puree.
2. Pour into the serving bowls and place in the refrigerator for 10 minutes.
3. Stir well and serve chilled.

74. Creamy Squash Soup

Preparation time: 35 minutes
Cooking time: 35 minutes
Servings: 8

Ingredients:

- 3 cups butternut squash, chopped
- 1 ½ cups unsweetened coconut milk
- 1 tbsp coconut oil
- 1 tsp dried onion flakes
- 1 tbsp curry powder
- 4 cups water
- 1 garlic clove
- 1 tsp kosher salt

Directions:

1. Add squash, coconut oil, onion flakes, curry powder, water, garlic, and salt into a large saucepan. Bring to boil over high heat.
2. Turn heat to medium and simmer for 20 minutes.
3. Puree the soup using a blender until smooth. Return soup to the saucepan and stir in coconut milk and cook for 2 minutes.
4. Stir well and serve hot.

75. Zucchini Soup

Preparation time: 20 minutes
Cooking time: 20 minutes
Servings: 8

Ingredients:

- 2 ½ lbs zucchini, peeled and sliced
- 1/3 cup basil leaves
- 4 cups vegetable stock
- 4 garlic cloves, chopped
- 2 tbsp olive oil
- 1 medium onion, diced
- Pepper
- Salt

Directions:

1. Heat olive oil in a pan over medium-low heat.
2. Add zucchini and onion and sauté until softened. Add garlic and sauté for a minute.
3. Add vegetable stock and simmer for 15 minutes.
4. Remove from heat. Stir in basil and puree the soup using a blender until smooth and creamy. Season with pepper and salt.
5. Stir well and serve.

76.Creamy Celery Soup

Preparation time: 40 minutes
Cooking time: 40 minutes
Servings: 4

Ingredients:

- 6 cups celery
- ½ tsp dill
- 2 cups water
- 1 cup coconut milk
- 1 onion, chopped

- Pinch of salt

Directions:

1. Add all ingredients into the electric pot and stir well.
2. Cover electric pot with the lid and select soup setting.
3. Release pressure using a quick release method than open the lid.
4. Puree the soup using an immersion blender until smooth and creamy.
5. Stir well and serve warm.

77.Avocado Cucumber Soup

Preparation time: 40 minutes
Cooking time: 40 minutes
Servings: 3

Ingredients:

- 1 large cucumber, peeled and sliced
- ¾ cup water
- ¼ cup lemon juice
- 2 garlic cloves
- 6 green onion
- 2 avocados, pitted
- ½ tsp black pepper
- ½ tsp pink salt

Directions:

1. Add all ingredients into the blender and blend until smooth and creamy.
2. Place in refrigerator for 30 minutes.
3. Stir well and serve chilled.

78.Creamy Garlic Onion Soup

Preparation time: 45 minutes
Cooking time: 25 minutes
Servings: 4

Ingredients:

- 1 onion, sliced
- 4 cups vegetable stock
- 1 1/2 tbsp olive oil
- 1 shallot, sliced
- 2 garlic clove, chopped
- 1 leek, sliced
- Salt

Directions:

1. Add stock and olive oil in a saucepan and bring to boil.
2. Add remaining ingredients and stir well.
3. Cover and simmer for 25 minutes.
4. Puree the soup using an immersion blender until smooth.
5. Stir well and serve warm.

79.Avocado Broccoli Soup

Preparation time: 20 minutes
Cooking time: 5 minutes
Servings: 4

Ingredients:

- 2 cups broccoli florets, chopped
- 5 cups vegetable broth
- 2 avocados, chopped
- Pepper
- Salt

Directions:

1. Cook broccoli in boiling water for 5 minutes. Drain well.
2. Add broccoli, vegetable broth, avocados, pepper, and salt to the blender and blend until smooth.
3. Stir well and serve warm.

80.Green Spinach Kale Soup

Preparation time: 10 minutes
Cooking time: 5 minutes
Servings: 6

Ingredients:

- 2 avocados
- 8 oz spinach
- 8 oz kale
- 1 fresh lime juice
- 1 cup water
- 3 1/3 cup coconut milk
- 3 oz olive oil
- 1/4 tsp pepper
- 1 tsp salt

Directions:

1. Heat olive oil in a saucepan over medium heat.
2. Add kale and spinach to the saucepan and sauté for 2-3 minutes. Remove saucepan from heat. Add coconut milk, spices, avocado, and water. Stir well.
3. Puree the soup using an immersion blender until smooth and creamy. Add fresh lime juice and stir well.
4. Serve and enjoy.

81.Cauliflower Asparagus Soup

Preparation time: 10 minutes
Cooking time: 30 minutes
Servings: 4

Ingredients:

- 20 asparagus spears, chopped
- 4 cups vegetable stock
- ½ cauliflower head, chopped
- 2 garlic cloves, chopped

- 1 tbsp coconut oil
- Pepper
- Salt

Directions:

1. Heat coconut oil in a large saucepan over medium heat.

2. Add garlic and sauté until softened.

3. Add cauliflower, vegetable stock, pepper, and salt. Stir well and bring to boil.

4. Reduce heat to low and simmer for 20 minutes.

5. Add chopped asparagus and cook until softened.

6. Puree the soup using an immersion blender until smooth and creamy.

7. Stir well and serve warm.

82.African Pineapple Peanut Stew

Preparation time: 10 minutes
Cooking time: 20 minutes
Servings: 4

Ingredients:

- 4 cups sliced kale
- 1 cup chopped onion
- 1/2 cup peanut butter
- 1 tbsp. hot pepper sauce or 1 tbsp. Tabasco sauce
- 2 minced garlic cloves
- 1/2 cup chopped cilantro
- 2 cups pineapple, undrained, canned & crushed
- 1 tbsp. vegetable oil

Directions:

1. In a saucepan (preferably covered), sauté the garlic and onions in the oil until the onions are lightly browned, approximately 10 minutes, stirring often.

2. Wash the kale, till the time the onions are sauté.

3. Get rid of the stems. Mound the leaves on a cutting surface & slice crosswise into slices (preferably 1" thick).

4. Now put the pineapple and juice to the onions & bring to a simmer. Stir the kale in, cover and simmer until just tender, stirring frequently, approximately 5 minutes.

5. Mix in the hot pepper sauce, peanut butter & simmer for more 5 minutes.

6. Add salt according to your taste.

83.Cabbage & Beet Stew

Preparation time: 20 minutes
Cooking time: 10 minutes
Servings: 4

Ingredients:

- 2 Tablespoons Olive Oil
- 3 Cups Vegetable Broth
- 2 Tablespoons Lemon Juice, Fresh
- ½ Teaspoon Garlic Powder
- ½ Cup Carrots, Shredded
- 2 Cups Cabbage, Shredded
- 1 Cup Beets, Shredded
- Dill for Garnish
- ½ Teaspoon Onion Powder
- Sea Salt & Black Pepper to Taste

Directions:

1. Heat oil in a pot, and then sauté your vegetables.

2. Pour your broth in, mixing in your seasoning. Simmer until it's cooked

through, and then top with dill.

3. Interesting Facts: This oil is the main source of dietary fat in a variety of diets. It contains many vitamins and minerals that play a part in reducing the risk of stroke and lowers cholesterol and high blood pressure and can also aid in weight loss. It is best consumed cold, as when it is heated it can lose some of its nutritive properties (although it is still great to cook with – extra virgin is best), many recommend taking a shot of cold oil olive daily! Bonus: if you don't like the taste or texture add a shot to your smoothie.

84.Basil Tomato Soup

Preparation time: 10 minutes
Cooking time: 10 minutes
Servings: 6

Ingredients:

- 28 oz can tomatoes
- ¼ cup basil pesto
- ¼ tsp dried basil leaves
- 1 tsp apple cider vinegar
- 2 tbsp erythritol
- ¼ tsp garlic powder
- ½ tsp onion powder
- 2 cups water
- 1 ½ tsp kosher salt

Directions:

1. Add tomatoes, garlic powder, onion powder, water, and salt in a saucepan.

2. Bring to boil over medium heat. Reduce heat and simmer for 2 minutes.

3. Remove saucepan from heat and puree the soup using a blender until smooth.

4. Stir in pesto, dried basil, vinegar, and erythritol.

5. Stir well and serve warm.

85.Mushroom & Broccoli Soup

Preparation time: 20 minutes
Cooking time: 45 minutes
Servings: 8

Ingredients:

- 1 bundle broccoli (around 1-1/2 pounds)
- 1 tablespoon canola oil
- 1/2 pound cut crisp mushrooms
- 1 tablespoon diminished sodium soy sauce
- 2 medium carrots, finely slashed
- 2 celery ribs, finely slashed
- 1/4 cup finely slashed onion
- 1 garlic clove, minced
- 1 container (32 ounces) vegetable juices
- 2 cups of water
- 2 tablespoons lemon juice

Directions:

1. Cut broccoli florets into reduced down pieces. Strip and hack stalks.

2. In an enormous pot, heat oil over medium-high warmth; saute mushrooms until delicate, 4-6 minutes. Mix in soy sauce; expel from skillet.

3. In the same container, join broccoli stalks, carrots, celery, onion, garlic, soup, and water; heat to the point of boiling. Diminish heat; stew, revealed, until vegetables are relaxed, 25-30 minutes.

4. Puree soup utilizing a drenching blender. Or then again, cool marginally and puree the soup in a blender; come back to the dish. Mix in florets and mushrooms; heat to the point of boiling. Lessen warmth to medium; cook until broccoli is delicate, 8-10 minutes, blending infrequently. Mix in lemon juice.

86. Creamy Cauliflower Pakora Soup

Preparation time: 20 minutes
Cooking time: 20 minutes
Servings: 8

Ingredients:

- 1 huge head cauliflower, cut into little florets
- 5 medium potatoes, stripped and diced
- 1 huge onion, diced
- 4 medium carrots, stripped and diced
- 2 celery ribs, diced
- 1 container (32 ounces) vegetable stock
- 1 teaspoon garam masala
- 1 teaspoon garlic powder
- 1 teaspoon ground coriander
- 1 teaspoon ground turmeric
- 1 teaspoon ground cumin
- 1 teaspoon pepper
- 1 teaspoon salt
- 1/2 teaspoon squashed red pepper chips
- Water or extra vegetable stock
- New cilantro leaves
- Lime wedges, discretionary

Directions:

1. In a Dutch stove over medium-high warmth, heat initial 14 fixings to the point of boiling. Cook and mix until vegetables are delicate, around 20 minutes. Expel from heat; cool marginally. Procedure in groups in a blender or nourishment processor until smooth. Modify consistency as wanted with water (or extra stock). Sprinkle with new cilantro. Serve hot, with lime wedges whenever wanted.

2. Stop alternative: Before including cilantro, solidify cooled soup in cooler compartments. To utilize, in part defrost in cooler medium-term. Warmth through in a pan, blending every so often and including a little water if fundamental. Sprinkle with cilantro. Whenever wanted, present with lime wedges.

87. Garden Vegetable and Herb Soup

Preparation time: 20 minutes
Cooking time: 30 minutes
Servings: 8

Ingredients:

- 2 tablespoons olive oil
- 2 medium onions, hacked
- 2 huge carrots, cut
- 1 pound red potatoes (around 3 medium), cubed
- 2 cups of water
- 1 can (14-1/2 ounces) diced tomatoes in sauce
- 1-1/2 cups vegetable soup
- 1-1/2 teaspoons garlic powder
- 1 teaspoon dried basil
- 1/2 teaspoon salt
- 1/2 teaspoon paprika
- 1/4 teaspoon dill weed

- 1/4 teaspoon pepper
- 1 medium yellow summer squash, split and cut
- 1 medium zucchini, split and cut

Directions:

1. In a huge pan, heat oil over medium warmth. Include onions and carrots; cook and mix until onions are delicate, 4-6 minutes. Include potatoes and cook 2 minutes. Mix in water, tomatoes, juices, and seasonings. Heat to the point of boiling. Diminish heat; stew, revealed, until potatoes and carrots are delicate, 9 minutes.

2. Include yellow squash and zucchini; cook until vegetables are delicate, 9 minutes longer. Serve or, whenever wanted, puree blend in clusters, including extra stock until desired consistency is accomplished.

88.Roasted Red Pepper and Cauliflower Soup Instant Pot

Preparation time: 10 minutes
Cooking time: 56 minutes
Servings: 9

Ingredients:

- 1 head cauliflower, cut into florets
- 5 garlic cloves, crushed
- 4 green onions, slashed
- 1 340 ml container of simmered red peppers, diced (approx. 3 peppers)
- 1 14oz container of finely slashed tomatoes (I utilized Solo Pomodoro Mutti tomatoes)
- 2 huge carrots, diced
- 2 red shepherd peppers, seeded + diced
- 1/4 cup greens of decision (I utilized swiss chard), cut up into little strings or diced
- 1 tbsp smoked paprika
- 1/2 tbsp onion powder
- 1/2 tbsp garlic powder
- 1/4 tsp dried cumin
- 2 tbsp apple juice vinegar
- 1/2-1 tsp ocean salt, dark salt or pink Himalayan salt
- 4 cups custom made stalk, bone stock or water
- Olive oil
- S+P to taste

Directions:

1. Attachment in the Instant Pot and press the "Sauté" work.

2. Include the olive oil, onions, carrots, shepherd peppers, and garlic to the pot and sauté until they start to mellow and turn translucent. Add a spot of salt to bring out flavors and discharge juices.

3. When the veggies are delicate mix in the flavors to cover.

4. Include the ACV and join well. Give the vinegar a chance to cook off for a moment or two, blending persistently. Scrape up any darker bits joined to the base of the pot.

5. Include the container of tomatoes and the cleaved up simmered red peppers to the pot, mix well, and let the tomato blend cook for a moment.

6. Add the greens to the pot just as the cauliflower florets, mix to consolidate, trailed by 4 cups of water (or stalk bone juices).

7. Press the "Keep Warm/Cancel" catch to stop the sauté mode.

8. Mix and afterward place the top on the Instant Pot and lock the top. Curve the steam discharge handle on the top to "Fixing".

9. Press the "Soup" catch to switch the cooking mode. The cooking time will set for 30 minutes. Note that the soup will cook for longer than 30 minutes as it requires some investment for the compel cooker to arrive at the wanted weight. The brief clock will begin once an appropriate weight is accomplished.

10. More directions to follow:

11. When the soup is finished cooking the Instant Pot will naturally change to the "Keep Warm" mode and will flag finished with signals. When you hear the blares, the soup has cooked for the full 30 minutes at full weight. Give the soup a chance to stay in the "Keep Warm" mode for 10 minutes and afterward press "Drop."

12. Curve the steam discharge handle on the top to "Venting". I generally put on my broiler glove as a safeguard as a limited quantity of steam will escape from the venting gap.

13. When the weight has discharged, cautiously open the Instant Pot.

14. Test for flavoring. Include progressively pink salt, fresh split pepper, and new pressed lemon juice to taste.

15. Utilize a potato masher to separate the lumps of cauliflower to arrive at desired consistency or mix for a smooth consistency.

16. Scoop soup into bowls. Top with some newly slashed chives and hot red pepper chips if so wants!

89. The Mediterranean Delight with Fresh Vinaigrette

Preparation Time: 5 minutes
Cooking Time: 10 minutes
Serving: 2

Ingredients:

- Herbed citrus vinaigrette:
- 1 tablespoon of lemon juice
- 2 tablespoons of orange juice
- ½ teaspoon of lemon zest
- ½ teaspoon of orange zest
- 2 tablespoons of olive oil
- 1 tablespoon of finely chopped fresh oregano leaves
- Salt to taste
- Black pepper to taste
- 2-3 tablespoons of freshly julienned mint leaves
- Salad:
- 1 freshly diced medium-sized cucumber
- 2 cups of cooked and rinsed chickpeas
- ½ cup of freshly diced red onion
- 2 freshly diced medium-sized tomatoes
- 1 freshly diced red bell pepper
- ¼ cup of green olives
- ½ cup of pomegranates

Directions:

1. In a large salad bowl, add the juice and zest of both the lemon and the orange along with oregano and olive oil. Whisk together so that they are mixed well. Season the vinaigrette with salt and pepper to taste.

2. After draining the chickpeas, add them to the dressing. Then, add the onions. Give them a thorough mix, so that the onion and chickpeas absorb

the flavors.

3. Now, chop the rest of the veggies and start adding them to the salad bowl. Give them a good toss.

4. Lastly, add the olives and fresh mint. Adjust the salt and pepper as required.

5. Serve this Mediterranean delight chilled — a cool summer salad that is good for the tummy and the soul.

90.Vegetable Broth Sans Sodium

Preparation Time: 5 minutes
Cooking Time: 60 minutes
Serving: 1 cup

Ingredients:

- 5 sprigs of dill
- 2 freshly sliced yellow onions
- 4 chives
- 6 freshly peeled and sliced carrots
- 10 cups of water
- 4 freshly sliced celery stalks
- 3 cloves of freshly minced garlic
- 4 sprigs of parsley

Directions:

1. Put a large pot on medium heat and stir the onions. Fry the onions for 1 minute until they become fragrant. Add the garlic, celery, carrots, and dill along with the chives and parsley and cook everything. You will know that the mix is ready when it becomes fragrant.

2. Add the water and allow the mixture to boil. Reduce the heat and allow everything to cook for 45 minutes.

3. Turn off the heat. The broth will cool in about 15 minutes.

4. Strain the broth with the help of a sieve so that you have a clear vegetable broth.

5. If you are not using the broth right away, store it as ice cubes. You can store the ice cubes for a week.

91.Amazing Chickpea and Noodle Soup

Preparation Time: 10 minutes
Cooking Time: 20 minutes
Serving: 1 cup

Ingredients:

- 1 freshly diced celery stalk
- ¼ cup of 'chicken' seasoning
- 1 cup of freshly diced onion
- 3 cloves of freshly crushed garlic
- 2 cups of cooked chickpeas
- 4 cups of vegetable broth
- Freshly chopped cilantro
- 2 freshly cubed medium-size potatoes
- Salt
- 2 freshly sliced carrots
- ½ teaspoon of dried thyme
- Pepper
- 2 cups of water
- 6 ounces of gluten-free spaghetti
- 'Chicken' seasoning
- 1 tablespoon of garlic powder
- 2 teaspoons of sea salt
- 1 1/3 cup of nutritional yeast
- 3 tablespoons of onion powder
- 1 teaspoon of oregano
- ½ teaspoon of turmeric
- 1 ½ tablespoons of dried basil

Directions:

1. Put a pot on medium heat and sauté the onion. It will soften within 3 minutes.

2. Add celery, potato, and carrots and sauté for another 3 minutes

3. Add the 'chicken' seasoning to the garlic, thyme, water, and vegetable broth.

4. Simmer the mix on medium-high heat. Cook the veggies for about 20 minutes until they soften.

5. Add the cooked pasta and chickpeas.

6. Add salt and pepper to taste.

7. Put the fresh cilantro on top and enjoy the fresh soup!

92. Lentil Soup the Vegan Way

Preparation Time: 5 minutes
Cooking Time: 20 minutes
Serving: 1 cup

Ingredients:

- 2 tablespoons of water
- 4 stalks of thinly sliced celery
- 2 cloves of freshly minced garlic
- 4 thinly sliced large carrots
- Sea salt
- 2 freshly diced small shallots
- Pepper
- 3 cups of red/yellow baby potatoes
- 2 cups of chopped sturdy greens
- 4 cups of vegetable broth
- 1 cup of uncooked brown or green lentils
- Fresh rosemary/thyme

Directions:

1. Put a large pot over medium heat. Once the pot is hot enough, add the shallots, garlic, celery, and carrots in water. Season the veggies with a little bit of pepper and salt.

2. Sauté the veggies for 5 minutes until they are tender. You will know that the veggies are ready when they have turned golden brown. Be careful with the garlic, because it can easily burn.

3. Add the potatoes and some more seasoning. Cook for 2 minutes.

4. Mix the vegetable broth with the rosemary. Now Increase the heat to medium-high. Allow the veggies to be in a rolling simmer. Add the lentils and give everything a thorough stir.

5. Once it starts to simmer again, decrease the heat and simmer for about 20 minutes without a cover. You will know that the veggies are ready when both the lentils and potatoes are soft

6. Add the greens. Cook for 4 minutes until they wilt. You can adjust the flavor with seasonings.

7. Enjoy this with rice or flatbread. The leftovers are equally tasty, so store them well to enjoy on a day when you are not in the mood to cook.

93. Beet and Kale Salad

Preparation Time: 5 minutes
Cooking Time: 5 minutes
Serving: 1

Ingredients:

- 8 ounces of beet and kale blend
- 1 tablespoon of olive oil
- 1 cucumber
- 13.4 ounce of chickpeas
- Salt

- 2 tablespoons of red wine vinegar
- Pepper
- ¼ cup of walnuts
- 2 ounces of dried cranberries
- Cashew cheese

Directions:

1. Cut the veggies and combine everything in a big salad bowl.
2. Serve the fresh salad and enjoy a hearty meal.

94. Kale and Cauliflower Salad

Preparation Time: 10 minutes
Cooking Time: 15 minutes
Serving: 1 portion

Ingredients:

- 6 ounces of Lacinato kale
- 8 ounces of cauliflower florets
- 1 lemon
- 1 tablespoon of Italian spice
- 2 radishes
- 13.4 ounce of butter beans
- Olive oil
- ¼ cup of walnuts
- ¼ cup of vegan Caesar dressing
- Pepper
- Salt

Directions:

1. Preheat the oven to 400°F. Put the cauliflower florets on a baking sheet, toss them with olive oil and spices, and add salt. Roast the cauliflower until it is brown. It will be done within 15-20 minutes.
2. De-stem the kale and slice the leaves.

Slice the radishes. Both kale and radish should be sliced thinly. Cut the lemon in half.

3. Put the kale in a large bowl and add the lemon juice and salt along with the pepper. Massage the kale so that it is properly covered with seasoning. The leaves will soon turn dark green. Mix the radishes.
4. Rinse the butter beans and pat them dry with a towel. On medium-high heat, put a large skillet, add some olive oil, and sauté the butter beans in a layer. Sprinkle some salt on top and shake the pan. The butter beans will be brown in places within 7 minutes.
5. Take two large plates and divide both the kale and beans equally. Put the walnuts and roasted cauliflower on top. Add the Caesar dressing on top and enjoy the amazing salad.

95. Asian Delight with Crunchy Dressing

Preparation Time: 20 minutes
Cooking Time: 10 minutes
Serving: 1 bowl

Ingredients:

- Salad Dressing
- ½ teaspoon of powdered ginger or 1 teaspoon of freshly chopped ginger
- 1 tablespoon of honey
- ¼ cup of rice wine vinegar
- 2 tablespoons of soy sauce
- 3 tablespoons of sesame oil
- 3 tablespoons of creamy peanut butter
- ¼ cup of vegetable oil
- 2 tablespoons of toasted sesame seeds
- Salad

- 1 finely shredded carrot
- 1 thinly sliced red bell pepper
- 6 cups of washed and dried spinach
- ¼ thinly sliced red onion
- 1 thinly sliced cucumber
- ½ pound of snap peas
- ½ cup of roasted peanuts
- 1 tablespoon of toasted sesame seeds

Directions:

1. In a medium bowl, mix the dressing ingredients and whisk them well. Do not put the sesame seeds in this dressing mixture.

2. Put some water in the pot and bring it to a boil. Add the sugar snap peas and cook them for about 5 minutes until they are crisp and tender. Drain and rinse them repeatedly in cold water so that the peas retain their crispy nature.

3. In a large bowl, add all the other ingredients for the salad. Put the salad dressing on top so that the veggies are well-coated. Add the toasted sesame seeds. Enjoy this salad when you are not in the mood for anything heavy.

96.Broccoli Salad the Thai Way

Preparation Time: 10 minutes
Cooking Time: 25 minutes
Serving: 1 portion

Ingredients

- 1 tablespoon of tamari
- ¾ cup of mung beans
- 1 lime
- 2 garlic cloves
- 3 tablespoons of cashew butter
- 1 cucumber
- ¼ ounce of fresh mint
- 1 tablespoon of chili-garlic sauce
- 1 head of artisan lettuce
- 3 Thai chilis
- 6 ounces of broccoli florets
- 2 tablespoons of olive oil
- Salt
- Pepper

Directions:

1. On high heat, add the mung beans to 3 cups of cold water. After they start boiling, reduce the heat to medium. Allow the beans to simmer, but stir them from time to time. The mung beans will be tender within 20 minutes. Drain the excess water and add some salt.

2. Mince the garlic and cut the lime in half. In a medium bowl, mix the lime juice, minced garlic, tamari, and cashew butter with chili-garlic sauce. Add 3 tablespoons of warm water. Whisk the mixture well.

3. Slice the cucumber, cut the broccoli into bite-size pieces, and chop the lettuce. Pick the mint leaves as well. Lastly, slice the Thai chilis.

4. On a non-stick skillet, put 2 tablespoons of olive oil. Turn the heat to medium-high. Once the oil is hot, add the broccoli florets and cook until they are brown. They will be crisp-tender. Add some pepper and salt to the broccoli and add the lime juice and Thai chilis.

5. In a shallow bowl, spread some cashew sauce. Add some chopped lettuce, mung beans, broccoli, and cucumber. Add mint leaves and mix the Thai chilies. Add some more cashew sauce and enjoy the salad!

97.Sweet Potato, Corn and Jalapeno Bisque

Preparation time: 10 minutes
Cooking time: 15 minutes
Servings: 4

Ingredients:

- 4 ears corn
- 1 seeded and chopped jalapeno
- 4 cups vegetable broth
- 1 tablespoon olive oil
- 3 peeled and cubed sweet potatoes
- 1 chopped onion
- ½ tablespoon salt
- ¼ teaspoon black pepper
- 1 minced garlic clove

Directions:

1. In a pan, heat the oil over medium flame and sauté onion and garlic in it and cook for around 3 minutes. Put broth and sweet potatoes in it and bring it to boil. Reduce the flame and cook it for an additional 10 minutes. Remove it from the stove and blend it with a blender. Again, put it on the stove and add corn, jalapeno, salt, and black pepper and serve it.

Nutrition: Carbohydrates 31g, protein 6g, fats 4g, sugar 11g.

98.Creamy Pea Soup with Olive Pesto

Preparation time: 20 minutes
Cooking time: 20 minutes
Servings: 4

Ingredients:

- 1 grated carrot
- 1 rinsed chopped leek
- 1 minced garlic clove
- 2 tablespoons olive oil
- 1 stem fresh thyme leaves
- 15 ounces rinsed and drained peas
- ½ tablespoon salt
- ¼ teaspoon ground black pepper
- 2 ½ cups vegetable broth
- ¼ cup parsley leaves
- 1 ¼ cups pitted green olives
- 1 teaspoon drained capers
- 1 garlic clove

Directions:

1. Take a pan with oil and put it over medium flame and whisk garlic, leek, thyme, and carrot in it. Cook it for around 4 minutes. Add broth, peas, salt, and pepper and increase the heat. When it starts boiling, lower down the heat and cook it with a lid on for around 15 minutes and remove from heat and blend it. For making pesto whisk parsley, olives, capers, and garlic and blend it in a way that it has little chunks. Top thc soup with thc scoop of olive pesto.

Nutrition: Carbohydrates 23g, protein 6g, fats 15g, sugar 4g, calories 230.

99.Spinach Soup with Dill and Basil

Preparation time: 10 minutes
Cooking time: 25 minutes
Servings: 8

Ingredients:

- 1 pound peeled and diced potatoes
- 1 tablespoon minced garlic
- 1 teaspoon dry mustard
- 6 cups vegetable broth
- 20 ounces chopped frozen spinach
- 2 cups chopped onion
- 1 ½ tablespoons salt
- ½ cup minced dill

- 1 cup basil
- ½ teaspoon ground black pepper

Directions:

1. Whisk onion, garlic, potatoes, broth, mustard, and salt in a pand cook it over medium flame. When it starts boiling, low down the heat and cover it with the lid and cook for 20 minutes. Add the remaining ingredients in it and blend it and cook it for few more minutes and serve it.

Nutrition: **Carbohydrates 12g, protein 13g, fats 1g, calories 165**.

100.Coconut Watercress Soup

Preparation time: 10 minutes
Cooking time: 20 minutes
Servings: 4

Ingredients:

- 1 teaspoon coconut oil
- 1 onion, diced
- ¾ cup coconut milk

Directions:

1. Preparing the ingredients.
2. Melt the coconut oil in a large pot over medium-high heat. Add the onion and cook until soft, about 5 minutes, then add the peas and the water. Bring to a boil, then lower the heat and add the watercress, mint, salt, and pepper.

3. Cover and simmer for 5 minutes. Stir in the coconut milk, and purée the soup until smooth in a blender or with an immersion blender.

4. Try this soup with any other fresh, leafy green—anything from spinach to collard greens to arugula to swiss chard.

101. Roasted Red Pepper and Butternut Squash Soup

Preparation time: 10 minutes
Cooking time: 45 minutes
Servings: 6

Ingredients:

- 1 small butternut squash
- 1 tablespoon olive oil
- 1 teaspoon sea salt
- 2 red bell peppers
- 1 yellow onion
- 1 head garlic
- 2 cups water, or vegetable broth
- Zest and juice of 1 lime
- 1 to 2 tablespoons tahini
- Pinch cayenne pepper
- ½ teaspoon ground coriander
- ½ teaspoon ground cumin
- Toasted squash seeds (optional)

Directions:

1. Preparing the ingredients.

2. Preheat the oven to 350°f.

3. Prepare the squash for roasting by cutting it in half lengthwise, scooping out the seeds, and poking some holes in the flesh with a fork. Reserve the seeds if desired.

4. Rub a small amount of oil over the flesh and skin, then rub with a bit of sea salt and put the halves skin-side down in a large baking dish. Put it in the oven while you prepare the rest of the vegetables.

5. Prepare the peppers the exact same way, except they do not need to be poked.

6. Slice the onion in half and rub oil on the exposed faces. Slice the top off the head of garlic and rub oil on the exposed flesh.

7. After the squash has cooked for 20 minutes, add the peppers, onion, and garlic, and roast for another 20 minutes. Optionally, you can toast the squash seeds by putting them in the oven in a separate baking dish 10 to 15 minutes before the vegetables are finished.

8. Keep a close eye on them. When the vegetables are cooked, take them out and let them cool before handling them. The squash will be very soft when poked with a fork.

9. Scoop the flesh out of the squash skin into a large pot (if you have an immersion blender) or into a blender.

10. Chop the pepper roughly, remove the onion skin and chop the onion roughly, and squeeze the garlic cloves out of the head, all into the pot or blender. Add the water, the lime zest and juice, and the tahini. Purée the soup, adding more water if you like, to your desired consistency. Season with

the salt, cayenne, coriander, and cumin. Serve garnished with toasted squash seeds (if using).

Nutrition: calories: 156; protein: 4g; total fat: 7g; saturated fat: 11g; carbohydrates: 22g; fiber: 5g

102.Tomato Pumpkin Soup

Preparation time: 25 minutes
Cooking time: 15 minutes
Servings: 4

Ingredients:

- 2 cups pumpkin, diced
- 1/2 cup tomato, chopped
- 1/2 cup onion, chopped
- 1 1/2 tsp curry powder
- 1/2 tsp paprika
- 2 cups vegetable stock
- 1 tsp olive oil
- 1/2 tsp garlic, minced

Directions:

1. In a saucepan, add oil, garlic, and onion and sauté for 3 minutes over medium heat.
2. Add remaining ingredients into the saucepan and bring to boil.
3. Reduce heat and cover and simmer for 10 minutes.
4. Puree the soup using a blender until smooth.
5. Stir well and serve warm.

103.Cauliflower Spinach Soup

Preparation time: 30 minutes
Cooking time: 25 minutes
Servings: 5

Ingredients:

- 1/2 cup unsweetened coconut milk
- 5 oz fresh spinach, chopped
- 5 watercress, chopped
- 8 cups vegetable stock
- 1 lb cauliflower, chopped
- Salt

Directions:

1. Add stock and cauliflower in a large saucepan and bring to boil over medium heat for 15 minutes.
2. Add spinach and watercress and cook for another 10 minutes.
3. Remove from heat and puree the soup using a blender until smooth.
4. Add coconut milk and stir well. Season with salt.
5. Stir well and serve hot.

104.Avocado Mint Soup

Preparation time: 10 minutes
Cooking time: 10 minutes
Servings: 2

Ingredients:

- 1 medium avocado, peeled, pitted, and cut into pieces
- 1 cup coconut milk
- 2 romaine lettuce leaves
- 20 fresh mint leaves
- 1 tbsp fresh lime juice
- 1/8 tsp salt

Directions:

1. Add all ingredients into the blender and blend until smooth. Soup should be thick not as a puree.
2. Pour into the serving bowls and place in the refrigerator for 10 minutes.
3. Stir well and serve chilled.

105.Creamy Squash Soup

Preparation time: 10 minutes
Cooking time: 25 minutes
Servings: 8

Ingredients:

- 3 cups butternut squash, chopped
- 1 ½ cups unsweetened coconut milk
- 1 tbsp coconut oil
- 1 tsp dried onion flakes
- 1 tbsp curry powder
- 4 cups water
- 1 garlic clove
- 1 tsp kosher salt

Directions:

1. Add squash, coconut oil, onion flakes, curry powder, water, garlic, and salt into a large saucepan. Bring to boil over high heat.
2. Turn heat to medium and simmer for 20 minutes.
3. Puree the soup using a blender until smooth. Return soup to the saucepan and stir in coconut milk and cook for 2 minutes.
4. Stir well and serve hot.

106.Zucchini Soup

Preparation time: 10 minutes
Cooking time: 15 minutes

Servings: 8

Ingredients:

- 2 ½ lbs zucchini, peeled and sliced
- 1/3 cup basil leaves
- 4 cups vegetable stock
- 4 garlic cloves, chopped
- 2 tbsp olive oil
- 1 medium onion, diced
- Pepper
- Salt

Directions:

1. Heat olive oil in a pan over medium-low heat.

2. Add zucchini and onion and sauté until softened. Add garlic and sauté for a minute.

3. Add vegetable stock and simmer for 15 minutes.

4. Remove from heat. Stir in basil and puree the soup using a blender until smooth and creamy. Season with pepper and salt.

5. Stir well and serve.

107.Creamy Celery Soup

Preparation time: 20 minutes
Cooking time: 20 minutes
Servings: 4

Ingredients:

- 6 cups celery
- ½ tsp dill
- 2 cups water
- 1 cup coconut milk
- 1 onion, chopped
- Pinch of salt

Directions:

1. Add all ingredients into the electric pot and stir well.

2. Cover electric pot with the lid and select soup setting.

3. Release pressure using a quick release method than open the lid.

4. Puree the soup using an immersion blender until smooth and creamy.

5. Stir well and serve warm.

108.Avocado Cucumber Soup

Preparation time: 20 minutes
Cooking time: 0 minutes
Servings: 3

Ingredients:

- 1 large cucumber, peeled and sliced
- ¾ cup water
- ¼ cup lemon juice
- 2 garlic cloves
- 6 green onion
- 2 avocados, pitted
- ½ tsp black pepper
- ½ tsp pink salt

Directions:

1. Add all ingredients into the blender and blend until smooth and creamy.
2. Place in refrigerator for 30 minutes.
3. Stir well and serve chilled.

109.Garden Vegetable Stew

Preparation time: 5 minutes
Cooking time: 60 minutes
Servings: 4

Ingredients:

- 2 tablespoons olive oil
- 1 medium red onion, chopped
- 1 medium carrot, cut into 1/4-inch slices
- 1/2 cup dry white wine
- 3 medium new potatoes, unpeeled and cut into 1-inch pieces
- 1 medium red bell pepper, cut into 1/2-inch dice
- 11/2 cups vegetable broth
- 1 tablespoon minced fresh savory or 1 teaspoon dried

Directions:

1. In a large saucepan, heat the oil over medium heat. Add the onion and carrot, cover, and cook until softened, 7 minutes. Add the wine and cook, uncovered, for 5 minutes. Stir in the potatoes, bell pepper, and broth and bring to a boil. Reduce the heat to medium and simmer for 15 minutes.

2. Add the zucchini, yellow squash, and tomatoes. Season with salt and black pepper to taste, cover, and simmer until the vegetables are tender, 20 to

30 minutes. Stir in the corn, peas, basil, parsley, and savory. Taste, adjusting seasonings if necessary. Simmer to blend flavors, about 10 minutes more. Serve immediately.

110.Moroccan Vermicelli Vegetable Soup

Preparation time: 5 minutes
Cooking time: 35 minutes
Servings: 4 to 6

Ingredients:

- 1 tablespoon olive oil

- 1 small onion, chopped

- 1 large carrot, chopped

- 1 celery rib, chopped

- 3 small zucchini, cut into 1/4-inch dice

- 1 (28-ounce) can diced tomatoes, drained

- 2 tablespoons tomato paste

- 11/2 cups cooked or 1 (15.5-ounce) can chickpeas, drained and rinsed

- 2 teaspoons smoked paprika

- 1 teaspoon ground cumin

- 1 teaspoon za'atar spice (optional)

- 1/4 teaspoon ground cayenne

- 6 cups vegetable broth, homemade (see light vegetable broth) or store-bought, or water

- Salt

- 4 ounces vermicelli

- 2 tablespoons minced fresh cilantro, for garnish

Directions:

1. In a large soup pot, heat the oil over medium heat. Add the onion, carrot, and celery. Cover and cook until softened, about 5 minutes. Stir in the zucchini, tomatoes, tomato paste, chickpeas, paprika, cumin, za'atar, and cayenne. Add the broth and salt to taste. Bring to a boil, then reduce heat to low and simmer, uncovered, until the vegetables are tender, about 30 minutes.

2. Shortly before serving, stir in the vermicelli and cook until the noodles are tender, about 5 minutes. Ladle the soup into bowls, garnish with cilantro, and serve.

111.Moroccan Vegetable Stew

Preparation time: 5 minutes
Cooking time: 35 minutes
Servings: 4

Ingredients:

- 1 tablespoon olive oil
- 2 medium yellow onions, chopped
- 2 medium carrots, cut into 1/2-inch dice
- 1/2 teaspoon ground cumin
- 1/2 teaspoon ground cinnamon or allspice
- 1/2 teaspoon ground ginger
- 1/2 teaspoon sweet or smoked paprika
- 1/2 teaspoon saffron or turmeric
- 1 (14.5-ounce) can diced tomatoes, undrained
- 8 ounces green beans, trimmed and cut into 1-inch pieces
- 2 cups peeled, seeded, and diced winter squash
- 1 large russet or other baking potato, peeled and cut into 1/2-inch dice
- 11/2 cups vegetable broth
- 11/2 cups cooked or 1 (15.5-ounce) can chickpeas, drained and rinsed
- ¾ cup frozen peas
- 1/2 cup pitted dried plums (prunes)
- 1 teaspoon lemon zest
- Salt and freshly ground black pepper
- 1/2 cup pitted green olives
- 1 tablespoon minced fresh cilantro or parsley, for garnish
- 1/2 cup toasted slivered almonds, for garnish

Directions:

1. In a large saucepan, heat the oil over medium heat. Add the onions and carrots, cover, and cook for 5 minutes. Stir in the cumin, cinnamon, ginger, paprika, and saffron. Cook, uncovered, stirring, for 30 seconds. Add the tomatoes, green beans, squash, potato, and broth and bring to a boil. Reduce heat to low, cover, and simmer until the vegetables are tender, about 20 minutes.

2. Add the chickpeas, peas, dried plums, and lemon zest. Season with salt and pepper to taste. Stir in the olives and simmer, uncovered, until the flavors are blended, about 10 minutes. Sprinkle with cilantro and almonds and serve immediately.

112. Basic Recipe for Vegetable Broth

Preparation Time: 10 Minutes
Cooking Time: 60 Minutes
Servings: Makes 2 Quarts

Ingredients:

- 8 cups Water
- 1 Onion, chopped
- 4 Garlic cloves, crushed
- 2 Celery Stalks, chopped
- Pinch of Salt
- 1 Carrot, chopped
- Dash of Pepper
- 1 Potato, medium & chopped
- 1 tbsp. Soy Sauce
- 3 Bay Leaves

Directions:

1. To make the vegetable broth, you need to place all of the ingredients in a deep saucepan.

2. Heat the pan over a medium-high heat. Bring the vegetable mixture to a boil.

3. Once it starts boiling, lower the heat to medium-low and allow it to simmer for at least an hour or so. Cover it with a lid.

4. When the time is up, pass it through a filter and strain the vegetables, garlic, and bay leaves.

5. Allow the stock to cool completely and store in an air-tight container.

113.Cucumber Dill Gazpacho

Preparation Time: 10 Minutes
Cooking Time: 2 hours
Serving Size: 4

Ingredients:

- 4 large cucumbers, peeled, deseeded, and chopped
- 1/8 tsp salt
- 1 tsp chopped fresh dill + more for

garnishing

- 2 tbsp freshly squeezed lemon juice
- 1 ½ cups green grape, seeds removed
- 3 tbsp extra virgin olive oil
- 1 garlic clove, minced

Directions:

1. Add all the ingredients to a food processor and blend until smooth.

2. Pour the soup into serving bowls and chill for 1 to 2 hours.

3. Garnish with dill and serve chilled.

114.Red Lentil Soup

Preparation Time: 5 Minutes
Cooking Time: 25 Minutes
Servings: Makes 6 cups

Ingredients:

- 2 tbsp. Nutritional Yeast
- 1 cup Red Lentil, washed
- ½ tbsp. Garlic, minced
- 4 cups Vegetable Stock
- 1 tsp. Salt
- 2 cups Kale, shredded
- 3 cups Mixed Vegetables

Directions:

1. To start with, place all ingredients needed to make the soup in a large

pot.

2. Heat the pot over medium-high heat and bring the mixture to a boil.

3. Once it starts boiling, lower the heat to low. Allow the soup to simmer.

4. Simmer it for 1o to 15 minutes or until cooked.

5. Serve and enjoy.

115.Spinach and Kale Soup

Preparation Time: 5 Minutes
Cooking Time: 5 Minutes
Serving: 2

Ingredients:

- 3 oz. vegan butter
- 1 cup fresh spinach, chopped coarsely
- 1 cup fresh kale, chopped coarsely
- 1 large avocado
- 3 tbsp chopped fresh mint leaves
- 3 ½ cups coconut cream
- 1 cup vegetable broth
- Salt and black pepper to taste
- 1 lime, juiced

Directions:

1. Melt the vegan butter in a medium pot over medium heat and sauté the kale and spinach until wilted, 3 minutes. Turn the heat off.

2. Stir in the remaining ingredients and using an immersion blender, puree

the soup until smooth.

3. Dish the soup and serve warm.

116.Coconut and Grilled Vegetable Soup

Preparation Time: 10 Minutes
Cooking Time: 45 Minutes
Serving: 4

Ingredients:

- 2 small red onions cut into wedges
- 2 garlic cloves
- 10 oz. butternut squash, peeled and chopped
- 10 oz. pumpkins, peeled and chopped
- 4 tbsp melted vegan butter
- Salt and black pepper to taste
- 1 cup of water
- 1 cup unsweetened coconut milk
- 1 lime juiced
- ¾ cup vegan mayonnaise
- Toasted pumpkin seeds for garnishing

Directions:

1. Preheat the oven to 400 F.

2. On a baking sheet, spread the onions, garlic, butternut squash, and pumpkins and drizzle half of the butter on top. Season with salt, black

pepper, and rub the seasoning well onto the vegetables. Roast in the oven for 45 minutes or until the vegetables are golden brown and softened.

3. Transfer the vegetables to a pot; add the remaining ingredients except for the pumpkin seeds and using an immersion blender puree the ingredients until smooth.

4. Dish the soup, garnish with the pumpkin seeds and serve warm.

117. Celery Dill Soup

Preparation Time: 5 Minutes
Cooking Time: 25 Minutes
Serving: 4

Ingredients:

- 2 tbsp coconut oil
- ½ lb celery root, trimmed
- 1 garlic clove
- 1 medium white onion
- ¼ cup fresh dill, roughly chopped
- 1 tsp cumin powder
- ¼ tsp nutmeg powder
- 1 small head cauliflower, cut into florets
- 3½ cups seasoned vegetable stock
- 5 oz. vegan butter

- Juice from 1 lemon
- ¼ cup coconut cream
- Salt and black pepper to taste

Directions:

1. Melt the coconut oil in a large pot and sauté the celery root, garlic, and onion until softened and fragrant, 5 minutes.

2. Stir in the dill, cumin, and nutmeg, and stir-fry for 1 minute. Mix in the cauliflower and vegetable stock. Allow the soup to boil for 15 minutes and turn the heat off.

3. Add the vegan butter and lemon juice, and puree the soup using an immersion blender.

4. Stir in the coconut cream, salt, black pepper, and dish the soup.

5. Serve warm.

118. Broccoli Fennel Soup

Preparation Time: 15 Minutes
Cooking Time: 10 Minutes
Serving: 4

Ingredients:

- 1 fennel bulb, white and green parts coarsely chopped
- 10 oz. broccoli, cut into florets
- 3 cups vegetable stock
- Salt and freshly ground black pepper

- 1 garlic clove
- 1 cup dairy-free cream cheese
- 3 oz. vegan butter
- ½ cup chopped fresh oregano

Directions:

1. In a medium pot, combine the fennel, broccoli, vegetable stock, salt, and black pepper. Bring to a boil until the vegetables soften, 10 to 15 minutes.

2. Stir in the remaining ingredients and simmer the soup for 3 to 5 minutes.

3. Adjust the taste with salt and black pepper, and dish the soup.

4. Serve warm.

119. Tofu Goulash Soup

Preparation Time: 35 Minutes
Cooking Time: 20 Minutes
Serving: 4

Ingredients:

- 4¼ oz. vegan butter
- 1 white onion, chopped
- 2 garlic cloves, minced
- 1 ½ cups butternut squash
- 1 red bell pepper, deseeded and chopped
- 1 tbsp paprika powder
- ¼ tsp red chili flakes

- 1 tbsp dried basil
- ½ tbsp crushed cardamom seeds
- Salt and black pepper to taste
- 1 ½ cups crushed tomatoes
- 3 cups vegetable broth
- 1½ tsp red wine vinegar
- Chopped parsley to serve

Directions:

1. Place the tofu between two paper towels and allow draining of water for 30 minutes. After, crumble the tofu and set aside.

2. Melt the vegan butter in a large pot over medium heat and sauté the onion and garlic until the veggies are fragrant and soft, 3 minutes.

3. Stir in the tofu and cook until golden brown, 3 minutes.

4. Add the butternut squash, bell pepper, paprika, red chili flakes, basil, cardamom seeds, salt, and black pepper. Cook for 2 minutes to release some flavor and mix in the tomatoes and 2 cups of vegetable broth.

5. Close the lid, bring the soup to a boil, and then simmer for 10 minutes.

6. Stir in the remaining vegetable broth, the red wine vinegar, and adjust the taste with salt and black pepper.

7. Dish the soup, garnish with the parsley and serve warm.

120. Pesto Pea Soup

Preparation Time: 10 Minutes
Cooking Time: 20 Minutes
Serving: 4

Ingredients:

- 2 cups Water

- 8 oz. Tortellini
- ¼ cup Pesto
- 1 Onion, small & finely chopped
- 1 lb. Peas, frozen
- 1 Carrot, medium & finely chopped
- 1 ¾ cup Vegetable Broth, less sodium
- 1 Celery Rib, medium & finely chopped

Directions:

1. To start with, boil the water in a large pot over a medium-high heat.

2. Next, stir in the tortellini to the pot and cook it following the instructions given in the packet.

3. In the meantime, cook the onion, celery, and carrot in a deep saucepan along with the water and broth.

4. Cook the celery-onion mixture for 6 minutes or until softened.

5. Now, spoon in the peas and allow it to simmer while keeping it uncovered.

6. Cook the peas for few minutes or until they are bright green and soft.

7. Then, spoon in the pesto to the peas mixture. Combine well.

8. Pour the mixture into a high-speed blender and blend for 2 to 3 minutes or until you get a rich, smooth soup.

9. Return the soup to the pan. Spoon in the cooked tortellini.

10. Finally, pour into a serving bowl and top with more cooked peas if desired.

11. Tip: If desired, you can season it with Maldon salt at the end.

121. Tofu and Mushroom Soup

Preparation Time: 15 Minutes
Cooking Time: 10 Minutes
Serving: 4

Ingredients:

- 2 tbsp olive oil
- 1 garlic clove, minced
- 1 large yellow onion, finely chopped
- 1 tsp freshly grated ginger
- 1 cup vegetable stock
- 2 small potatoes, peeled and chopped
- ¼ tsp salt
- ¼ tsp black pepper
- 2 (14 oz) silken tofu, drained and rinsed
- 2/3 cup baby Bella mushrooms, sliced
- 1 tbsp chopped fresh oregano
- 2 tbsp chopped fresh parsley to garnish

Directions:

1. Heat the olive oil in a medium pot over medium heat and sauté the garlic, onion, and ginger until soft and

fragrant.

2. Pour in the vegetable stock, potatoes, salt, and black pepper. Cook until the potatoes soften, 12 minutes.

3. Stir in the tofu and using an immersion blender, puree the ingredients until smooth.

4. Mix in the mushrooms and simmer with the pot covered until the mushrooms warm up while occasionally stirring to ensure that the tofu doesn't curdle, 7 minutes.

5. Stir oregano, and dish the soup.

6. Garnish with the parsley and serve warm.

122.Avocado Green Soup

Preparation Time: 5 Minutes
Cooking Time: 5 Minutes
Serving: 4

Ingredients:

- 2 tbsp olive oil
- 1 ½ cup fresh kale, chopped coarsely
- 1 ½ cup fresh spinach, chopped coarsely
- 3 large avocados, halved, pitted and pulp extracted

- 2 cups of soy milk
- 2 cups no-sodium vegetable broth
- 3 tbsp chopped fresh mint leaves
- ¼ tsp salt
- ¼ tsp black pepper
- 2 limes, juiced

Directions:

1. Heat the olive oil in a medium saucepan over medium heat and mix in the kale and spinach. Cook until wilted, 3 minutes and turn off the heat.

2. Add the remaining ingredients and using an immersion blender, puree the soup until smooth.

3. Dish the soup and serve immediately.

123.Black Bean Nacho Soup

Preparation Time: 5 Minutes
Cooking Time: 30 Minutes
Serving: 4

Ingredients:

- 30 oz. Black Bean
- 1 tbsp. Olive Oil
- 2 cups Vegetable Stock
- ½ of 1 Onion, large & chopped
- 2 ½ cups Water

- 3 Garlic cloves, minced
- 14 oz. Mild Green Chillies, diced
- 1 tsp. Cumin
- 1 cup Salsa
- ½ tsp. Salt
- 16 oz. Tomato Paste
- ½ tsp. Black Pepper

Directions:

1. For making this delicious fare, heat oil in a large pot over medium-high heat.

2. Once the oil becomes hot, stir in onion and garlic to it.

3. Sauté for 4 minutes or until the onion is softened.

4. Next, spoon in chilli powder, salt, cumin, and pepper to the pot. Mix well.

5. Then, stir in tomato paste, salsa, water, green chillies, and vegetable stock to onion mixture. Combine.

6. Bing the mixture to a boil. Allow the veggies to simmer.

7. When the mixture starts simmering, add the beans.

8. Bring the veggie mixture to a simmer again and lower the heat to low.

9. Finally, cook for 15 to 20 minutes and check for seasoning. Add more salt and pepper if needed.

10. Garnish with the topping of your choice. Serve it hot.

124.Potato Leek Soup

Preparation Time: 5 Minutes
Cooking Time: 5 Minutes
Serving: 4

Ingredients:

- 1 cup fresh cilantro leaves
- 6 garlic cloves, peeled
- 3 tbsp vegetable oil
- 3 leeks, white and green parts chopped
- 2 lb russet potatoes, peeled and chopped
- 1 tsp cumin powder
- ¼ tsp salt
- ¼ tsp black pepper
- 2 bay leaves
- 6 cups no-sodium vegetable broth

Directions:

1. In a spice blender, process the cilantro and garlic until smooth paste forms.

2. Heat the vegetable oil in a large pot and sauté the garlic mixture and leeks until the leeks are tender, 5 minutes.

3. Mix in the remaining ingredients and

allow boiling until the potatoes soften, 15 minutes.

4. Turn the heat off, open the lid, remove and discard the bay leaves.

5. Using an immersion blender, puree the soup until smooth.

6. Dish the food and serve warm.

125.Lentil Soup

Preparation Time: 15 Minutes
Cooking Time: 25 Minutes
Serving: 4

Ingredients:

- 1 tbsp. Olive Oil
- 4 cups Vegetable Stock
- 1 Onion, finely chopped
- 2 Carrots, medium
- 1 cup Lentils, dried
- 1 tsp. Cumin

Directions:

1. To make this healthy soup, first, you need to heat the oil in a medium-sized skillet over medium heat.

2. Once the oil becomes hot, stir in the cumin and then the onions.

3. Sauté them for 3 minutes or until the onion is slightly transparent and

cooked.

4. To this, add the carrots and toss them well.

5. Next, stir in the lentils. Mix well.

6. Now, pour in the vegetable stock and give a good stir until everything comes together.

7. As the soup mixture starts to boil, reduce the heat and allow it to simmer for 10 minutes while keeping the pan covered.

8. Turn off the heat and then transfer the mixture to a bowl.

9. Finally, blend it with an immersion blender or in a high-speed blender for 1 minute or until you get a rich, smooth mixture.

10. Serve it hot and enjoy.

126.Kale White Bean Soup

Preparation Time: 10 Minutes
Cooking Time: 45 Minutes
Serving: 4

Ingredients:

- 1 Onion, medium & finely sliced
- 3 cups Kale, coarsely chopped
- 2 tsp. Olive Oil
- 15 oz. White Beans

- 4 cups Vegetable Broth
- 4 Garlic Cloves, minced
- Sea Salt & Pepper, as needed
- 2 tsp. Rosemary, fresh & chopped
- 1 lb. White Potatoes, cubed

Directions:

1. Begin by taking a large saucepan and heat it over a medium-high heat.

2. Once the pan becomes hot, spoon in the oil.

3. Next, stir in the onion and sauté for 8 to 9 minutes or until the onions are cooked and lightly browned.

4. Then, add the garlic and rosemary to the pan.

5. Sauté for a further minute or until aromatic.

6. Now, pour in the broth along with the potatoes, black pepper, and salt. Mix well.

7. Bring the mixture to a boil, and when it starts boiling, lower the heat.

8. Allow it to simmer for 32 to 35 minutes or until the potatoes are cooked and tender.

9. After that, mash the potatoes slightly by using the back of the spoon.

10. Finally, add the kale and beans to the soup and cook for 8 minutes or until the kale is wilted.

11. Check the seasoning. Add more salt and pepper if needed.

12. Serve hot.

127. Black Bean Mushroom Soup

Preparation Time: 10 Minutes
Cooking Time: 40 Minutes
Serving: 2

Ingredients:

- 2 tbsp. Olive Oil
- 1 clove of Garlic, peeled & minced
- ½ cup Vegetable Stock
- 1 tsp. Thyme, dried
- 15 oz. Black Beans
- 1 2/3 cup Water, hot
  - o   oz. Mushrooms
- 1 Onion, finely chopped
- 4 Sourdough Bread Slices
- Vegan Butter, to serve

Directions:

1. To begin with, spoon the oil into a medium-sized deep saucepan over a medium heat.

2. Once the oil becomes hot, stir in the onion and garlic.

3. Sauté for 5 minutes or until the onion is translucent.

4. Next, spoon in the mushrooms and

thyme. Mix well.

5. Cook for another 5 minutes or until dark brown.

6. Then, pour the water into the mixture along with the stock and beans.

7. Allow it to simmer for 20 minutes or until the mushroom is soft.

8. Pour the mixture to a high-speed blender and pulse for 1 to 2 minutes until it is smooth yet grainy.

9. Serve and enjoy.

128.Broccoli Soup

Preparation Time: 5 Minutes
Cooking Time: 15 Minutes
Serving: 2

Ingredients:

- 3 cup Vegetable Broth
- 2 Green Chili
- 2 cups Broccoli Florets
- 1 tbsp. Chia Seeds
- 1 cup Spinach
- 1 tsp. Oil
- 4 Celery Stalk
- 1 Potato, medium & cubed
- 4 Garlic cloves
- Salt, as needed
- Juice of ½ of 1 Lemon

Directions:

1. First, heat the oil in a large sauté pan over a medium-high heat.

2. Once the oil becomes hot, add the potatoes to it.

3. When the potatoes become soft, stir all the remaining ingredients into the pan, excluding the spinach, chia seeds, and lemon.

4. Cook until the broccoli is soft, and then add the spinach and chia seed to the pan.

5. Turn off the heat after cooking for 2 minutes.

6. Allow the spinach mixture to cool slightly. Pour the mixture into a high-speed blender and blend for two minutes or until smooth.

7. Pour the lemon juice over the soup. Stir and serve immediately.

8. Enjoy.

129.Squash Lentil Soup

Preparation Time: 10 Minutes
Cooking Time: 35 Minutes
Serving: 4

Ingredients:

- 7 cups Vegetable Broth
- 2 tbsp. Olive Oil
- 2 tsp, Sage dried
- 1 Yellow Onion, medium & diced.
- Salt & Pepper t0 taste
- 1 Butternut Squash
- 1 ½ cup Red Lentils

Directions:

1. Start by heating the oil in a large saucepan, and stir in the onions.

2. Sauté the onions for to 2 to 3 minutes or until softened.

3. Once cooked, stir in squash and sage while stirring continuously.

4. Then, spoon in the lentils, salt, and pepper.

5. Bring the lentil mixture to a boil for about 30 minutes. Lower the heat.

6. Then, allow the soup to cool down until the lentils are soft.

7. Finally, transfer the mixture to a high-speed blender and blend for 3 to 4 minutes or until smooth.

8. Serve hot.

130.Mexican Soup

Preparation Time: 10 Minutes
Cooking Time: 45 Minutes
Serving: 6

Ingredients:

- 2 tbsp. Extra Virgin Olive Oil
- 8 oz. can of Diced Tomatoes & Chilies
- 1 Yellow Onion, diced
- 2 cups Green Lentils
- ½ tsp. Salt
- 2 Celery Stalks, diced
- 8 cups Vegetable Broth
- 2 Carrots, peeled & diced
- 2 cups Diced Tomatoes & Juices
- 3 Garlic cloves, minced
- 1 Red Bell Pepper, diced
- 1 tsp. Oregano
- 1 tbsp. Cumin
- ¼ tsp. Smoked Paprika
- 1 Avocado, pitted & diced

Directions:

1. Heat oil in a large-sized pot over a medium heat.

2. Once the oil becomes hot, stir in the onion, bell pepper, carrot, and celery into the pot.

3. Cook the onion mixture for 5 minutes or until the veggies are soft.

4. Then, spoon in garlic, oregano, cumin, and paprika into it and sauté for one minute or until aromatic.

5. Next, add the tomatoes, salt, chilies, broth, and lentils to the mixture.

6. Now, bring the tomato-chili mixture to a boil and allow it to simmer for 32 to 40 minutes or until the lentils become soft.

7. Check the seasoning and add more if needed.

8. Serve along with avocado and hot sauce.

131.Celery Dill Soup

Preparation Time: 10 Minutes
Cooking Time: 20 Minutes
Serving: 4

Ingredients:

- 2 tbsp coconut oil
- ½ lb celery root, trimmed
- 1 garlic clove
- 1 medium white onion
- ¼ cup fresh dill, roughly chopped
- 1 tsp cumin powder
- ¼ tsp nutmeg powder
- 1 small head cauliflower, cut into florets
- 3½ cups seasoned vegetable stock
- 5 oz. vegan butter
- Juice from 1 lemon
- ¼ cup coconut cream
- Salt and black pepper to taste

Directions:

1. Melt the coconut oil in a large pot and sauté the celery root, garlic, and onion until softened and fragrant, 5 minutes.
2. Stir in the dill, cumin, and nutmeg, and stir-fry for 1 minute. Mix in the cauliflower and vegetable stock. Allow the soup to boil for 15 minutes and

turn the heat off.
3. Add the vegan butter and lemon juice, and puree the soup using an immersion blender.
4. Stir in the coconut cream, salt, black pepper, and dish the soup.
5. Serve warm.

132. Medley of Mushroom Soup

Preparation Time: 10 Minutes
Cooking Time: 20 Minutes
Serving: 4

Ingredients:

- 4 oz. unsalted vegan butter
- 1 small onion, finely chopped
- 1 garlic clove, minced
- 2 cups sliced mixed mushrooms
- ½ lb celery root, chopped
- ½ tsp dried rosemary
- 3 cups of water
- 1 vegan stock cube, crushed
- 1 tbsp plain vinegar
- 1 cup coconut cream
- 6 leaves basil, chopped

Directions:

1. Melt the vegan butter in a medium pot and sauté the onion, garlic, mushrooms, celery, and rosemary until the vegetables soften, 5 minutes.
2. Stir in the water, stock cube, and vinegar. Cover the pot, allow boiling, and then, simmer for 10 minutes.
3. Mix in the coconut cream and puree the ingredients using an immersion blender until smooth. Simmer for 2 minutes.
4. Dish the soup and serve warm.

PASTA & NOODLES

133.Coconut Curry Noodle

Preparation time: 10 minutes
Cooking time: 30 minutes
Servings: 4

Ingredients

- ½ tablespoon oil
- 3 garlic cloves, minced
- 2 tablespoons lemongrass, minced
- 1 tablespoon fresh ginger, grated
- 2 tablespoons red curry paste
- 1 (14 oz) can coconut milk
- 1 tablespoon brown sugar
- 2 tablespoons soy sauce
- 2 tablespoons fresh lime juice
- 1 tablespoon hot chili paste
- 12 oz linguine
- 2 cups broccoli florets
- 1 cup carrots, shredded
- 1 cup edamame, shelled
- 1 red bell pepper, sliced

Directions:

1. Fill a suitably-sized pot with salted water and boil it on high heat.

2. Add pasta to the boiling water and cook until it is al dente then rinse under cold water.

3. Now place a medium-sized saucepan over medium heat and add oil.

4. Stir in ginger, garlic, and lemongrass, then sauté for 30 seconds.

5. Add coconut milk, soy sauce, curry paste, brown sugar, chili paste, and lime juice.

6. Stir this curry mixture for 10 minutes, or until it thickens.

7. Toss in carrots, broccoli, edamame, bell pepper, and cooked pasta.

8. Mix well, then serve warm.

134.Collard Green Pasta

Preparation time: 10 minutes
Cooking time: 20 minutes
Servings: 4

Ingredients

- 2 tablespoons olive oil
- 4 garlic cloves, minced
- 8 oz whole wheat pasta
- ½ cup panko bread crumbs
- 1 tablespoon nutritional yeast
- 1 teaspoon red pepper flakes
- 1 large bunch collard greens

- 1 large lemon, zest and juiced

Directions:

1. Fill a suitable pot with salted water and boil it on high heat.
2. Add pasta to the boiling water and cook until it is al dente, then rinse under cold water.
3. Reserve ½ cup of the cooking liquid from the pasta.
4. Place a non-stick pan over medium heat and add 1 tablespoon olive oil.
5. Stir in half of the garlic, then sauté for 30 seconds.
6. Add breadcrumbs and sauté for approximately 5 minutes.
7. Toss in red pepper flakes and nutritional yeast then mix well.
8. Transfer the breadcrumbs mixture to a plate and clean the pan.
9. Add the remaining tablespoon oil to the nonstick pan.
10. Stir in the garlic clove, salt, black pepper, and chard leaves.
11. Cook for 5 minutes until the leaves are wilted.
12. Add pasta along with the reserved pasta liquid.
13. Mix well, then add garlic crumbs, lemon juice, and zest.
14. Toss well, then serve warm.

135. Jalapeno Rice Noodles

Preparation time: 10 minutes
Cooking time: 25 minutes
Servings: 4

Ingredients

- ¼ cup soy sauce
- 1 tablespoon brown sugar
- 2 teaspoons sriracha
- 3 tablespoons lime juice
- 8 oz rice noodles
- 3 teaspoons toasted sesame oil
- 1 package extra-firm tofu, pressed
- 1 onion, sliced
- 2 cups green cabbage, shredded
- 1 small jalapeno, minced
- 1 red bell pepper, sliced
- 1 yellow bell pepper, sliced
- 3 garlic cloves, minced
- 3 scallions, sliced
- 1 cup Thai basil leaves, roughly chopped
- Lime wedges for serving

Directions:

1. Fill a suitably-sized pot with salted water and boil it on high heat.
2. Add pasta to the boiling water and cook until it is al dente, then rinse under cold water.

3. Put lime juice, soy sauce, sriracha, and brown sugar in a bowl then mix well.

4. Place a large wok over medium heat then add 1 teaspoon sesame oil.

5. Toss in tofu and stir for 5 minutes until golden-brown.

6. Transfer the golden-brown tofu to a plate and add 2 teaspoons oil to the wok.

7. Stir in scallions, garlic, peppers, cabbage, and onion.

8. Sauté for 2 minutes, then add cooked noodles and prepared sauce.

9. Cook for 2 minutes, then garnish with lime wedges and basil leaves.

10. Serve fresh.

136.Rainbow Soba Noodles

Preparation time: 10 minutes
Cooking time: 20 minutes
Servings: 4

Ingredients

- 8 oz tofu, pressed and crumbled
- 1 teaspoon olive oil
- ½ teaspoon red pepper flakes
- 10 oz package buckwheat soba noodles, cooked
- 1 package broccoli slaw
- 2 cups cabbage, shredded

- ¼ cup very red onion, thinly sliced
- Peanut Sauce
- ¼ cup peanut butter
- ¾ cup hot water
- 2 tablespoons apple cider vinegar
- 1 tablespoon maple syrup
- 1–2 garlic cloves, minced
- 1 lime, zest, and juice
- Salt and crushed red pepper flakes, to taste
- Cilantro, for garnish
- Crushed peanuts, for garnish

Directions:

1. Crumble tofu on a baking sheet and toss in 1 teaspoon oil and 1 teaspoon red pepper flakes.

2. Bake the tofu for 20 minutes at 400ºF in a preheated oven.

3. Meanwhile, whisk peanut butter with hot water, garlic cloves, maple syrup, cider vinegar, lime zest, salt, lime juice, and pepper flakes in a large bowl.

4. Toss in cooked noodles, broccoli slaw, cabbages, and onion.

5. Mix well, then stir in tofu, cilantro, and peanuts.

6. Enjoy.

137.Spicy Pad Thai Pasta

Preparation time: 10 minutes
Cooking time: 10 minutes
Servings: 4

Ingredients

- Spicy Tofu
- 1 lb extra-firm tofu, sliced
- 1 tablespoon peanut butter
- 3 tablespoons soy sauce
- 2 tablespoons Sriracha
- 2 tablespoons rice vinegar
- 2 teaspoons sesame oil
- 2 teaspoons ginger, grated
- Pad Thai
- 8 oz brown rice noodles
- 2 teaspoons coconut oil
- 1 red pepper, sliced
- ½ white onion, sliced
- 2 carrots, sliced
- 1 Thai chili, chopped
- ½ cup peanuts, chopped
- ½ cup cilantro, chopped
- Spicy Pad Thai Sauce
- 3 tablespoons soy sauce
- 3 tablespoons fresh lime juice
- 1 tablespoon Sriracha
- 3 tablespoons brown sugar
- 3 tablespoons vegetable broth
- 1 teaspoon garlic-chili paste
- 2 garlic cloves, minced

Directions:

1. Fill a suitably-sized pot with water and soak rice noodles in it.
2. Press the tofu to squeeze excess liquid out of it.
3. Place a non-stick pan over medium-high heat and add tofu.
4. Sear the tofu for 2-3 minutes per side until brown.
5. Whisk all the ingredients for tofu crumbles in a large bowl.
6. Stir in tofu and mix well.
7. Separately mix the pad Thai sauce in a bowl and add to the tofu.
8. Place a wok over medium heat and add 1 teaspoon oil.
9. Toss in chili, carrots, onion, and red pepper, then sauté for 3 minutes.
10. Transfer the veggies to the tofu bowl.
11. Add more oil to the same pan and stir in drained noodles, then stir cook for 1 minute.
12. Transfer the noodles to the tofu and toss it all well.
13. Add cilantro and peanuts.
14. Serve fresh.

138.Spinach Pasta

Preparation time: 10 minutes
Cooking time: 12 minutes
Servings: 4

Ingredients

- 2 tablespoons olive oil
- 3 shallots, chopped
- 2 garlic cloves, minced
- ¼ teaspoon red pepper flakes
- 8 oz spinach leaves
- 8 oz linguine
- ¼ cup vegan parmesan cheese

Directions:

1. Fill a suitably-sized pot with salted water and bring it to a boil on high heat.
2. Add pasta to the boiling water then cook until it is al dente, then rinse under cold water.
3. Place a suitably-sized pan over medium heat and add oil.
4. Toss in shallots then sauté for 5 minutes.
5. Stir in red pepper flakes, salt, black pepper, garlic, and spinach.
6. Cook for 1 minute then add the drained pasta to the pan.
7. Toss well then garnish with parmesan cheese.
8. Serve warm.

139.Linguine with Wine Sauce

Preparation time: 10 minutes
Cooking time: 18 minutes
Servings: 4

Ingredients

- 1 tablespoon olive oil
- 5 garlic cloves, minced
- 16 oz shiitake, chopped
- ¼ teaspoon salt
- ¼ teaspoon ground pepper
- 1 pinch red pepper flakes
- ½ cup dry white wine
- 12 oz linguine
- 2 teaspoons vegan butter
- ¼ cup Italian parsley, finely chopped

Directions:

1. Fill a suitably-sized pot with salted water and bring it to a boil on high heat.
2. Add pasta to the boiling water then cook until it is al dente, then rinse under cold water.
3. Place a non-stick skillet over medium-high heat then add olive oil.
4. Stir in garlic and sauté for 1 minute.
5. Stir in mushrooms and cook for 10 minutes.
6. Add salt, red pepper flakes, and black

pepper for seasoning.

7. Toss in the cooked pasta and mix well.

8. Garnish with parsley and butter.

9. Enjoy.

140. Cheesy Macaroni with Broccoli

Preparation time: 10 minutes
Cooking time: 25 minutes
Servings: 6

Ingredients

- 1/3 cup melted coconut oil
- ¼ cup nutritional yeast
- 1 tablespoon tomato paste
- 1 tablespoon dried mustard
- 2 garlic cloves, minced
- 1 ½ teaspoons salt
- ½ teaspoon ground turmeric
- 4 ½ cups almond milk
- 3 cups cauliflower florets, chopped
- 1 cup raw cashews, chopped
- 1 lb shell pasta
- 1 tablespoon white vinegar
- 3 cups broccoli florets

Directions:

1. Place a suitably-sized saucepan over medium heat and add coconut oil.

2. Stir in mustard, yeast, garlic, salt, tomato paste, and turmeric.

3. Cook for 1 minute then add almond milk, cashews, and cauliflower florets.

4. Continue cooking for 20 minutes on a simmer.

5. Transfer the cauliflower mixture to a blender jug then blend until smooth.

6. Stir in vinegar and blend until creamy.

7. Fill a suitably-sized pot with salted water and bring it to a boil on high heat.

8. Add pasta to the boiling water.

9. Place a steamer basket over the boiling water and add broccoli to the basket.

10. Cook until the pasta is al dente. Drain and rinse the pasta and transfer the broccoli to a bowl.

11. Add the cooked pasta to the cauliflower-cashews sauce.

12. Toss in broccoli florets, salt, and black pepper.

13. Mix well then serve.

141. Soba Noodles with Tofu

Preparation time: 10 minutes
Cooking time: 38 minutes
Servings: 4

Ingredients

- Marinated Tofu

- 2 tablespoons olive oil
- 8 oz firm tofu, pressed and drained
- ¼ cup cilantro, finely chopped
- ¼ cup mint, finely chopped
- 1-inch fresh ginger, grated
- Soba Noodles
- 8 oz soba noodles
- ¾ cup edamame
- 2 cucumbers, peeled and julienned
- 1 large carrot, peeled and julienned
- 2 tablespoons black sesame seeds
- 2 tablespoons white sesame seeds
- 2 scallions, chopped
- Ginger-Soy Sauce
- 2 tablespoons fresh lime juice
- 2 tablespoons soy sauce
- 1 tablespoon brown sugar
- 1 tablespoon fresh ginger, grated
- 2 tablespoons sesame oil
- ½ tablespoon garlic chili sauce

Directions:

1. Blend herbs, ginger, salt, black pepper, and olive oil in a blender.
2. Add the spice mixture to the tofu and toss it well to coat.
3. Allow the tofu to marinate for 30 minutes at room temperature.
4. Fill a suitably-sized pot with salted water and bring it to a boil on high heat.
5. Add pasta to the boiling water then cook until it is al dente, then rinse under cold water.
6. Place a large wok over medium heat and add marinated tofu.

7. Sauté for 5–8 minutes until golden-brown, then transfer to a large bowl.
8. Add veggies to the same wok and stir until veggies are soft.
9. Transfer the veggies to the tofu and add cooked noodles.
10. Toss well, then serve warm.
11. Enjoy.

142. Pasta with Roasted Red Pepper Sauce

Preparation time: 10 minutes
Cooking time: 12 minutes
Servings: 4

Ingredients

- ¾ cup soy milk
- 1 tablespoon olive oil
- ¾ teaspoon salt
- 1 (12 oz) jar roasted red pepper
- 4 garlic cloves, chopped
- 2 tablespoons tahini
- 2 tablespoons nutritional yeast
- ½ teaspoon red pepper flakes
- 12 oz penne pasta

Directions:

1. Fill a suitably-sized pot with salted water and bring it to a boil on high heat.

2. Add pasta to the boiling water and cook until it is al-dente, then rinse under cold water.

3. Add drained roasted red peppers, garlic, salt, olive oil, soy milk, tahini, nutritional yeast, and red pepper flakes to a blender then puree until smooth.

4. Add the pepper puree to a pan along with salt and black pepper.

5. Cook the puree for 5 minutes on a simmer.

6. Add cooked pasta to the sauce and mix well.

7. Serve warm.

143.Pasta with White Beans and Olives

Preparation time: 20 minutes
Cooking time: 10 minutes
Servings: 2

Ingredients:

- Basil, fresh, ground, one quarter cup
- Black olives, two tablespoons chop
- Black pepper, one half teaspoon
- Cannellini beans, one fifteen ounce can, drain and rinse
- Garlic, minced, one tablespoon
- Olive oil, one tablespoon
- Romano cheese, fresh, grated, two tablespoons
- Tomatoes, two medium-sized diced
- Ziti or rigatoni, whole wheat, four ounces

Directions:

1. Follow the instructions on the packaging to cook the quinoa. Cook the beans and garlic in hot oil for five

minutes. Remove the pan from the heat. Add to the beans and garlic the basil, olives, pepper, and tomatoes and mix well. Place the cooked pasta on two plates divided evenly and tops the pasta with the tomato and bean mix, then sprinkle on the cheese and serve.

144.Plant Based Keto Lo Mein

Preparation Time: 10 minutes
Cooking Time: 10 minutes
Servings: 2

Ingredients:

- 2 tablespoons carrots, shredded
- 1 package kelp noodles, soaked in water
- 1 cup broccoli, frozen
- For the Sauce
- 1 tablespoon sesame oil
- 2 tablespoons tamari
- ½ teaspoon ground ginger
- ¼ teaspoon Sriracha
- ½ teaspoon garlic powder

Directions:

1. Put the broccoli in a saucepan on medium low heat and add the sauce ingredients.

2. Cook for about 5 minutes and add the noodles after draining water.

3. Allow to simmer about 10 minutes, occasionally stirring to avoid burning.

4. When the noodles have softened, mix everything well and dish out to serve.

145.Vegetarian Chowmein

Preparation Time: 20 minutes
Cooking Time: 30 minutes

Servings: 2

Ingredients:

- ½ large onion, chopped
- ½ small leek, chopped
- ½ tablespoon ginger paste
- ½ tablespoon Worcester sauce
- ½ tablespoon Oriental seasoning
- ½ teaspoon parsley
- Salt and black pepper, to taste
- ½ pound noodles
- 2 large carrots, diced
- 2 celery sticks, chopped
- 1 tablespoon olive oil
- ½ teaspoon garlic paste
- 1½ tablespoons soy sauce
- 1 tablespoon Chinese five spice
- ½ teaspoon coriander
- 2 cups water

Directions:

1. Put olive oil, ginger, garlic paste, and onion in a pot on medium heat and sauté for about 5 minutes.
2. Stir in all the vegetables and cook for about5 minutes.
3. Add rest of the ingredients and combine well.
4. Secure the lid and cook on medium heat for about 20 minutes, stirring occasionally.
5. Open the lid and dish out to serve hot.

146.Veggie Noodles

Preparation Time: 10 minutes
Cooking Time: 5 minutes
Servings: 2

Ingredients:

- 2 tablespoons vegetable oil
- 4 spring onions, divided
- 1 cup snap pea
- 2 tablespoons brown sugar
- 9 oz. dried rice noodles, cooked
- 5 garlic cloves, minced
- 2 carrots, cut into small sticks
- 3 tablespoons soy sauce

Directions:

1. Heat vegetable oil in a skillet over medium heat and add garlic and 3 spring onions.
2. Cook for about 3 minutes and add the carrots, peas, brown sugar and soy sauce.
3. Add rice noodles and cook for about 2 minutes.
4. Season with salt and black pepper and top with remaining spring onion to serve.

147.Stir Fry Noodles

Preparation Time: 10 minutes
Cooking Time: 8 minutes
Servings: 4

Ingredients:

- 1 cup broccoli, chopped
- 1 cup red bell pepper, chopped
- 1 cup mushrooms, chopped
- 1 large onion, chopped
- 1 batch Stir Fry Sauce, prepared
- Salt and black pepper, to taste
- 2 cups spaghetti, cooked
- 4 garlic cloves, minced

- 2 tablespoons sesame oil

Directions:

1. Heat sesame oil in a pan over medium heat and add garlic, onions, bell pepper, broccoli, mushrooms.
2. Sauté for about 5 minutes and add spaghetti noodles and stir fry sauce.
3. Mix well and cook for 3 more minutes.
4. Dish out in plates and serve to enjoy.

148.Spicy Sweet Chili Veggie Noodles

Preparation Time: 10 minutes
Cooking Time:7 minutes
Servings: 2

Ingredients:

- 1 head of broccoli, cut into bite sized florets
- 1 onion, finely sliced
- 1 tablespoon olive oil
- 1 courgette, halved
- 2 nests of whole-wheat noodles
- 150g mushrooms, sliced
- For Sauce
- 3 tablespoons soy sauce
- ¼ cup sweet chili sauce
- 1 teaspoon Sriracha
- 1 tablespoon peanut butter
- 2 tablespoons boiled water
- For Topping
- 2 teaspoons sesame seeds
- 2 teaspoons dried chili flakes

Directions:

1. Heat olive oil on medium heat in a saucepan and add onions.

2. Sauté for about 2 minutes and add broccoli, courgette and mushrooms.
3. Cook for about 5 minutes, stirring occasionally.
4. Whisk sweet chili sauce, soy sauce, Sriracha, water and peanut butter in a bowl.
5. Cook the noodles according to packet instructions and add to the vegetables.
6. Stir in the sauce and top with dried chili flakes and sesame seeds to serve.

149.Creamy Vegan Mushroom Pasta

Preparation Time: 10 minutes
Cooking Time: 30 minutes
Servings: 6

Ingredients:

- 2 cups frozen peas, thawed
- 3 tablespoons flour, unbleached
- 3 cups almond breeze, unsweetened
- 1 tablespoon nutritional yeast
- ⅓ cup fresh parsley, chopped, plus extra for garnish
- ¼ cup olive oil
- 1 pound pasta of choice
- 4 cloves garlic, minced
- ⅔ cup shallots, chopped
- 8 cups mixed mushrooms, sliced
- Salt and black pepper, to taste

Directions:

1. Take a bowl and boil pasta in salted water.
2. Heat olive oil in a pan over medium heat.
3. Add mushrooms, garlic, shallots and ½ tsp salt and cook for 15 minutes.

4. Sprinkle flour on the vegetables and stir for a minute while cooking.

5. Add almond beverage, stir constantly.

6. Let it simmer for 5 minutes and add pepper to it.

7. Cook for 3 more minutes and remove from heat.

8. Stir in nutritional yeast.

9. Add peas, salt, and pepper.

10. Cook for another minute and add

11. Add pasta to this sauce.

12. Garnish and serve!

150. Vegan Chinese Noodles

Preparation Time: 15 minutes
Cooking Time: 8 minutes
Servings: 4

Ingredients:

- 300 g mixed oriental mushrooms, such as oyster, shiitake and enoki, cleaned and sliced

- 200 g thin rice noodles, cooked according to packet instructions and drained

- 2 garlic cloves, minced

- 1 fresh red chili

- 200 g courgettes, sliced

- 6 spring onions, reserving the green part

- 1 teaspoon corn flour

- 1 tablespoon agave syrup

- 1 teaspoon sesame oil

- 100 g baby spinach, chopped

- Hot chili sauce, to serve

- 2(1-inch) pieces of ginger

- ½ bunch fresh coriander, chopped

- 4 tablespoons vegetable oil

- 2 tablespoons low-salt soy sauce

- ½ tablespoon rice wine

- 2 limes, to serve

Directions:

1. Heat sesame oil over high heat in a large wok and add the mushrooms.

2. Sauté for about 4 minutes and add garlic, chili, ginger, courgette, coriander stalks and the white part of the spring onions.

3. Sauté for about 3 minutes until softened and lightly golden.

4. Meanwhile, combine the corn flour and 2 tablespoons of water in a bowl.

5. Add soy sauce, agave syrup, sesame oil and rice wine to the corn flour mixture.

6. Put this mixture in the pan to the veggie mixture and cook for about 3 minutes until thickened.

7. Add the spinach and noodles and mix well.

8. Stir in the coriander leaves and top with lime wedges, hot chili sauce and reserved spring onions to serve.

151. Vegetable Penne Pasta

Preparation Time: 15 minutes
Cooking Time: 20 minutes
Servings: 6

Ingredients:

- ½ large onion, chopped

- 2 celery sticks, chopped

- ½ tablespoon ginger paste

- ½ cup green bell pepper

- 1½ tablespoons soy sauce

- ½ teaspoon parsley
- Salt and black pepper, to taste
- ½ pound penne pasta, cooked
- 2 large carrots, diced
- ½ small leek, chopped
- 1 tablespoon olive oil
- ½ teaspoon garlic paste
- ½ tablespoon Worcester sauce
- ½ teaspoon coriander
- 1 cup water

Directions:

1. Heat olive oil in a wok on medium heat and add onions, garlic and ginger paste.
2. Sauté for about 3 minutes and stir in all bell pepper, celery sticks, carrots and leek.
3. Sauté for about 5 minutes and add remaining ingredients except for pasta.
4. Cover the lid and cook for about 12 minutes.
5. Stir in the cooked pasta and dish out to serve warm.

152.Spaghetti in Spicy Tomato Sauce

Preparation Time: 15 minutes
Cooking Time: 40 minutes
Servings: 4

Ingredients:

- 1 pound dried spaghetti
- 1 red bell pepper, diced
- 4 garlic cloves, minced
- 1 teaspoon red pepper flakes, crushed
- 2 (14-ounce) cans diced tomatoes

- 1 (6-ounce) can tomato paste
- 2 teaspoons vegan sugar, granulated
- 2 tablespoons olive oil
- 1 medium onion, diced
- 1 cup dry red wine
- 1 teaspoon dried thyme
- ½ teaspoon fennel seed, crushed
- 1½ cups coconut milk, full-fat
- Salt and black pepper, to taste

Directions:

1. Boil water in a large pot and add pasta.
2. Cook according to the package directions and drain the pasta into a colander.
3. Dish out the pasta in a large serving bowl and add a dash of olive oil to prevent sticking.
4. Heat 2 tablespoons of olive oil over medium heat in a large pot and add garlic, onion and bell pepper.
5. Sauté for about 5 minutes and stir in the wine, thyme, fennel and red pepper flakes.
6. Allow to simmer on high heat for about 5 minutes until the liquid is reduced by about half.
7. Add diced tomatoes and tomato paste and allow to simmer for about 20 minutes, stirring occasionally.
8. Stir in the coconut milk and sugar and simmer for about 10 more minutes.
9. Season with salt and black pepper and pour the sauce over the pasta.
10. Toss to coat well and dish out in plates to serve.

153.20 Minutes Vegetarian Pasta

Preparation Time: 5 minutes
Cooking Time: 16 minutes
Servings: 4

Ingredients:

- 3 shallots, chopped
- ¼ teaspoon red pepper flakes
- ¼ cup vegan parmesan cheese
- 2 tablespoons olive oil
- 2 garlic cloves, minced
- 8-ounces spinach leaves
- 8-ounces linguine pasta
- 1 pinch salt
- 1 pinch black pepper

Directions:

1. Boil salted water in a large pot and add pasta.
2. Cook for about 6 minutes and drain the pasta in a colander.
3. Heat olive oil over medium heat in a large skillet and add the shallots.
4. Cook for about 5 minutes until soft and caramelized and stir in the spinach, garlic, red pepper flakes, salt and black pepper.
5. Cook for about 5 minutes and add pasta and 2 ladles of pasta water.
6. Stir in the parmesan cheese and dish out in a bowl to serve.

154.Creamy Vegan Pumpkin Pasta

Preparation Time: 15 minutes
Cooking Time: 5 minutes
Servings: 6

Ingredients:

- 1 tablespoon olive oil
- 1 cup raw cashews, soaked in water 4-

8 hours, drained and rinsed

- 12 ounces dried penne pasta
- 1 cup pumpkin puree, canned
- 1 cup almond milk, plus more as needed
- 3 garlic cloves
- ¼ teaspoon ground nutmeg
- Fresh parsley, for garnish
- 1 tablespoon lemon juice
- ¾ teaspoon salt
- 1 tablespoon fresh sage, chopped

Directions:

1. Boil salted water in a large pot and add pasta.
2. Cook according to the package directions and drain the pasta into a colander.
3. Dish out the pasta in a large serving bowl and add a dash of olive oil to prevent sticking.
4. Put the pumpkin, cashews, milk, lemon juice, garlic, salt and nutmeg into the food processor and blend until smooth.
5. Stir in the sauce and sage over the pasta and toss to coat well.
6. Garnish with fresh parsley and dish out to serve hot.

155.Loaded Creamy Vegan Pesto Pasta

Preparation Time: 15 minutes
Cooking Time:10 minutes
Servings: 6

Ingredients:

- ¼ onion, finely chopped
- 8 romaine lettuce leaves

- 1 celery stalk, thinly sliced
- ½ cup blue cheese, crumbled
- 1 tablespoon olive oil, plus a dash
- 1 cup almond milk, unflavored and unsweetened
- ½ cup vegan pesto
- 1 cup chickpeas, cooked
- 1 cup fresh arugula, packed
- 2 tablespoons lemon juice
- Salt and black pepper, to taste
- 6-ounces orecchiette pasta, dried
- 1 cup full-fat coconut milk
- 2 tablespoons whole wheat flour
- 1½ cups cherry tomatoes, halved
- ½ cup Kalamata olives, halved
- Red pepper flakes, to taste

Directions:

1. Boil salted water in a large pot and add pasta.
2. Cook according to the package directions and drain the pasta into a colander.
3. Dish out the pasta in a large serving bowl and add a dash of olive oil to prevent sticking.
4. Put olive oil over medium heat in a large pot and whisk in the flour.
5. Cook for about 4 minutes, until the mixture begins to smell nutty and stir in the coconut milk and almond milk.
6. Let the sauce simmer for about 1 minute and add the chickpeas, olives and arugula.
7. Stir well and season with lemon juice, red pepper flakes, and salt and black pepper.
8. Dish out into plates and serve hot.

156.Creamy Vegan Spinach Pasta

Preparation Time: 20 minutes
Cooking Time: 5 minutes
Servings: 4

Ingredients:

- 1 cup raw cashews, soaked in water for 8 hours
- 2 tablespoons lemon juice
- 1 tablespoon olive oil
- 1½ cups vegetable broth
- 2 tablespoons fresh dill, chopped
- Red pepper flakes, to taste
- 10 ounces dried fusilli
- ½ cup almond milk, unflavored and unsweetened
- 2 tablespoons white miso paste
- 4 garlic cloves, divided
- 8-ounces fresh spinach, finely chopped
- ¼ cup scallions, chopped
- Salt and black pepper, to taste

Directions:

1. Boil salted water in a large pot and add pasta.
2. Cook according to the package directions and drain the pasta into a colander.
3. Dish out the pasta in a large serving bowl and add a dash of olive oil to prevent sticking.
4. Put the cashews, milk, miso, lemon juice, and 1 garlic clove into the food processor and blend until smooth.
5. Put olive oil over medium heat in a large pot and add the remaining 3 cloves of garlic.
6. Sauté for about 1 minute and stir in

the spinach and broth.

7. Raise the heat and allow to simmer for about 4 minutes until the spinach is bright green and wilted.

8. Stir in the pasta and cashew mixture and season with salt and black pepper.

9. Top with scallions and dill and dish out into plates to serve.

157. Vegan Bake Pasta with Bolognese Sauce and Cashew Cream

Preparation Time: 1 hour 10 minutes
Cooking Time: 20 minutes
Servings: 8

Ingredients:

- For the Pasta:
- 1 packet penne pasta
- For the Bolognese Sauce:
- 1 tablespoon soy sauce
- 1 small can lentils
- 1 tablespoon brown sugar
- ½ cup tomato paste
- 1 teaspoon garlic, crushed
- 1 tablespoon olive oil
- 2 tomatoes, chopped
- 1 onion, chopped
- 2 cups mushrooms, sliced
- Salt, to taste
- Pepper, to taste
- For the Cashew Cream:
- 1 cup raw cashews
- ½ lemon, squeezed
- ½ teaspoon salt
- ½ cup water

- For the White Sauce:
- 1 teaspoon black pepper
- 1 teaspoon Dijon mustard
- ¼ cup nutritional yeast
- Sea salt, as required
- 2 cups coconut milk
- 3 tablespoons vegan butter
- 2 tablespoons all-purpose flour
- 1/3 cup vegetable broth

Directions:

1. Take a pot and boil water, add pasta to it, boil for 3 minutes and set aside.

2. Fry onion and garlic, mushroom in olive oil and add soy sauce to it.

3. Add in sugar tomato paste, lentils, and canned tomato to it and let it simmer, Bolognese sauce is prepared.

4. Season it with salt and black pepper.

5. Add the lemon juice, cashews, water and salt to the blender, blend for 2 minutes.

6. Add this to the sauce you have prepared and stir pasta in it.

7. Melt the vegan butter in a saucepan, add in the flour and stir.

8. Add vegetable stock and coconut milk to it and whisk well.

9. Stir continuously and let it boil for about 5 minutes, then remove from heat.

10. Add Dijon mustard, nutritional yeast, black pepper, and sea salt.

11. Preheat the oven to 430 degrees F.

12. Prepare rectangular oven-safe dish by placing pasta and Bolognese sauce to it.

13. Pour the white sauce on it and bake

for a time period of 20-25 minutes.

158.Asian Veggie Noodles

Preparation Time: 10 minutes
Cooking Time: 20 minutes
Servings: 4

Ingredients:

- ½ cup peas
- 1 teaspoon rice vinegar
- 3 carrots, chopped
- 1 small packet vermicelli
- 3 tablespoons sesame oil
- 1 red pepper, chopped in small cubes
- 1 can baby corn
- 1 clove garlic, chopped
- 2 tablespoons soy sauce
- 1 teaspoon ginger powder
- ½ teaspoon curry powder
- Salt and black pepper, to taste

Directions:

1. Take a bowl and add ginger powder, vinegar, soy sauce, curry powder, and a pinch of salt to it.
2. Cook the noodles according to the instructions and drain them.
3. Heat the sesame oil and cook vegetables in it for 10 minutes on medium heat.
4. Add noodles to it and cook for 3 more minutes.
5. Remove from heat and serve to enjoy.

159. Ingredients Pasta

Preparation Time: 15 minutes
Cooking Time: 25 minutes
Servings: 5

Ingredients:

- 1 (25 oz.) jar marinara sauce
- Olive oil, as needed
- 1 pound dry vegan pasta
- 1 pound assorted vegetables, like red onion, zucchini and tomatoes
- ¼ cup prepared hummus
- Salt, to taste

Instructions:

1. Preheat the oven to 400 degrees F and grease a large baking sheet.
2. Arrange the vegetables in a single layer on the baking sheet and sprinkle with olive oil and salt.
3. Transfer into the oven and roast the vegetables for about 15 minutes.
4. Boil salted water in a large pot and cook the pasta according to the package directions.
5. Drain the water when the pasta is tender and put the pasta in a colander.
6. Mix together the marinara sauce and hummus in a large pot to make a creamy sauce.
7. Stir in the cooked vegetables and pasta to the sauce and toss to coat well.
8. Dish out in a bowl and serve warm.

160.Salads

Avocado Grapefruit Couscous Salad with Lime and Honey Dressing

Preparation time: 15 minutes

Cooking time: 0 minutes

Servings: 4

Ingredients:

- Salad

- Avocados, two large peeled, pitted and diced
- Cilantro, fresh chop, three tablespoons
- Feta cheese, crumbled, one half cup
- Grapefruit, red, two large, peel apart the sections and cut into bite-size chunks
- Mint, fresh chop, three tablespoons
- Vegetable broth, three-fourths cup
- White beans, one fifteen ounce can, drain and rinse
- Whole wheat couscous, uncooked, three-fourths cup
- Dressing
- Honey, two tablespoons
- Lime juice, three tablespoons
- Olive oil, two tablespoons
- Salt, one quarter teaspoon

Directions:

1. Into a small saucepan pour the vegetable broth over medium heat and let it boil. Remove the pan off the heat and blend in the couscous, then cover the pot and let it sit for five minutes. Mix together in a small-sized bowl the salt, olive oil, honey, and lime juice for the dressing and mix them together well. Into a large bowl pour the couscous and mix in the beans, stirring to combine well. Then dump the dressing over the top of the beans and couscous and mix this all together well. Then blend in the cilantro, mint, feta, grapefruit, and avocado and mix everything gently but thoroughly. Serve either at room temperature or well chilled.

161.Lentil, Lemon & Mushroom

Salad

Preparation time: 10 minutes
Cooking time: 0 minutes
Servings: 2

Ingredients:

- ½ cup dry lentils of choice
- 2 cups vegetable broth
- 3 cups mushrooms, thickly sliced
- 1 cup sweet or purple onion, chopped
- 4 tsp. extra virgin olive oil
- 2 tbsp. garlic powder
- ¼ tsp. chili flakes
- 1 tbsp. lemon juice
- 2 tbsp. cilantro, chopped
- ½ cup arugula
- Salt and pepper

Directions:

1. Sprout the lentils according the method. (Don't cook them).

2. Place the vegetable stock in a deep saucepan and bring it to a boil.

3. Add the lentils to the boiling broth, cover the pan, and cook for about 5 minutes over low heat until the lentils are a bit tender.

4. Remove the pan from heat and drain the excess water.

5. Put a frying pan over high heat and add 2 tablespoons of olive oil.

6. Add the onions, garlic, and chili flakes, and cook until the onions are almost translucent, around 5 to 10 minutes while stirring.

7. Add the mushrooms to the frying pan and mix in thoroughly. Continue cooking until the onions are completely translucent and the

mushrooms have softened; remove the pan from the heat.

8. Mix the lentils, onions, mushrooms, and garlic in a large bowl.

9. Add the lemon juice and the remaining olive oil. Toss or stir to combine everything thoroughly.

10. Serve the mushroom/onion mixture over some arugala in bowl, adding salt and pepper to taste, or, store and enjoy later!

162. Sweet Potato & Black Bean Protein Salad

Preparation time: 15 minutes
Cooking time: 0 minutes
Servings: 2

Ingredients:

- 1 cup dry black beans
- 4 cups of spinach
- 1 medium sweet potato
- 1 cup purple onion, chopped
- 2 tbsp. olive oil
- 2 tbsp. lime juice
- 1 tbsp. minced garlic
- ½ tbsp. chili powder
- ¼ tsp. cayenne
- ¼ cup parsley
- Salt and pepper to taste

Directions:

1. Prepare the black beans according to the method.

2. Preheat the oven to 400°F.

3. Cut the sweet potato into ¼-inch cubes and put these in a medium-sized bowl. Add the onions, 1 tablespoon of olive oil, and salt to taste.

4. Toss the ingredients until the sweet potatoes and onions are completely coated.

5. Transfer the ingredients to a baking sheet lined with parchment paper and spread them out in a single layer.

6. Put the baking sheet in the oven and roast until the sweet potatoes are starting to turn brown and crispy, around 40 minutes.

7. Meanwhile, combine the remaining olive oil, lime juice, garlic, chili powder, and cayenne thoroughly in a large bowl, until no lumps remain.

8. Remove the sweet potatoes and onions from the oven and transfer them to the large bowl.

9. Add the cooked black beans, parsley, and a pinch of salt.

10. Toss everything until well combined.

11. Then mix in the spinach, and serve in desired portions with additional salt and pepper.

12. Store or enjoy!

163. Super Summer Salad

Preparation time: 10 minutes
Cooking time: 0 minutes
Servings: 2

Ingredients:

- Dressing:
- 1 tbsp. olive oil
- ¼ cup chopped basil
- 1 tsp. lemon juice
- Salt to taste
- 1 medium avocado, halved, diced
- ¼ cup water

- Salad:
- ¼ cup dry chickpeas
- ¼ cup dry red kidney beans
- 4 cups raw kale, shredded
- 2 cups Brussel sprouts, shredded
- 2 radishes, thinly sliced
- 1 tbsp. walnuts, chopped
- 1 tsp. flax seeds
- Salt and pepper to taste

Directions:

1. Prepare the chickpeas and kidney beans according to the method.

2. Soak the flax seeds according the method, and then drain excess water.

3. Prepare the dressing by adding the olive oil, basil, lemon juice, salt, and half of the avocado to a food processor or blender, and pulse on low speed.

4. Keep adding small amounts of water until the dressing is creamy and smooth.

5. Transfer the dressing to a small bowl and set it aside.

6. Combine the kale, Brussel sprouts, cooked chickpeas, kidney beans, radishes, walnuts, and remaining avocado in a large bowl and mix thoroughly.

7. Store the mixture, or, serve with the dressing and flax seeds, and enjoy!

164.Roasted Almond Protein Salad

Preparation time: 30 minutes
Cooking time: 0 minutes
Servings: 4

Ingredients:

- ½ cup dry quinoa

- ½ cup dry navy beans
- ½ cup dry chickpeas
- ½ cup raw whole almonds
- 1 tsp. extra virgin olive oil
- ½ tsp. salt
- ½ tsp. paprika
- ½ tsp. cayenne
- Dash of chili powder
- 4 cups spinach, fresh or frozen
- ¼ cup purple onion, chopped

Directions:

1. Prepare the quinoa according to the recipe. Store in the fridge for now.

2. Prepare the beans according to the method. Store in the fridge for now.

3. Toss the almonds, olive oil, salt, and spices in a large bowl, and stir until the ingredients are evenly coated.

4. Put a skillet over medium-high heat, and transfer the almond mixture to the heated skillet.

5. Roast while stirring until the almonds are browned, around 5 minutes. You may hear the ingredients pop and crackle in the pan as they warm up. Stir frequently to prevent burning.

6. Turn off the heat and toss the cooked and chilled quinoa and beans, onions, and spinach or mixed greens in the skillet. Stir well before transferring the roasted almond salad to a bowl.

7. Enjoy the salad with a dressing of choice, or, store for later!

165.Lentil Radish Salad

Preparation time: 15 minutes
Cooking time: 0 minutes
Servings: 3

Ingredients:

- Dressing:
- 1 tbsp. extra virgin olive oil
- 1 tbsp. lemon juice
- 1 tbsp. maple syrup
- 1 tbsp. water
- ½ tbsp. sesame oil
- 1 tbsp. miso paste, yellow or white
- ¼ tsp. salt
- Pepper to taste
- Salad:
- ½ cup dry chickpeas
- ¼ cup dry green or brown lentils
- 1 14-oz. pack of silken tofu
- 5 cups mixed greens, fresh or frozen
- 2 radishes, thinly sliced
- ½ cup cherry tomatoes, halved
- ¼ cup roasted sesame seeds

Directions:

1. Prepare the chickpeas according to the method.

2. Prepare the lentils according to the method.

3. Put all the ingredients for the dressing in a blender or food processor. Mix on low until smooth, while adding water until it reaches the desired consistency.

4. Add salt, pepper (to taste), and optionally more water to the dressing; set aside.

5. Cut the tofu into bite-sized cubes.

6. Combine the mixed greens, tofu, lentils, chickpeas, radishes, and tomatoes in a large bowl.

7. Add the dressing and mix everything

until it is coated evenly.

8. Top with the optional roasted sesame seeds, if desired.

9. Refrigerate before serving and enjoy, or, store for later!

166.Southwest Style Salad

Preparation time: 10 minutes
Cooking time: 0 minutes
Servings: 2

Ingredients:

- ½ cup dry black beans
- ½ cup dry chickpeas
- 1/3 cup purple onion, diced
- 1 red bell pepper, pitted, sliced
- 4 cups mixed greens, fresh or frozen, chopped
- 1 cup cherry tomatoes, halved or quartered
- 1 medium avocado, peeled, pitted, and cubed
- 1 cup sweet kernel corn, canned, drained
- ½ tsp. chili powder
- ¼ tsp. cumin
- Salt and pepper to taste
- 2 tsp. olive oil
- 1 tbsp. vinegar

Directions:

1. Prepare the black beans and chickpeas according to the method.

2. Put all of the ingredients into a large bowl.

3. Toss the mix of veggies and spices until combined thoroughly.

4. Store, or serve chilled with some olive

oil and vinegar on top!

167.Shaved Brussel Sprout Salad

Preparation time: 25 minutes
Cooking time: 0 minutes
Servings: 4
Ingredients:

- Dressing:
- 1 tbsp. brown mustard
- 1 tbsp. maple syrup
- 2 tbsp. apple cider vinegar
- 2 tbsp. extra virgin olive oil
- ½ tbsp. garlic minced
- Salad:
- ½ cup dry red kidney beans
- ¼ cup dry chickpeas
- 2 cups Brussel sprouts
- 1 cup purple onion
- 1 small sour apple
- ½ cup slivered almonds, crushed
- ½ cup walnuts, crushed
- ½ cup cranberries, dried
- Salt and pepper to taste

Directions:

1. Prepare the beans according to the method.

2. Combine all dressing ingredients in a bowl and stir well until combined.

3. Refrigerate the dressing for up to one hour before serving.

4. Use a grater, mandolin, or knife to thinly slice each Brussel sprout. Repeat this with the apple and onion.

5. Take a large bowl to mix the chickpeas, beans, sprouts, apples, onions, cranberries, and nuts.

6. Drizzle the cold dressing over the salad to coat.

7. Serve with salt and pepper to taste, or, store for later!

168.Colorful Protein Power Salad

Preparation time: 20 minutes
Cooking time: 0 minutes
Servings: 2

Ingredients:

- ½ cup dry quinoa
- 2 cups dry navy beans
- 1 green onion, chopped
- 2 tsp. garlic, minced
- 3 cups green or purple cabbage, chopped
- 4 cups kale, fresh or frozen, chopped
- 1 cup shredded carrot, chopped
- 2 tbsp. extra virgin olive oil
- 1 tsp. lemon juice
- Salt and pepper to taste

Directions:

1. Prepare the quinoa according to the recipe.

2. Prepare the beans according to the method.

3. Heat up 1 tablespoon of the olive oil in a frying pan over medium heat.

4. Add the chopped green onion, garlic, and cabbage, and sauté for 2-3 minutes.

5. Add the kale, the remaining 1 tablespoon of olive oil, and salt. Lower the heat and cover until the greens have wilted, around 5 minutes. Remove the pan from the stove and set aside.

6. Take a large bowl and mix the remaining ingredients with the kale and cabbage mixture once it has cooled down. Add more salt and pepper to taste.

7. Mix until everything is distributed evenly.

8. Serve topped with a dressing, or, store for later!

169. Edamame & Ginger Citrus Salad

Preparation time: 15 minutes
Cooking time: 0 minutes
Servings: 3

Ingredients:

- Dressing:
- ¼ cup orange juice
- 1 tsp. lime juice
- ½ tbsp. maple syrup
- ½ tsp. ginger, finely minced
- ½ tbsp. sesame oil
- Salad:
- ½ cup dry green lentils
- 2 cups carrots, shredded
- 4 cups kale, fresh or frozen, chopped
- 1 cup edamame, shelled
- 1 tablespoon roasted sesame seeds
- 2 tsp. mint, chopped
- Salt and pepper to taste
- 1 small avocado, peeled, pitted, diced

Directions:

1. Prepare the lentils according to the method.

2. Combine the orange and lime juices, maple syrup, and ginger in a small bowl. Mix with a whisk while slowly adding the sesame oil.

3. Add the cooked lentils, carrots, kale, edamame, sesame seeds, and mint to a large bowl.

4. Add the dressing and stir well until all the ingredients are coated evenly.

5. Store or serve topped with avocado and an additional sprinkle of mint.

170. Taco Tempeh Salad

Preparation time: 25 minutes
Cooking time: 0 minutes
Servings: 3

Ingredients:

1. 1 cup dry black beans
2. 1 8-oz. package tempeh
3. 1 tbsp. lime or lemon juice
4. 2 tbsp. extra virgin olive oil
5. 1 tsp. maple syrup
6. ½ tsp. chili powder
7. ¼ tsp. cumin
8. ¼ tsp. paprika
9. 1 large bunch of kale, fresh or frozen, chopped
10. 1 large avocado, peeled, pitted, diced
11. ½ cup salsa

171. Salt and pepper

Directions:

1. Prepare the beans according to the method.

2. Cut the tempeh into ¼-inch cubes, place in a bowl, and then add the lime or lemon juice, 1 tablespoon of olive oil, maple syrup, chili powder, cumin, and paprika.

3. Stir well and let the tempeh marinate

in the fridge for at least 1 hour, up to 12 hours.

4. Heat the remaining 1 tablespoon of olive oil in a frying pan over medium heat.

5. Add the marinated tempeh mixture and cook until brown and crispy on both sides, around 10 minutes.

6. Put the chopped kale in a bowl with the cooked beans and prepared tempeh.

7. Store, or serve the salad immediately, topped with salsa, avocado, and salt and pepper to taste.

172.Tangy Chickpea Soup with a Hint of Lemon

Preparation Time: 10 minutes
Cooking Time: 30 minutes
Serving: 6

Ingredients:

- 2 cups of freshly diced onion
- 3 freshly minced large garlic cloves
- Water
- ½ cup of freshly diced celery
- ¾ teaspoon of sea salt
- Freshly ground black pepper to taste
- 1 teaspoon of mustard seeds
- ½ teaspoon of dried oregano
- 1 teaspoon of cumin seeds
- ½ teaspoon of paprika
- 1 ½ teaspoons of dried thyme
- 3 ½ cups of cooked chickpeas
- 1 cup of dried red lentils
- 3 cups of vegetable stock
- 2 dried bay leaves
- 2 cups of freshly chopped tomatoes or zucchini
- 2 cups of water
- ¼ to 1/3 cup of fresh lemon juice

Directions:

1. Put a large pot on the stove on medium heat.

2. Add onion, water, salt, celery, garlic, pepper, cumin, and mustard seeds along with thyme, oregano, and paprika. Stir everything to combine well.

3. Cover the pot and cook for about 7 minutes, stirring occasionally.

4. Rinse the lentils.

5. Add the lentils along with 2 ½ cups of chickpeas, zucchini/tomatoes, stock, bay leaves, and water. Stir everything to combine well.

6. Increase the heat to bring to a boil.

7. Once the ingredients start to boil, cover the pot, lower the heat, and simmer for 20-25 minutes.

8. You will know that the soup is ready when the lentils are tender.

9. After removing the bay leaves, add the lemon juice.

10. Once the ingredients have cooled down, use a hand blender to puree the ingredients, but keep a somewhat coarse texture instead of having a smooth puree.

11. Add the remaining chickpeas. Taste the soup and adjust the salt, pepper, and lemon juice to taste.

12. Enjoy this amazing soup with your favorite bread.

173.Quinoa Soup with a Dash of Kale

Preparation Time: 15 minutes
Cooking Time: 45 minutes
Serving: 6

Ingredients:

- 3 carrots freshly peeled and chopped
- 3 tablespoons of extra virgin olive oil
- 6 freshly minced or pressed garlic cloves
- 2 freshly chopped celery stalks
- 1 freshly chopped medium-sized white or yellow onion
- 1-2 cups of seasonal veggies: butternut squash, yellow squash, zucchini, sweet potato, bell pepper
- ½ teaspoon of dried thyme
- 1 cup of rinsed quinoa
- 1 can of diced tomatoes
- 2 cups of water
- 2 bay leaves
- 4 cups of vegetable broth
- 1 teaspoon of salt
- Freshly ground black pepper to taste
- 1 cup of freshly chopped kale or collard greens
- Red pepper flakes
- 1-2 teaspoons of lemon juice
- 1 can of rinsed and dried great northern beans or chickpeas
- Freshly grated parmesan cheese

Directions:

1. On medium heat, warm the olive oil in a soup pot. Once the oil starts to shimmer, start adding the carrot, onion, celery, and seasonal veggies, along with salt. Cook everything until the onion softens. You will know that the veggies have become tender when the onions become translucent. This will take about 6-8 minutes.

2. Add the thyme and garlic to the veggies. After cooking for about 1 minute, it will turn fragrant. Add the diced tomatoes and cook everything for a few more minutes.

3. Add the quinoa, water, and broth.

4. Add the bay leaves along with 1 teaspoon of salt and red pepper flakes. Increase the heat and bring everything to boil. Cover the pot partially and lower the heat so that the ingredients continue to simmer.

5. Simmer for about 25 minutes.

6. Uncover the pot, and add the greens and beans. Simmer for another 5 minutes. Let the greens soften a bit.

7. Remove the pot from the heat, and remove the bay leaves. Add 1 teaspoon of lemon juice.

8. Taste the soup and add salt and pepper to taste. Divide the warm, hearty soup equally in bowls and top with parmesan cheese. Dig in and enjoy a bowl full of happiness.

174. Tasty Salad with Lentil & Red Onion and a Dash of Roasted Cumin

Preparation Time: 10 minutes
Cooking Time: 35 minutes
Serving: 3

Ingredients:

- 2 cans of green lentils
- 70 g of watercress
- 20 g of coriander
- 4 carrots
- 2 teaspoons of fennel seeds
- 2 red onions

- 2 teaspoons of cumin seeds
- 50 g of pine nuts
- Olive oil
- Cashew cheese:
- 1 freshly juiced lemon
- Salt
- 150 g of cashew nuts
- Pepper
- 5 tablespoons of water

Directions:

1. Preheat the oven to 180o C. Peel the carrots and slice them diagonally. Roughly chop the onions.

2. Put the carrots and onion on a baking tray and sprinkle with cumin and fennel seeds. Do not forget a good dose of olive oil on the top. Top with salt and pepper. Roast everything in the oven for half an hour.

3. Heat a pan and fry the pine nuts without oil. Once they start to brown, take them off the stove and allow them to cool.

4. Put all of the ingredients for the cashew cheese in a blender and create a smooth puree.

5. Once the veggies are cooked, rinse the lentils and add them to a warm pan. They should be slightly warm. Add the carrots and onion with the seeds. Scoop some oil from the baking tray and include it in this mixture as well.

6. Chop the coriander roughly and add it to the lentil mixture. Season with salt and pepper to taste.

7. Remove the pan from the heat and add the watercress. Plate the salad with a good sprinkle of pine nuts on top.

8. Top the salad with some good cashew cheese and enjoy this fresh, amazing salad, which is the best remedy for an empty stomach.

175.Health is Wealth Salad: Dash of Chickpea and Tomato

Preparation Time: 10 minutes
Cooking Time: 10 minutes
Serving: 3-4

Ingredients:

- 1 freshly chopped red pepper
- 2 cups of cooked chickpeas
- 1/3 cup of freshly chopped parsley
- 5 freshly chopped spring onions
- 1 cup of rinsed baby spinach leaves
- ½ a lemon, juiced
- 5 freshly chopped medium tomatoes
- 1 tablespoon of balsamic vinegar
- 2 tablespoons of sesame seeds
- ½ thinly sliced hot pepper
- 2 tablespoons of olive oil
- 2 tablespoons of flax seeds

Directions:

1. Thoroughly clean and chop all the vegetables. Do not chop the baby spinach.

2. In a big salad bowl, mix together the chickpeas, onions, tomatoes, pepper, spinach, and parsley.

3. Toss with the sesame seeds and sprinkle the flax seeds.

4. Drizzle with olive oil, lemon juice, and balsamic vinegar. Give all of the ingredients a thorough mix.

5. Add salt and pepper to taste and serve this summer staple. It is fresh and

healthy, and you cannot say no to this delicious salad.

176.The Mediterranean Delight with Fresh Vinaigrette

Preparation Time: 5 minutes
Cooking Time: 10 minutes
Serving: 2

- Ingredients:
- Herbed citrus vinaigrette:
- 1 tablespoon of lemon juice
- 2 tablespoons of orange juice
- ½ teaspoon of lemon zest
- ½ teaspoon of orange zest
- 2 tablespoons of olive oil
- 1 tablespoon of finely chopped fresh oregano leaves
- Salt to taste
- Black pepper to taste
- 2-3 tablespoons of freshly julienned mint leaves
- Salad:
- 1 freshly diced medium-sized cucumber
- 2 cups of cooked and rinsed chickpeas
- ½ cup of freshly diced red onion
- 2 freshly diced medium-sized tomatoes
- 1 freshly diced red bell pepper
- ¼ cup of green olives
- ½ cup of pomegranates

Directions:

1. In a large salad bowl, add the juice and zest of both the lemon and the orange along with oregano and olive oil. Whisk together so that they are mixed well. Season the vinaigrette

with salt and pepper to taste.

2. After draining the chickpeas, add them to the dressing. Then, add the onions. Give them a thorough mix, so that the onion and chickpeas absorb the flavors.

3. Now, chop the rest of the veggies and start adding them to the salad bowl. Give them a good toss.

4. Lastly, add the olives and fresh mint. Adjust the salt and pepper as required.

5. Serve this Mediterranean delight chilled — a cool summer salad that is good for the tummy and the soul.

177.Smashing Sweet Potato Burger with Quinoa

Preparation Time: 20 minutes
Cooking Time: 60 minutes
Serving: 12

Ingredients:

- 1 15-ounce can of rinsed black beans
- 2 tablespoons of finely diced jalapeno
- 2 cups of mashed roasted sweet potatoes
- ½ cup of freshly diced purple onion
- 1/3 cup of roasted sunflower seeds
- 2 cups of cooked quinoa
- ¼ cup of oat flour
- 2 teaspoons of garlic powder
- 1 teaspoon of olive oil
- 1 tablespoon of ground cumin
- ¼ teaspoon of sea salt

Directions:

1. Preheat the oven to 375o F. Spray some coconut oil on a baking sheet.

2. After cutting the sweet potatoes in half, arrange them on the baking sheet with a drizzle of olive oil.

3. Make perforations with a fork. Put them skin-side down on the tray, and bake them for about an hour.

4. Mix all of the other ingredients in a large bowl while the potatoes are roasting.

5. Allow the potatoes to cool for 10 minutes. Scoop out the flesh with a spoon. Mash the flesh with a spoon, and mix it with the rest of the ingredients.

6. Preheat the oven again to 375o F. Spray some coconut oil on the baking sheet.

7. In order to create burger patties, you need to scoop some of the sweet potato mixture and form a 1-inch patty with the mashed mix. You can moisten your hands to shape the patty properly. Put them in the oven, and bake them for 15 minutes.

8. Once the burgers are baked, heat some olive oil in a skillet.

9. Put the patties in the oil for 4-5 minutes, flipping half way through the cooking time. You will know that the patties are ready when both sides are golden brown.

10. Once the patties are ready, top with your favorite salad and toppings, and enjoy your healthy burgers.

178.Famous Veg Caprese Bowl

Preparation Time: 15 minutes
Cooking Time: 35 minutes
Serving: 4

Ingredients:

- 1 medium-sized zucchini
- 2 tablespoons of olive oil
- 1 cup of freshly chopped yellow onion
- 16 ounces of freshly sliced cremini mushrooms
- 1 tablespoon of finely chopped garlic
- 1 tablespoon of unsalted tomato paste
- 1 teaspoon of freshly ground black pepper
- 1 can of fire-roasted, diced, unsalted tomatoes, undrained
- 5 ounces of fresh baby spinach
- ¼ cup of fresh basil
- 1 teaspoon of freshly ground black pepper
- ¾ cup of part-skim mozzarella cheese
- ½ cup of part-skim ricotta cheese

Directions:

1. Cut long strips of zucchini. In a colander, mix some salt with the zucchini. Allow it to stand for some time.

2. Over medium-high heat, warm some oil. Add the onion and garlic and cook until they are fragrant and tender. This will take about 3 minutes.

3. Add the mushrooms and stir. Cook the mushrooms until they are brown; this will take about 5 minutes.

4. Add the tomato paste and cook everything for 1 minute.

5. Add the pepper, tomatoes, and salt.

6. Decrease the heat to medium-low, and allow the veggies to simmer, stirring them until the ingredients have reduced. This will take about 6 minutes.

7. Add the spinach, cover the pot, and allow the spinach leaves to wilt. This will take another 3 minutes.

8. Remove the pot from the stove and

add the zucchini strips.

9. In a small bowl, mix the mozzarella and ricotta cheese and microwave for about 30 seconds. Now top the mixture with the warmed cheese and some basil.

179. Tempting Tempeh BLT

Preparation Time: 15 minutes
Cooking Time: 20 minutes
Serving: 4-6

Ingredients:

- 1 tablespoon of pure maple syrup
- 1 ½ teaspoons of black pepper
- 1 ½ tablespoons of reduced sodium tamari
- 2 teaspoons of smoked paprika
- 1 package of tempeh cut into 16 slices
- 8 whole-wheat bread slices
- ½ cup of wild blackberry wood chips
- 5 teaspoons of canola mayonnaise
- 8 romaine lettuce leaves
- 1 heirloom tomato

Directions:

1. Preheat the oven to 400o F. In a bowl, whisk together the maple syrup, tamari sauce, and smoked paprika. Add 1 teaspoon of pepper.

2. Place the tempeh on a baking sheet and lather both sides with the prepared mixture.

3. Take a disposable aluminum foil pan and pierce 10 holes in the bottom.

4. Put the wood chips on top of the holes and allow the holed side to sit on a stopover burner. The temperature should be medium-high.

5. Heat until the wood chips begin to smoke. This will take about 1 minute. Remove from the heat.

6. Put a wire rack on the baking sheet and bake the tempeh at 400o F. You will know that the tempeh is ready when the slices are golden brown and slightly crispy. You should flip them once halfway through cooking.

7. Put the bread slices on the oven rack, and toast them for about 5 minutes.

8. Spread ¼ teaspoon of mayo on one side of the bread. Sprinkle some pepper on top. Now add the tomato slices, followed by lettuce, and then top it with tempeh. Finally, add the other toasted bread slice to form the BLT.

9. This is a perfect antidote for your hunger, and you can even enjoy this snack away from home.

180. Vegan Mac n Cheese

Preparation Time: 10 minutes
Cooking Time: 20 minutes
Serving: 6

Ingredients:

- 3 cups of vegetable broth
  - cups of rinsed quinoa
- 1 8.5 ounce jar of drained and sliced sun-dried tomatoes
- Salt
- 1 tablespoon of minced garlic
- Pepper
- 4 cups of deboned kale
- 1-2 tablespoons of EVOO
- Cheese sauce:
- 2 tablespoons of corn starch
- 2 cups of Blue Diamond Almond Breeze, preferably the unsweetened

version

- 2 cups of shredded mozzarella cheese

Directions:

1. Boil the quinoa and vegetable broth in a medium-sized pot. Reduce the heat, cover the pot, and allow the quinoa to simmer for about 15 minutes or until it soaks up all of the liquid.

2. In the meantime, drain the tomatoes and slice them, but do not rinse them. After deboning the kale, chop it into bite-sized portions.

3. In a frying pan, add the EVOO, tomatoes, garlic, and kale and sauté for about 5 minutes. You will know that it is ready when the kale is wilted.

4. In a medium-sized pot, add 2 cups of almond milk and 2 tablespoons of corn starch, and bring to a boil. Reduce the heat to medium, and allow the ingredients to cook for 8 minutes. As the milk thickens, you can add the shredded cheese to form a smooth substance. Do not stop stirring.

5. In a large bowl, mix the quinoa, cheese sauce, and veggies. Dig into this one-of-a-kind mac n cheese!

181. Amazing Cavatappi with Pesto & Carrots

Preparation Time: 10 minutes
Cooking Time: 30 minutes
Serving: 2

Ingredients:

- 10 ounces of asparagus
- 1 lemon
- 8 ounces of carrots
- 2 cloves of garlic
- ¼ cup of soy-free vegan parmesan

- 1 box of Banza Cavatappi
- 4 ounces of baby arugula
- ½ cup of almonds
- Pepper
  - tablespoons of olive oil
- Salt to taste

Directions:

1. Preheat the oven to 400o F.

2. Peel and slice the carrots, and trim the end of each asparagus. Chop the asparagus stalks into 1-inch pieces. Peel the garlic.

3. Put the carrots on a baking sheet, drizzle some olive oil over them, and sprinkle with salt and pepper. Roast the carrots until you can insert a fork through them. This will take about 10-12 minutes.

4. Put 1 cup of Cavatappi aside, and add the rest of the Cavatappi to the water. Bring to a boil, then reduce the heat and cook until al dente. The entire process will be done within 6-8 minutes. Remove ½ cup of pasta water, and drain the pasta.

5. In a food processor, add half of the lemon juice, garlic, carrots, and almonds along with ½ cup of arugula, water, salt, and 2 tablespoons of parmesan. Adjust salt to taste. Pulse the ingredients. Add some olive oil, and make a smooth puree.

6. Put the pot back on medium-high heat, and warm 2 tablespoons of olive oil. Add the chopped asparagus, and cook until they are crisp-tender. This will take about 2-3 minutes. Add the carrot pesto, Cavatappi, reserved water with remaining arugula, and the rest of the lemon juice. Stir everything so that the ingredients do not stick to the pot.

7. You will know that the dish is almost ready when the arugula wilts. Adjust the salt and pepper, and divide it into bowls. Sprinkle some more parmesan on the top, and enjoy this amazing pasta.

182.Thai-Style Eggplant

Preparation Time: 10 minutes
Cooking Time: 25 minutes
Serving: 2

Ingredients:

- 1 eggplant
- ¾ cup of jasmine rice
- 1 shallot
    - ounces of coconut milk
- 3 cloves of garlic
- 1 red bell pepper
- 1 jalapeno
- 1 tablespoon of rice vinegar
- 2 scallions
- 2 tablespoons of tamari
- Salt to taste
- 4 teaspoons of turbinado sugar
    - tablespoons of olive oil

Directions:

1. Mix the jasmine rice with coconut milk and ½ cup of water with salt to cook the rice. Bring to a boil and then reduce the heat to cook the rice until the water is absorbed and the rice is fluffy. This will take about 15-20 minutes.

2. Chop the eggplant into 1-inch cubes. Mince the garlic and the shallot. Roughly chop the bell pepper. Chop the scallions into 2-inch pieces. Lastly, mince the jalapeno.

3. On medium-high heat, add 2 tablespoons of vegetable oil to a non-stick skillet. After the oil is warm, add the eggplant and cook until brown. The entire process will take about 4 minutes. You can transfer the eggplant to a plate.

4. Add 1 tablespoon of vegetable oil, and cook the garlic, shallot, and jalapeno. Stir occasionally. You will have fragrant aromatics in about 4 minutes.

5. Now, add the pepper, eggplant, scallions, tamari, turbinado sugar, and rice vinegar with ¼ cup of water.

6. Once the sauce starts to coat the eggplant (in about 1-2 minutes), adjust the seasoning.

7. Enjoy your jasmine rice with Thai-style eggplant curry!

183.Celery Salad

Preparation time: 10 minutes
Cooking time: 0 minutes
Servings: 6

Ingredients:

- 6 cups celery, sliced
- ¼ tsp celery seed
- 1 tbsp lemon juice
- 2 tsp lemon zest, grated
- 1 tbsp parsley, chopped
- 1 tbsp olive oil
- Sea salt

Directions:

1. Add all ingredients into the large mixing bowl and toss well.

2. Serve immediately and enjoy.

184.Ginger Avocado Kale Salad

Preparation time: 15 minutes
Cooking time: 0 minutes
Servings: 4

Ingredients:

- 1 avocado, peeled and sliced
- 1 tbsp ginger, grated
- 1/2 lb kale, chopped
- 1/4 cup parsley, chopped
- 2 fresh scallions, chopped

Directions:

1. Add all ingredients into the mixing bowl and toss well.
2. Serve and enjoy.

185.Avocado Cabbage Salad

Preparation time: 20 minutes
Cooking time: 0 minutes
Servings: 4
Ingredients:

- 2 avocados, diced
- 4 cups cabbage, shredded
- 3 tbsp fresh parsley, chopped
- 2 tbsp apple cider vinegar
- 4 tbsp olive oil
- 1 cup cherry tomatoes, halved
- 1/2 tsp pepper
- 1 1/2 tsp sea salt

Directions:

1. Add cabbage, avocados, and tomatoes to a medium bowl and mix well.
2. In a small bowl, whisk together oil, parsley, vinegar, pepper, and salt.
3. Pour dressing over vegetables and mix well.
4. Serve and enjoy.

186.Vegetable Salad

Preparation time: 15 minutes
Cooking time: 0 minutes
Servings: 6

Ingredients:

- 2 cups cauliflower florets
- 2 cups carrots, chopped
- 2 cups cherry tomatoes, halved
- 2 tbsp shallots, minced
- 1 bell pepper, seeded and chopped
- 1 cucumber, seeded and chopped
- For dressing:
- 2 garlic cloves, minced
- 1/2 cup red wine vinegar
- 1/2 cup olive oil
- Pepper
- Salt

Directions:

1. In a small bowl, combine together all dressing ingredients.
2. Add all salad ingredients to the large bowl and toss well.
3. Pour dressing over salad and toss well.
4. Place salad bowl in refrigerator for 4 hours.
5. Serve chilled and enjoy.

187.Refreshing Cucumber Salad

Preparation time: 10 minutes
Cooking time: 0 minutes
Servings: 4

Ingredients:

- 1/3 cup cucumber basil ranch
- 1 cucumber, chopped

- 3 tomatoes, chopped
- 3 tbsp fresh herbs, chopped
- ½ onion, sliced

Directions:

1. Add all ingredients into the large mixing bowl and toss well.
2. Serve immediately and enjoy.

188.Avocado Almond Cabbage Salad

Preparation time: 15 minutes
Cooking time: 0 minutes
Servings: 3

Ingredients:

- 3 cups savoy cabbage, shredded
- ½ cup blanched almonds
- 1 avocado, chopped
- ¼ tsp pepper
- ¼ tsp sea salt
- For dressing:
- 1 tsp coconut aminos
- ½ tsp Dijon mustard
- 1 tbsp lemon juice
- 3 tbsp olive oil
- Pepper
- Salt

Directions:

1. In a small bowl, mix together all dressing ingredients and set aside.
2. Add all salad ingredients to the large bowl and mix well.
3. Pour dressing over salad and toss well.
4. Serve immediately and enjoy.

189.Tuna Salad

Preparation time: 10 minutes
Cooking time: 10 minutes
Servings: 4

Ingredients

- 1 teaspoon of garlic powder
- ½ a teaspoon of maple syrup
- 1 ½ teaspoons of freshly squeezed lemon juice
- 2 tablespoons of Dijon mustard
- ¼ cup of chopped celery
- ½ a cup of chopped red onion
- 1 pitted and peeled avocado
- A head of romaine lettuce, sliced

Directions

1. Combine the avocado and chickpeas in a large bowl and use a potato masher to smash them down.
2. Add the garlic powder, maple syrup, lemon juice, mustard, celery and onion and stir to combine.
3. Divide the lettuce onto plates, spoon the tuna salad over the top and serve.

190.Southwest Spinach Salad

Preparation time: 10 minutes
Cooking time: 10 minutes
Servings: 2

Ingredients

- ½ a tablespoon of flaxseeds
- ½ a cup of corn
- ½ a cup of cooked brown rice
- ½ a cup of cooked black beans
- 8 ounces of fresh spinach
- ¼ teaspoon of red pepper flakes

- ½ a teaspoon of smoked paprika
- ½ a teaspoon of BBQ sauce
- ½ a teaspoon of balsamic vinegar

Directions

1. Combine the BBQ sauce, red pepper flakes, paprika and vinegar in a large bowl and whisk to combine.
2. Add the corn, rice, black beans and spinach and toss to coat.
3. Divide onto plates, top with flaxseed and serve.

191.Kale and Lemon Salad

Preparation time: 10 minutes
Cooking time: 10 minutes
Servings: 4

Ingredients

- 5 cups of chopped kale
- 1 teaspoon of minced garlic
- ½ a tablespoon of maple syrup
- 2 tablespoons of lemon juice, freshly squeezed

Directions

1. Combine the garlic, maple syrup and lemon juice in a large bowl and whisk to combine.
2. Add the kale and massage the dressing into it for two minutes before serving.

192.Mango Jicama Basil Salad

Preparation time: 10 minutes
Cooking time: 1 hour 15 minutes
Servings: 6

Ingredients

- 1 jicama, grated and peeled

- 1 peeled and sliced mango
- ¼ cup of non-dairy milk
- 2 tablespoons of chopped, fresh basil
- 1 large chopped scallion
- ¼ teaspoon of sea salt
- 1 ½ tablespoons of tahini (optional)
- Fresh greens (to serve)
- Chopped cashews (to serve, optional)
- Cheesy sprinkle (to serve, optional)

Directions

1. Place the jicama into a large bowl.
2. Add the milk and mango to a food processor and blend until smooth.
3. Add the scallions, basil, tahini and salt and continue to blend.
4. Add the dressing to the jicama, stir to combine, put a lid on the bowl and refrigerate for an hour.
5. Arrange the greens on a plate, add the jicama and sprinkle the cheesy sprinkle and cashews over the top and serve.

193.Avocado and Roasted Beet Salad

Preparation time: 10 minutes
Cooking time: 40 minutes
Servings: 2

Ingredients

- 2 beets, thinly sliced and peeled
- 1 teaspoon of olive oil
- A pinch of sea salt
- 1 avocado
- 2 cups of mixed greens
- 4 tablespoons of creamy Balsamic Dressing

- 2 tablespoons of chopped almonds

Directions

1. Prepare the oven by preheating it to 450 degrees F.

2. In a large bowl, combine the oil, beets and salt, massage with your hands.

3. Arrange the beets in a single layer on a baking dish and bake them for 30 minutes.

4. Slice the avocado in half and remove the seed.

5. Scoop out the avocado flesh in one piece and slice it into crescents.

6. Once the beets are cooked, remove them from the oven and arrange the slices onto plates.

7. Top the beets with a slice of avocado, a handful of salad and drizzle the dressing over the top, coat with some chopped almonds and serve.

194.Kale Salad With Creamy Avocado

Preparation time: 10 minutes
Cooking time: 30 minutes
Servings: 4

Ingredients for the Dressing

- 1 peeled and pitted avocado
- 1 tablespoon of fresh lemon juice
- 1 tablespoon of fresh dill
- 1 small clove of garlic, pressed
- 1 chopped scallion
- A pinch of sea salt
- ¼ cup of water
- Ingredients for the Salad
- 8 large leaves of kale
- ½ a cup of chopped green beans

- 1 cup of halved cherry tomatoes
- 1 chopped, bell pepper
- 2 chopped scallions
- 2 cups of cooked millet
- Hummus (optional)
- Directions to Make the Dressing
- Transfer all the ingredients into a food processor, and blend until smooth.
- You can add more salt if you need to.

Directions:

1. Remove the stems from the kale and chop the leaves. Add a pinch of salt and massage with your fingers to soften the kale.

2. In a large bowl combine the millet, scallions, bell pepper, cherry tomatoes, green beans, kale and the dressing, toss to combine all ingredients.

3. Arrange the salad onto plates, if using hummus, place a spoonful on the side of each plate.

195.Aubergine Moroccan Salad

Preparation time: 10 minutes
Cooking time: 45 minutes
Servings: 2

Ingredients

- 1 teaspoon of olive oil
- 1 diced egg plant
- ½ a teaspoon of ground cumin
- ½ a teaspoon of ground ginger
- ¼ teaspoon of turmeric
- ¼ teaspoon of ground nutmeg
- A pinch of sea salt
- The juice and zest of half a lemon

- Half a lemon sliced into wedges
- 2 tablespoons of capers
- 1 tablespoon of green olives chopped
- 1 clove of garlic, pressed
- A handful of finely chopped fresh mint
- 2 cups of chopped spinach

Directions

1. In a large frying pan, heat the oil over a medium temperature.
2. Sauté the eggplant for 5 minutes and then add the nutmeg, turmeric, ginger, cumin and salt, and stir to combine. Continue to cook for about 10 minutes until the eggplant becomes extremely soft.
3. Add the mint, garlic, olives, capers, lemon juice and zest.
4. Arrange a handful of spinach onto each plate and top with the eggplant mixture.
5. Squeeze a wedge of lemon over the top and serve.

196. Potato and Dill Salad

Preparation time: 10 minutes
Cooking time: 35 minutes
Servings: 4

Ingredients

- 6 medium potatoes sliced into cubes
- 1 zucchini sliced into cubes
- ¼ cup of fresh dill, chopped
- 2 teaspoons of Dijon mustard
- 1/8 teaspoon of sea salt
- Ground black pepper
- 1 teaspoon of nutritional yeast (optional)
- Milk – the non-dairy kind (optional)

- 3 chopped stalks of celery
- 1 bell pepper chopped and seeded
- 1 tablespoon of scallions, chopped

Directions

1. Boil a large pot of water, add the potatoes and boil for 10 minutes.
2. Add the zucchini and boil for a further 10 minutes.
3. Take the saucepan off the fire, drain the water, but save one cup of the water.
4. Transfer the potatoes and zucchini in a bowl and set to one side to cool down.
5. Put ½ a cup of the potatoes and zucchini into a food processor, add the water from step 3, nutritional yeast (if using), salt, pepper, mustard, dill, non-dairy milk (if using) and blend until smooth.
6. Add the chives, bell pepper and celery to the rest of the zucchini and potatoes, pour the dressing over the top, arrange onto plates and serve.

197. White Bean Tuscan Salad

Preparation time: 10 minutes
Cooking time: 40 minutes
Servings: 2

Ingredients

- 1 tablespoon of olive oil
- 2 tablespoons of balsamic vinegar
- 1 tablespoon of scallions, minced
- 1 clove of minced garlic
- 1 tablespoon of chopped, fresh rosemary
- 1 tablespoon of chopped, fresh oregano

- A pinch of salt

- Ingredients for The Salad

- 1 can of cannellini beans, rinsed and drained

- 6 thinly sliced mushrooms

- 1 diced zucchini

- 2 diced carrots

- 2 tablespoons of chopped, fresh basil

Directions

1. To make the dressing, add all the ingredients into a food processor and blend until smooth.

2. Arrange the salad in a plastic container, pour the dressing over the top, toss to combine, cover and refrigerate for 30 minutes before serving.

198.Edamame and Black Rice Salad

Preparation time: 10 minutes
Cooking time: 40 minutes
Servings: 4

Ingredients

- 1 cup of black rice

- 2 cups of water

- A pinch of sea salt

- 1 large sweet potato

- 1 teaspoon of olive oil

- 1 cup of edamame beans

- 1 chopped and seeded bell pepper

- ½ a head of chopped broccoli

- 4 chopped scallions

- Chopped fresh cilantro

- Sesame seeds

- Ingredients for The Dressing

- The juice of ½ an orange

- 1 tablespoon of soy sauce

- 1 tablespoon of apple cider vinegar

- 2 teaspoons of maple syrup

- 2 teaspoons of sesame oil

Directions

1. Prepare the oven by preheating it to 400 degrees F.

2. Cook the rice according to the instructions on the packet. Once the rice is cooked, remove it from the stove, drain and rinse the rice and set it to one side to cool down.

3. Peel the sweet potato, dice it and toss olive oil over the top.

4. Arrange the sweet potato over a baking dish and bake for 20 minutes. Once cooked, remove them from the oven and leave them to cool down.

5. Transfer all the ingredients for the dressing into a jar and shake to combine.

6. In a large bowl, add the scallions, broccoli, bell pepper, edamame, sweet potato and rice and toss to combine.

7. Arrange onto plates, drizzle the dressing over the top, and garnish with sesame seeds and fresh cilantro.

199.Sweet Dill Dressing

Preparation time: 10 minutes
Cooking time: 5 minutes
Servings: 1

Ingredients

- 3 tablespoons of water

- ¼ teaspoon of garlic powder

- 1 teaspoon of dried dill

- 1 tablespoon of apple cider vinegar

- 1 tablespoon of agave nectar
- 3 tablespoons of veganaise
- ¼ cup of nutritional yeast

Directions

1. Combine all the ingredients in a food processor and blend until smooth.

200.Cherry Tomato Dressing

Preparation time: 10 minutes
Cooking time: 5 minutes
Servings: 1

Ingredients

- ¼ teaspoon of black pepper
- ¼ teaspoon of salt
- ¼ teaspoon of garlic powder
- ½ teaspoon of onion powder
- ½ a teaspoon of paprika
- 1 tablespoon of agave nectar
- ¼ cup of olive oil
- ¼ cup of balsamic vinegar
- Cherry tomatoes

Directions

1. Combine all the ingredients in a food processor and blend until smooth.

201.Greek Dressing

Preparation time: 10 minutes
Cooking time: 5 minutes
Servings: 1

Ingredients

- ¼ teaspoon of black pepper
- ¼ teaspoon of salt
- ¼ teaspoon of garlic powder
- ½ teaspoon of dried oregano

- 1 tablespoon of Dijon mustard
- ¼ cup of lemon juice
- ¼ cup of olive oil

Directions

1. Combine all the ingredients in a food processor and blend until smooth.

202.Mustard Maple Dressing

Preparation time: 10 minutes
Cooking time: 5 minutes
Servings: 1

Ingredients

- ¼ teaspoon of garlic powder
- 1 tablespoon of lemon juice
- 2 tablespoons of Dijon mustard
- 2 tablespoons of maple syrup
- ¼ cup of olive oil

Directions

1. Combine all the ingredients into a food processor and blend until smooth.

203.Zucchini & Lentil Salad

Preparation Time: 10 Minutes
Cooking Time: 20 Minutes
Serving: 1

Ingredients:

- ½ cup Brown Lentils, dried & cooked
- 15 Cherry Tomatoes, quartered
- 2 Zucchini, rinsed and ends discarded
- For the dressing:
- 15 Capers
- 1 Avocado, small & ripe
- ¼ cup Water

- ½ cup Parsley, fresh
- ½ tsp. Garlic Powder
- Juice of ½ of 1 Lemon
- 1 tbsp. Extra Virgin Olive Oil

Directions:

1. For making this healthy salad, you need to make zucchini ribbons by running the vegetable peeler down the entire length of the veggie while pressing it down lightly.

2. Now, combine the zucchini ribbons and quartered cherry tomatoes in a large mixing bowl.

3. Next, blend all the ingredients needed to make the dressing in a high-speed blender for two minutes or until you get a smooth one.

4. Then, check for seasoning and add more as needed.

5. Finally, stir in the cooked lentils and spoon in the dressing over it.

6. Serve and enjoy.

204. Greek Salad

Preparation Time: 5 Minutes
Cooking Time: 5 Minutes
Serving: 2

Ingredients:

- For the salad:
- ½ yellow bell pepper, seeded and cut into bite-size pieces
- ½ red onion, peeled and sliced thinly
- ½ cup tofu cheese, cut into bite-size squares
- 10 Kalamata olives pitted
- 3 large tomatoes cut into bite-size pieces
- ½ cucumber, cut into bite-size pieces

- For the dressing:
- 4 tbsp olive oil
- ½ tbsp red wine vinegar
- 2 tsp dried oregano
- Salt and black pepper to taste

Directions:

1. In a salad bowl, combine all the salad's ingredients until well combined

2. In a small bowl, mix the dressing's ingredients and toss into the salad.

3. Dish the salad and enjoy!

205. Cashew Salad with Peanut Sauce

Preparation Time: 10 Minutes
Cooking Time: 25 Minutes
Serving: 4

Ingredients:

- 4 Green Onions, diced
- ½ cup Quinoa, raw
- 2 tbsp. Cilantro
- ½ of 1 Red Bell Pepper, thinly sliced
- ¼ cup Basil, chopped
- 1 Carrot, large & shaved
- ½ cup Cashew, roasted
- 2 cup Kale, packed loosely
- ¾ cup Edamame
- For the Thai peanut sauce:
- 2 tbsp. Water
- ¼ cup Natural Peanut Butter
- Pinch of Cayenne
- 2 tbsp. Sesame Oil
- Juice of ½ of 1 Lemon

- 2 tbsp. Soy Sauce
- 1 tsp. Maple Syrup
- 1 tbsp. Rice Vinegar
- 2 Garlic cloves, minced
- 2 tsp. Ginger, fresh & grated

Directions:

1. First, place quinoa and one cup of water in a deep saucepan over medium-high heat and bring the mixture to a boil.

2. Reduce the heat once the mixture starts boiling and allow it to simmer.

3. Simmer the quinoa for 20 to 25 minutes or until all the water has been absorbed.

4. Next, fluff the cooked quinoa with a fork. Set it aside to cool. Once cooled, place the quinoa in the refrigerator.

5. In the meantime, toss all the remaining ingredients together in a large mixing bowl.

6. After that, make the dressing by mixing all the ingredients needed to make the dressing in a large bowl, excluding the water with an immersion blender or blend in a high-speed blender.

7. Blend until you get a smooth, thickened sauce.

8. Add water as needed to get the consistency you desire.

9. Finally, combine the cooled quinoa with the salad and drizzle the peanut sauce over it.

10. Toss well and serve immediately.

206. Rainbow Vegetables Salad

Preparation time: 5 minutes
Cooking time: 20 minutes
Servings: 4

Ingredients:

- 1 medium red bell pepper, deseeded, diced
- 1/2 of medium sweet onion, cut into wedges
- 1 medium yellow summer squash, diced
- 1 zucchini, diced
- 4 ounces mushrooms, halved
- 1/3 teaspoon ground black pepper
- 2/3 teaspoon salt
- 1 tablespoon olive oil

Directions:

1. Switch on the air fryer, insert the fryer basket, then shut it with the lid, set the frying temperature 350 degrees F, and let it preheat for 5 minutes.

2. Meanwhile, take a large bowl, place all the vegetables in it, drizzle with oil, season with salt and black pepper and toss until coated.

3. Open the preheated fryer, place vegetables in it, close the lid and cook for 20 minutes until golden brown and cooked, shaking halfway.

4. When done, the air fryer will beep, open the lid and transfer vegetables to a dish.

5. Serve straight away.

207. Vegetable Salad with Chimichurri Vinaigrette

Preparation time: 5 minutes
Cooking time: 30 minutes
Servings: 4

Ingredients:

- For the Salad:
- 1/2 head of medium purple

cauliflower, cut into small florets

- 2 cups baby arugula
- 3 small red beets, peeled, 1/4-inch thick diced
- 1/2 head of medium white cauliflower, cut into small florets
- 1 medium head of frisee, torn into small pieces
- 1/2 head of medium yellow cauliflower, cut into small florets
- 6 breakfast radishes, peeled, sliced
- 1 1/3 teaspoon salt
- ¾ teaspoon ground black pepper
- 1 small bunch of mint, slivered
- Olive oil spray
- For the Vinaigrette:
- 1 clove of garlic, peeled
- 1/2 bunch of chives, chopped
- 1 lemon, juiced
- 1 bunch of cilantro, leaves chopped
- 1 medium shallot, peeled, chopped
- 1 bunch parsley, leaves chopped
- 1/3 teaspoon ground black pepper
- 1/8 teaspoon red pepper flakes
- 2/3 teaspoon salt
- 1/2 cup olive oil
- 1/4 cup red wine vinegar

Directions:

1. Switch on the air fryer, insert the fryer basket, then shut it with the lid, set the frying temperature 360 degrees F, and let it preheat for 5 minutes.

2. Meanwhile, place white, yellow, and purple cauliflower in separate large bowls, place beets in another bowl, then season all the cauliflower and beets with salt and black pepper, drizzle with oil and toss until well coated.

3. Open the preheated fryer, place seasoned white cauliflower in it in a single layer, close the lid and cook for 8 minutes until golden brown and cooked, shaking halfway.

4. When done, the air fryer will beep, open the lid, transfer florets to a dish and then cook yellow cauliflower and purple cauliflower separately in the same manner.

5. When cauliflowers have roasted, add beets into the fryer basket in a single layer, close the lid and cook for 14 minutes until golden brown and cooked, shaking halfway.

6. Meanwhile, prepare the vinaigrette and for this, place all of its ingredients in a food processor, except for oil, pulse for 1 minute and then slowly blend in oil until smooth.

7. Assemble the salad and for this, place all the roasted vegetables in a large bowl, pour in vinaigrette, and toss until well coated.

8. Then add remaining vegetables, toss until mixed, garnish with mint and serve.

208.Roasted Vegetable and Pasta Salad

Preparation time: 10 minutes
Cooking time: 1 hour and 35 minutes
Servings: 16

Ingredients:

- 4 cups whole-grain pasta, cooked
- 3 small eggplants, destemmed
- 2 medium green bell peppers, deseeded, chopped

- 4 medium tomatoes, cut in eighths
- 3 medium zucchini, trimmed
- 1 cup cherry tomatoes, sliced
- 2 teaspoons salt
- ½ cup Italian dressing
- 2 tablespoons olive oil
- 8 tablespoons grated parmesan cheese
- Olive oil spray

Directions:

1. Switch on the air fryer, insert the fryer basket, then shut it with the lid, set the frying temperature 350 degrees F, and let it preheat for 5 minutes.

2. Meanwhile, cut the eggplant into ½-inch thick round slices, place them in a bowl, drizzle with 1 tablespoon oil and toss until coated.

3. Open the preheated fryer, place eggplant pieces in it, close the lid, and cook for 40 minutes until cooked and very tender, shaking halfway.

4. Meanwhile, cut zucchini into ½-inch thick round slices, place them in a bowl, drizzle with 1 tablespoon oil and toss until coated.

5. When done, the air fryer will beep, open the lid and transfer eggplant to a dish.

6. Place zucchini into the fryer basket, close the lid, and cook for 25 minutes until cooked and very tender, shaking halfway.

7. When done, the air fryer will beep, open the lid and transfer zucchini to a dish containing eggplant.

8. Place tomato slices into the fryer basket, spray with olive oil, close the lid and cook for 30 minutes until cooked and very tender, shaking halfway.

9. Then take a large salad bowl, place peppers in it, then add cherry tomatoes and all the roasted vegetables, add remaining ingredients and toss until well mixed.

10. Chill the salad for 20 minutes in the refrigerated and then serve straight away.

209. Taco Salad Bowl

Preparation time: 10 minutes
Cooking time: 7 minutes
Servings: 4

Ingredients:

- 1 flour tortilla, burrito size
- Olive oil spray
- Taco filling as needed
- Method:
- Switch on the air fryer, then shut it with the lid, set the frying temperature 400 degrees F, and let it preheat for 5 minutes.
- Meanwhile, spray tortilla with oil on both sides, then double over with a large piece of foil on both sides; it should be slightly larger than a tortilla, press it into the fryer basket and shape it into a bowl by placing ramekins in the middle.
- Open the preheated fryer, insert the fryer basket, close the lid and cook for 5 minutes, then remove the ramekin and foil and continue cooking for 2 minutes until the edges of the tortilla are golden brown.
- When done, the air fryer will beep, open the lid, and lift out the taco bowl.
- Let it cool for 10 minutes, then fill it with favorite stuffing and serve.

210. Roasted Butternut Squash Salad

Preparation time: 10 minutes
Cooking time: 15 minutes
Servings: 4

Ingredients:

- 1 small shallot, peeled, minced
- 1 small butternut squash, peeled, deseeded, 1-inch cubed
- 1 small apple, cored, sliced
- 6 ounces arugula
- 1/4 teaspoon salt
- 1/4 teaspoon cayenne pepper
- 1 teaspoon all-purpose seasoning
- 2 tablespoons lemon juice
- 4 tablespoons olive oil
- 1/2 cup toasted sliced almonds
- 1/2 cup grated vegan Parmesan cheese

Directions:

1. Switch on the air fryer, insert the fryer basket, then shut it with the lid, set the frying temperature 400 degrees F, and let it preheat for 5 minutes.

2. Meanwhile, take a large bowl, place squash in it, seasoning with all-purpose seasoning and cayenne pepper, drizzle with 2 tablespoons oil and toss until coated.

3. Open the preheated fryer, place squash in it, close the lid and cook for 15 minutes until golden brown and cooked, shaking halfway.

4. Meanwhile, take a large bowl, place shallots in it, season with salt, drizzle with lemon juice and remaining olive oil, whisk until combined, add arugula and toss until coated.

5. When done, the air fryer will beep and then open the lid and transfer squash to a plate.

6. Assemble the salad and for this, distribute arugula between four plates, top with apples and roasted squash and then sprinkle with cheese and almonds.

7. Chill the salad for 15 minutes in the refrigerator and then serve straight away.

211. Fried Chickpea Salad

Preparation time: 5 minutes
Cooking time: 10 minutes
Servings: 4

Ingredients:

- 1 1/2 cups cooked chickpeas
- 1/2 teaspoon onion powder
- 1/8 teaspoon salt
- 2 teaspoons nutritional yeast
- Olive oil spray
- For the Salad:
- ¼ cup chopped green onion
- ¼ cup chopped tomatoes
- 2 tablespoons chopped green chilies

Directions:

1. Switch on the air fryer, insert the fryer basket, then shut it with the lid, set the frying temperature 400 degrees F, and let it preheat for 5 minutes.

2. Meanwhile, take a bowl, add chickpeas in it, spray generously with oil, add onion, salt and yeast and toss until mixed.

3. Open the preheated fryer, place chickpeas in it, close the lid and cook for 7 minutes until golden brown and cooked, shaking halfway.

4. When done, the air fryer will beep, then open the lid and transfer chickpeas to a salad bowl.

5. Cool chickpeas for 10 minutes, then add all the ingredients for the salad in it and toss until mixed.

6. Serve straight away.

212.Sweet Potato Croutons Salad

Preparation time: 5 minutes
Cooking time: 20 minutes
Servings: 4

Ingredients:

- 12s-ounce baked sweet potato, skin-on, cut into pieces
- 2 mandarin oranges, peeled, segmented, halved
- 1-pound mixed salad greens and vegetables
- 1 sweet apple, cored, diced, air fried
- 2 tablespoons balsamic vinegar
- 1/3 cup pomegranate seeds

Directions:

1. Switch on the air fryer, insert the fryer basket, then shut it with the lid, set the frying temperature 350 degrees F, and let it preheat for 5 minutes.

2. Meanwhile, prepare sweet potatoes, and for this, dice them into small pieces.

3. Open the preheated fryer, place sweet potatoes in it in a single layer, spray with olive oil, close the lid and cook for 20 minutes until golden brown and cooked, shaking halfway.

4. When done, the air fryer will beep, open the lid, and then transfer sweet potato croutons to a salad bowl.

5. Add remaining ingredients, gently stir

until combined, and then serve.

213.Brussel sprouts Salad

Preparation time: 5 minutes
Cooking time: 9 minutes
Servings: 2

Ingredients:

- 12 Brussel sprouts, cored, leaves removed
- 1 ½ tablespoons capers
- 2 tablespoons toasted sliced almonds
- 2 teaspoons chopped parsley
- 1/8 teaspoon ground black pepper
- 1/8 teaspoon red chili flakes
- 1/8 teaspoon salt
- 1 ½ tablespoon red wine vinegar
- 2 teaspoons and 1 ½ tablespoon olive oil

Directions:

1. Switch on the air fryer, insert the fryer basket, then shut it with the lid, set the frying temperature 400 degrees F, and let it preheat for 5 minutes.

2. Meanwhile, take a large bowl, place sprouts in it, add 1 ½ tablespoon olive oil and toss until coated.

3. Open the preheated fryer, place sprouts in it in, close the lid and cook for 9 minutes until golden brown and cooked, shaking halfway.

4. When done, the air fryer will beep, open the lid, and transfer sprouts to a dish lined with paper towels to remove excess oil.

5. Then remove the paper towels, add remaining ingredients, and toss until combined.

6. Serve straight away.

214.Garlic and Lemon Mushroom Salad

Preparation time: 5 minutes
Cooking time: 10 minutes
Servings: 2

Ingredients:

- 8 ounces mushrooms
- 1/2 teaspoon garlic powder
- 1 tablespoon chopped parsley
- 1 teaspoon soy sauce
- ½ teaspoon salt
- 1/3 teaspoon ground black pepper
- 2 tablespoons olive oil
- 2 wedges of lemon for serving

Directions:

1. Switch on the air fryer, insert the fryer basket, then shut it with the lid, set the frying temperature 380 degrees F, and let it preheat for 5 minutes.

2. Meanwhile, cut mushrooms in quarters, then place them in a bowl, add remaining ingredients, except for lemon wedges and toss until coated.

3. Open the preheated fryer, place mushrooms in it, close the lid and cook for 10 minutes until golden brown and cooked, shaking halfway.

4. When done, the air fryer will beep, open the lid, and transfer mushrooms to the salad bowls.

5. Let mushroom cool for 10 minutes and then serve straight away.

215.Italian Tofu Salad

Preparation time: 5 minutes
Cooking time: 10 minutes
Servings: 2

Ingredients:

- 8 ounces tofu, extra-firm, pressed, drained
- 1/2 teaspoon dried oregano
- 1/4 teaspoon onion powder
- 1/2 teaspoon garlic powder
- 1/2 teaspoon dried basil
- ¼ teaspoon ground black pepper
- 1 tablespoon soy sauce
- 1 tablespoon chickpeas liquid

Directions:

1. Switch on the air fryer, insert the fryer basket, then shut it with the lid, set the frying temperature 350 degrees F, and let it preheat for 5 minutes.

2. Meanwhile, paper tofu and for this, cut tofu into ten cubed, place them in a plastic bag, add remaining ingredients, seal the bag and shake well until coated.

3. Open the preheated fryer, place tofu in it in a single layer, close the lid and cook for 10 minutes until golden brown and cooked, turning halfway.

4. When done, the air fryer will beep and then open the lid and transfer tofu to a salad bowl.

5. Serve straight away.

6. Stir-Fried, Grilled Vegetables

216.Crusty Grilled Corn

Preparation time: 10 minutes
Cooking time: 15 minutes
Servings: 4

Ingredients

- 2 corn cobs
- 1/3 cup Vegenaise

- 1 small handful cilantro
- ½ cup breadcrumbs
- 1 teaspoon lemon juice

Directions:

1. Preheat the gas grill on high heat.
2. Add corn grill to the grill and continue grilling until it turns golden-brown on all sides.
3. Mix the Vegenaise, cilantro, breadcrumbs, and lemon juice in a bowl.
4. Add grilled corn cobs to the crumbs mixture.
5. Toss well then serve.

217. Grilled Carrots with Chickpea Salad

Preparation time: 10 minutes
Cooking time: 10 minutes
Servings: 8
Ingredients

- Carrots
- 8 large carrots
- 1 tablespoon oil
- 1 ½ teaspoon salt
- 1 teaspoon dried oregano
- 1 teaspoon dried thyme
- 2 teaspoon paprika powder
- 1 ½ tablespoon soy sauce
- ½ cup of water
- Chickpea Salad
- 14 oz canned chickpeas
- 3 medium pickles
- 1 small onion
- A big handful of lettuce

- 1 teaspoon apple cider vinegar
- ½ teaspoon dried oregano
- ½ teaspoon salt
- Ground black pepper, to taste
- ½ cup vegan cream

Directions:

1. Toss the carrots with all of its ingredients in a bowl.
2. Thread one carrot on a stick and place it on a plate.
3. Preheat the grill over high heat.
4. Grill the carrots for 2 minutes per side on the grill.
5. Toss the ingredients for the salad in a large salad bowl.
6. Slice grilled carrots and add them on top of the salad.
7. Serve fresh.

218. Grilled Avocado Guacamole

Preparation time: 10 minutes
Cooking time: 20 minutes
Servings: 4

Ingredients

- ½ teaspoon olive oil
- 1 lime, halved
- ½ onion, halved
- 1 serrano chile, halved, stemmed, and seeded
- 3 Haas avocados, skin on
- 2–3 tablespoons fresh cilantro, chopped
- ½ teaspoon smoked salt

Directions:

1. Preheat the grill over medium heat.

2. Brush the grilling grates with olive oil and place chile, onion, and lime on it.

3. Grill the onion for 10 minutes, chile for 5 minutes, and lime for 2 minutes.

4. Transfer the veggies to a large bowl.

5. Now cut the avocados in half and grill them for 5 minutes.

6. Mash the flesh of the grilled avocado in a bowl.

7. Chop the other grilled veggies and add them to the avocado mash.

8. Stir in remaining ingredients and mix well.

9. Serve.

219. Grilled Fajitas with Jalapeño Sauce

Preparation time: 10 minutes
Cooking time: 25 minutes
Servings: 4

Ingredients

- Marinade
- ¼ cup olive oil
- ¼ cup lime juice
- 2 garlic cloves, minced
- 1 teaspoon chili powder
- 1 teaspoon ground cumin
- 1 teaspoon dried oregano
- ½ teaspoon salt
- ½ teaspoon black pepper
- Jalapeño Sauce
- 6 jalapeno peppers stemmed, halved, and seeded
- 1–2 teaspoons olive oil
- 1 cup raw cashews, soaked and drained
- ½ cup almond milk
- ¼ cup water
- ¼ cup lime juice
- 2 teaspoons agaves
- ½ cup fresh cilantro
- Salt, to taste
- Grilled Vegetables
- ½ lb asparagus spears, trimmed
- 2 large portobello mushrooms, sliced
- 1 large zucchini, sliced
- 1 red bell pepper, sliced
- 1 red onion, sliced

Directions:

1. Dump all the ingredients for the marinade in a large bowl.

2. Toss in all the veggies and mix well to marinate for 1 hour.

3. Meanwhile, prepare the sauce and brush the jalapenos with oil.

4. Grill the jalapenos for 5 minutes per side until slightly charred.

5. Blend the grilled jalapenos with other ingredients for the sauce in a blender.

6. Transfer this sauce to a separate bowl and keep it aside.

7. Now grill the marinated veggies in the grill until soft and slightly charred on all sides.

8. Pour the prepared sauce over the

grilled veggies.

9. Serve.

220. Grilled Ratatouille Kebabs

Preparation time: 10 minutes
Cooking time: 20 minutes
Servings: 6

Ingredients

- 3 tablespoons soy sauce
- 3 tablespoons balsamic vinegar
- 1 teaspoon dried thyme leaves
- 2 tablespoons extra virgin olive oil
- Veggies
- 1 zucchini, diced
- ½ red onion, diced
- ½ red capsicum, diced
- 2 tomatoes, diced
- 1 small eggplant, diced
- 8 button mushrooms, diced

Directions:

1. Toss the veggies with soy sauce, olive oil, thyme, and balsamic vinegar in a large bowl.

2. Thread the veggies alternately on the wooden skewers and reserve the remaining marinade.

3. Marinate these skewers for 1 hour in the refrigerator.

4. Preheat the grill over medium heat.

5. Grill the marinated skewers for 5 minutes per side while basting with the reserved marinade.

6. Serve fresh.

221. Tofu Hoagie Rolls

Preparation time: 10 minutes
Cooking time: 20 minutes
Servings: 06

Ingredients:

- ½ cup vegetable broth
- ¼ cup hot sauce
- 1 tablespoon vegan butter
- 1 (16 ounce) package tofu, pressed and diced
- 4 cups cabbage, shredded
- 2 medium apples, grated
- 1 medium shallot, grated
- 6 tablespoons vegan mayonnaise
- 1 tablespoon apple cider vinegar
- Salt and black pepper
- 4 6-inch hoagie rolls, toasted

Directions:

1. In a saucepan, combine broth with butter and hot sauce and bring to a boil.

2. Add tofu and reduce the heat to a simmer.

3. Cook for 10 minutes then remove from heat and let sit for 10 minutes to marinate.

4. Toss cabbage and rest of the ingredients in a salad bowl.

5. Prepare and set up a grill on medium heat.

6. Drain the tofu and grill for 5 minutes per side.

7. Lay out the toasted hoagie rolls and add grilled tofu to each hoagie

8. Add the cabbage mixture evenly between them then close it.

9. Serve.

222 Grilled Avocado with Tomatoes

Preparation time: 10 minutes
Cooking time: 15 minutes
Servings: 06

Ingredients:

- 3 avocados, halved and pitted
- 3 limes, wedged
- 1½ cup grape tomatoes
- 1 cup fresh corn
- 1 cup onion, chopped
- 3 serrano peppers
- 2 garlic cloves, peeled

- ¼ cup cilantro leaves, chopped
- 1 tablespoon olive oil
- Salt and black pepper to taste

Directions:

1. Prepare and set a grill over medium heat.

2. Brush the avocado with oil and grill it for 5 minutes per side.

3. Meanwhile, toss the garlic, onion, corn, tomatoes, and pepper in a baking sheet.

4. At 550 degrees F, roast the vegetables for 5 minutes.

5. Toss the veggie mix and stir in salt, cilantro, and black pepper.

6. Mix well then fill the grilled avocadoes with the mixture.

7. Garnish with lime.

8. Serve.

223. Grilled Tofu with Chimichurri Sauce

Preparation time: 10 minutes
Cooking time: 12 minutes
Servings: 04

Ingredients:

- 2 tablespoons plus 1 teaspoon olive oil

- 1 teaspoon dried oregano
- 1 cup parsley leaves
- ½ cup cilantro leaves
- 2 Fresno peppers, seeded and chopped
- 2 tablespoons white wine vinegar
- 2 tablespoons water
- 1 tablespoon fresh lime juice
- Salt and black pepper
- 1 cup couscous, cooked
- 1 teaspoon lime zest
- ¼ cup toasted pumpkin seeds
- 1 cup fresh spinach, chopped
- 1 (15.5 ounce) can kidney beans, rinsed and drained
- 1 (14 to 16 ounce) block tofu, diced
- 2 summer squashes, diced
- 3 spring onions, quartered

Directions:

1. In a saucepan, heat 2 tablespoons oil and add oregano over medium heat.
2. After 30 seconds add parsley, chili pepper, cilantro, lime juice, 2 tablespoons water, vinegar, salt and black pepper.
3. Mix well then blend in a blender.
4. Add the remining oil, pumpkin seeds, beans and spinach and cook for 3 minutes.
5. Stir in couscous and adjust seasoning with salt and black pepper.
6. Prepare and set up a grill on medium heat.
7. Thread the tofu, squash, and onions on the skewer in an alternating pattern.

8. Grill these skewers for 4 minutes per side while basting with the green sauce.
9. Serve the skewers on top of the couscous with green sauce.
10. Enjoy.

224. Grilled Seitan with Creole Sauce

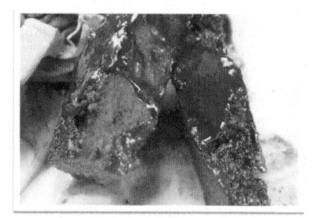

Preparation time: 10 minutes
Cooking time: 14 minutes
Servings: 4

Ingredients:

- Grilled Seitan Kebabs:
- 4 cups seitan, diced
- 2 medium onions, diced into squares
- 8 bamboo skewers
- 1 can coconut milk
- 2½ tablespoons creole spice
- 2 tablespoons tomato paste
- 2 cloves of garlic
- Creole Spice Mix:
- 2 tablespoons paprika
- 12 dried peri peri chili peppers
- 1 tablespoon salt
- 1 tablespoon freshly ground pepper
- 2 teaspoons dried thyme

- 2 teaspoons dried oregano

Directions:

1. Prepare the creole seasoning by blending all its ingredients and preserve in a sealable jar.

2. Thread seitan and onion on the bamboo skewers in an alternating pattern.

3. On a baking sheet, mix coconut milk with creole seasoning, tomato paste and garlic.

4. Soak the skewers in the milk marinade for 2 hours.

5. Prepare and set up a grill over medium heat.

6. Grill the skewers for 7 minutes per side.

7. Serve.

225.Mushroom Steaks

Preparation time: 10 minutes
Cooking time: 24 minutes
Servings: 4

Ingredients:

- 1 tablespoon vegan butter
- ½ cup vegetable broth
- ½ small yellow onion, diced
- 1 large garlic clove, minced
- 3 tablespoons balsamic vinegar
- 1 tablespoon mirin
- ½ tablespoon soy sauce
- ½ tablespoon tomato paste
- 1 teaspoon dried thyme
- ½ teaspoon dried basil
- A dash of ground black pepper
- 2 large, whole portobello mushrooms

Directions:

1. Melt butter in a saucepan over medium heat and stir in half of the broth.

2. Bring to a simmer then add garlic and onion. Cook for 8 minutes.

3. Whisk the rest of the ingredients except the mushrooms in a bowl.

4. Add this mixture to the onion in the pan and mix well.

5. Bring this filling to a simmer then remove from the heat.

6. Clean the mushroom caps inside and out and divide the filling between the mushrooms.

7. Place the mushrooms on a baking sheet and top them with remaining sauce and broth.

8. Cover with foil then place it on a grill to smoke.

9. Cover the grill and broil for 16 minutes over indirect heat.

10. Serve warm.

226.Zucchini Boats with Garlic Sauce

Preparation time: 10 minutes
Cooking time: 10 minutes
Servings: 2

Ingredients:

- 1 zucchini
- 1 tbsp olive oil
- Salt, to taste
- Black pepper, to taste
- Filling:
- 1 cup organic walnuts
- 2 tablespoons olive oil
- ½ teaspoon smoked paprika
- ½ teaspoon ground cumin
- 1 pinch salt
- Sauce:
- ½ cup cashews
- ½ cup water
- 2 teaspoons olive oil
- 2 teaspoons lemon juice
- 1 clove garlic
- ⅛ teaspoon salt

Directions:

1. Cut the zucchini squash in half and scoop out some flesh from the center to make boats.
2. Rub the zucchini boats with oil, salt, and black pepper.
3. Prepare and set up a grill over medium heat.
4. Grill the boats for 5 minutes per side.
5. In a blender, add all the filling ingredients and blend them well.
6. Divide the filling between the zucchini boats.
7. Blend all of the sauce ingredients until it is lump free.
8. Pour the sauce over the zucchini boats.
9. Serve.

227. Grilled Eggplant with Pecan Butter Sauce

Preparation time: 10 minutes
Cooking time: 31 minutes
Servings: 02

Ingredients:

- Marinated Eggplant:
- 1 eggplant, sliced
- Salt to taste
- 4 tablespoons olive oil
- ¼ teaspoon smoked paprika
- ¼ teaspoon ground turmeric

- Black Bean and Pecan Sauce:
- ⅓ cup vegetable broth
- ⅓ cup red wine
- ⅓ cup red wine vinegar
- 1 large shallot, chopped
- 1 teaspoon ground coriander
- 2 teaspoons minced cilantro
- ½ cup pecan pieces, toasted
- 2 roasted garlic cloves
- 4 small banana peppers, seeded, and diced
- 8 tablespoons butter
- 1 tablespoon chives, chopped
- 1 (15.5 ounce) can black beans, rinsed and drained
- Salt and black pepper to taste
- 1 teaspoon fresh lime juice

Directions:

1. In a saucepan, add broth, wine, vinegar, shallots, coriander, cilantro and garlic.
2. Cook while stirring for 20 minutes on a simmer.
3. Meanwhile blend butter with chives, pepper, and pecans in a blender.
4. Add this mixture to the broth along with salt, lime juice, black pepper, and beans.
5. Mix well and cook for 5 minutes.
6. Rub the eggplant with salt and spices.
7. Prepare and set up the grill over medium heat.
8. Grill the eggplant slices for 6 minutes per side.
9. Serve the eggplant with prepared sauce.

10. Enjoy.

228.Sweet Potato Grilled Sandwich

Preparation time: 10 minutes
Cooking time: 12 minutes
Servings: 02

Ingredients:

- 1 small sweet potato, sliced
- ½ cup sweet bell peppers, sliced
- 1 cup canned black beans, roughly mashed
- ½ cup salsa
- 1 avocado, peeled and sliced
- 4 slices bread
- 1-2 tablespoons vegan butter

Directions:

1. Prepare and set up the grill over medium heat.
2. Grill the sweet potato slices for 5 minutes and the bell pepper slices for 3 minutes.
3. Spread each slice of bread liberally with butter.
4. On two of the bread slices, layer sweet potato slices, bell peppers, beans, salsa and avocado slices.
5. Place the other two slices of bread on top to make two sandwiches.
6. Cut them in half diagonally then grill the sandwiches for 1 minute per side.
7. Serve.

229.Grilled Eggplant

Preparation time: 10 minutes
Cooking time: 10 minutes
Servings: 04

Ingredients:

- 2 tablespoons salt
- 1 cup water
- 3 medium eggplants, sliced
- ⅓ cup olive oil

Directions:

1. Mix water with salt in a bowl and soak eggplants for 10 minutes.
2. Drain the eggplant and leave them in a colander.
3. Pat them dry with a paper towel.
4. Prepare and set up the grill at medium heat.
5. Toss the eggplant slices in olive oil.
6. Grill them for 5 minutes per side.
7. Serve.

230Grilled Portobello

Preparation time: 10 minutes

Cooking time: 8 minutes

Servings: 04

Ingredients:

- 4 portobello mushrooms
- ¼ cup soy sauce
- ¼ cup tomato sauce
- 2 tablespoons maple syrup
- 1 tablespoon molasses
- 2 tablespoons minced garlic
- 1 tablespoon onion powder
- 1 pinch salt and pepper

Directions:

1. Mix all the ingredients except mushrooms in a bowl.
2. Add mushrooms to this marinade and mix well to coat.
3. Cover and marinate for 1 hour.
4. Prepare and set up the grill at medium heat. Grease it with cooking spray.
5. Grill the mushroom for 4 minutes per side.
6. Serve.

231.Ginger Sweet Tofu

Preparation time: 10 minutes
Cooking time: 15 minutes
Servings: 04

Ingredients:

- ½ pound firm tofu, drained and diced
- 2 tablespoons peanut oil
- 1-inch piece ginger, sliced
- ⅓ pound bok choy, leaves separated
- 1 tablespoon shao sing rice wine
- 1 tablespoon rice vinegar
- ½ teaspoon dried chili flakes
- Marinade:
- 1 tablespoon grated ginger
- 1 teaspoon dark soy sauce
- 2 tablespoons light soy sauce
- 1 tablespoon brown sugar

Directions:

1. Toss the tofu cubes with the marinade ingredients and marinate for 15 minutes.
2. In a wok, add half of the oil and ginger, then sauté for 30 secs.
3. Toss in bok choy and cook for 2 minutes.
4. Add a splash of water and steam for 2 minutes.

5. Transfer the bok choy to a bowl.
6. Add remaining oil and tofu to the pan then sauté for 10 minutes.
7. Add the tofu to the bok choy.
8. Serve.

232.Singapore Tofu

Preparation time: 10 minutes
Cooking time: 8 minutes
Servings: 04

Ingredients:

- ounces fine rice noodles, boiled
- 4 ounces firm tofu, boiled
- 2 tablespoons sunflower oil
- 3 spring onions, shredded
- 1 small piece of ginger, chopped
- 1 red pepper, thinly sliced
  - ounces snap peas
  - ounces beansprouts
- 1 teaspoon tikka masala paste
- 2 teaspoons reduced-salt soy sauce
- 1 tablespoon sweet chili sauce
- Chopped coriander and lime
- Lime wedges, to serve

Directions:

1. In a wok, add 1 tablespoon oil and the tofu then sauté for 5 minutes.

2. Transfer the sautéed tofu to a bowl.

3. Add more oil and the rest of the ingredients except noodles to the wok.

4. Stir fry for 3 minutes then add the tofu.

5. Toss well and then add noodles.

6. Mix and serve with lime wedges.

233.Wok Fried Broccoli

Preparation time: 10 minutes
Cooking time: 16 minutes
Servings: 02

Ingredients:

- 3 ounces whole, blanched peanuts
- 2 tablespoons olive oil
- 1 banana shallot, sliced
- 10 ounces broccoli, trimmed and cut into florets
- ¼ red pepper, julienned
- ½ yellow pepper, julienned
- 1 teaspoon soy sauce

Directions:

1. Toast peanuts on a baking sheet for 15 minutes at 350 degrees F.

2. In a wok, add oil and shallots and sauté for 10 minutes.

3. Toss in broccoli and peppers.

4. Stir fry for 3 minutes then add the rest of the ingredients.

5. Cook for 3 additional minutes and serve.

234.Broccoli & Brown Rice Satay

Preparation time: 10 minutes
Cooking time: 10 minutes
Servings: 4

Ingredients:

6 trimmed broccoli florets, halved

1-inch piece of ginger, shredded

2 garlic cloves, shredded

1 red onion, sliced

1 roasted red pepper, cut into cubes

2 teaspoons olive oil

1 teaspoon mild chili powder

1 tablespoon reduced salt soy sauce

1 tablespoon maple syrup

1 cup cooked brown rice

Directions:

Boil broccoli in water for 4 minutes then drain immediately.

In a pan add olive oil, ginger, onion, and garlic.

Stir fry for 2 minutes then add the rest of the ingredients.

Cook for 3 minutes then serve.

235.Sautéed Sesame Spinach

Preparation time: 1 hr. 10 minutes
Cooking time: 3 minutes
Servings: 04

Ingredients:

- 1 tablespoon toasted sesame oil
- ½ tablespoon soy sauce
- ½ teaspoon toasted sesame seeds, crushed
- ½ teaspoon rice vinegar
- ½ teaspoon golden caster sugar
- 1 garlic clove, grated
- 8 ounces spinach, stem ends trimmed

Directions:

1. Sauté spinach in a pan until it is wilted.
2. Whisk the sesame oil, garlic, sugar, vinegar, sesame seeds, soy sauce and black pepper together in a bowl.
3. Stir in spinach and mix well.
4. Cover and refrigerate for 1 hour.
5. Serve.

SNACKS

236.Hummus without Oil

Preparation Time: 5 minutes
Cooking Time: 0 minutes
Serving: 6

Ingredients

- 2 tablespoons of lemon juice
- 1 15-ounce can of chickpeas
- 2 tablespoons of tahini
- 1-2 freshly chopped/minced garlic cloves
- Red pepper hummus
- 2 tablespoons of almond milk pepper

Directions:

1. Rinse the chickpeas and put them in a high-speed blender with garlic. Blend them until they break into fine pieces.
2. Add the other ingredients and blend everything until you have a smooth paste. Add some water if you want a less thick consistency.
3. Your homemade hummus dip is ready to be served with eatables!

237.Quick Peanut Butter Bars

Preparation Time: 10 minutes
Cooking Time: 0 minutes
Serving: 1

Ingredients:

- 20 soft-pitted Medjool dates
- 1 cup of raw almonds
- 1 ¼ cup of crushed pretzels
- 1/3 cup of natural peanut butter

Directions:

1. Put the almonds in a food processor

and mix them until they are broken.

2. Add the peanut butter and the dates. Blend them until you have a thick dough

3. Crush the pretzels and put them in the processor. Pulse enough to mix them with the rest of the ingredients. You can also give them a good stir with a spoon.

4. Take a small, square pan and line it with parchment paper. Press the dough onto the pan, flattening it with your hands or a spoon.

5. Put it in the freezer for about 2 hours or in the fridge for about 4 hours.

6. Once it is fully set, cut it into bars. Store them and enjoy them when you are hungry. Just remember to store them in a sealed container.

238. Healthy Cauliflower Popcorn

Preparation Time: 10 minutes
Cooking Time: 12 hours
Serving: 2

Ingredients:

- 2 heads of cauliflower
- Spicy Sauce
- ½ cup of filtered water
- ½ teaspoon of turmeric
- 1 cup of dates
- 2-3 tablespoons of nutritional yeast
- ¼ cup of sun-dried tomatoes
- 2 tablespoons of raw tahini
- 1-2 teaspoons of cayenne pepper
- 2 teaspoons of onion powder
- 1 tablespoon of apple cider vinegar
- 2 teaspoons of garlic powder

Directions:

1. Chop the cauliflower into small pieces so that you can have crunchy popcorn.

2. Put all the ingredients for the spicy sauce in a blender and create a mixture with a smooth consistency.

3. Coat the cauliflower florets in the sauce. See that each piece is properly covered.

4. Put the spicy florets in a dehydrator tray.

5. Add some salt and your favorite herb if you want.

6. Dehydrate the cauliflower for 12 hours at 115°F. Keep dehydrating until it is crunchy.

7. Enjoy the cauliflower popcorn, which is a healthier alternative!

239. Crisp Balls Made with Peanut Butter

Preparation Time: 29 minutes
Cooking Time: 0 minutes
Serving: 16 balls

Ingredients:

- ¼ cup of wheat germ
- ½ cup of natural peanut butter
- 1/3 cup of rolled oats
- ¼ cup of unsweetened flaked coconut
- ¼ cup of whole quick oats
- ½ teaspoon of ground cinnamon
- ¼ cup of brown rice crisp cereal
- 1 tablespoon of maple syrup
- ¼ cup of apple cider vinegar

Directions:

1. In a bowl, mix all the ingredients apart from the rice cereal. Combine

everything properly.

2. Create 16 balls out of the mixture. Each ball should be 1 inch in diameter.

3. In a shallow dish, add the rice cereal and roll each ball on the crispies. See that the balls are properly coated.

4. Enjoy your no-bake crisp balls.

5. Store them in a refrigerator for later use.

240. Tempting Quinoa Tabbouleh

Preparation Time: 10 minutes
Cooking Time: 10 minutes
Serving: 6

Ingredients

- 1 cup of well-rinsed quinoa
- 1 finely minced garlic clove
- ½ teaspoon of kosher salt
- ½ cup of extra virgin olive oil
- 2 tablespoons of fresh lemon juice
- Freshly ground black pepper
- 2 Persian cucumbers, cut into ¼-inch pieces
- 2 thinly sliced scallions
- 1 pint of halved cherry tomatoes
- ½ cup of chopped fresh mint
- 2/3 cup of chopped parsley

Directions:

1. Put a medium saucepan on high heat and boil the quinoa mixed with salt in 1 ¼ cups of water. Decrease the heat to medium-low, cover the pot, and simmer everything until the quinoa is tender. The entire process will take 10 minutes. Remove the quinoa from heat and allow it to stand for 5 minutes. Fluff it with a fork.

2. In a small bowl, whisk the garlic with the lemon juice. Add the olive oil gradually. Mix the salt and pepper to taste.

3. On a baking sheet, spread the quinoa and allow it to cool. Shift it to a large bowl and mix ¼ of the dressing.

4. Add the tomatoes, scallions, herbs, and cucumber. Give them a good toss and season everything with pepper and salt. Add the remaining dressing.

241. Hummus Made with Sweet Potato

Preparation Time: 15 minutes
Cooking Time: 55 minutes
Serving: 3-4 cups

Ingredients:

- 2 cups of cooked chickpeas
- 2 medium sweet potatoes
- 3 tablespoons of tahini
- 3 tablespoons of olive oil
- 3 freshly peeled garlic gloves
- Freshly squeezed lemon juice
- Ground sea salt
- ¼ teaspoon of cumin
- Zest from half a lemon
- ½ teaspoon of smoked paprika
- 1 ½ teaspoons of cayenne pepper

Directions:

1. Preheat the oven to 400°F. Put the sweet potatoes on the middle rack of the oven and bake them for about 45 minutes. You can also bake the potatoes in a baking dish. You will know that they are ready when they become soft and squishy.

2. Allow the sweet potatoes to cool

down. Blend all the other ingredients in a food processor.

3. After the sweet potatoes have sufficiently cooled down, use a knife to peel off the skin.

4. Add the sweet potatoes to a blender and blend well with the rest of the ingredients.

5. Once you have a potato mash, sprinkle some sesame seeds and cayenne pepper and serve it!

242. Healthy Protein Bars

Preparation Time: 19 minutes
Cooking Time: 0 minutes
Servings: 12 balls

Ingredients:

- 1 large banana
- 1 cup of rolled oats
- 1 serving of vegan vanilla protein powder

Directions:

1. In a food processor, blend the protein powder and rolled oats.

2. Blend them for 1 minute until you have a semi-coarse mixture. The oats should be slightly chopped, but not powdered.

3. Add the banana and form a pliable and coarse dough.

4. Shape into either balls or small bars and store them in a container.

5. Eat one and store the rest in an airtight container in the refrigerator!

243. Chocolate Avocado Mousse

Preparation time: 10 minutes
Cooking time: 10 minutes
Servings: 6

Ingredients:

- 1¼ cups almond milk, unsweetened
- 1 lb. dairy-free dark chocolate, coarsely chopped
- 4 small ripe avocados, pitted, peeled, and chopped
- ¼ cup agave syrup
- 1 tbsp orange zest, finely grated
- 2 tbsp puffed quinoa
- 2 tsp Maldon sea salt
- 2 tsp Aleppo pepper flakes
- 1 tbsp extra virgin olive oil

Directions:

1. Heat almond milk in a saucepan. After 5 to 10 minutes, add in chopped chocolate.

2. Take all remaining ingredients and blend them until smooth.

3. Mix both and let cool for a while.

4. Refrigerate for about 2 hours before serving.

244. Fudge

Preparation time: 10 minutes
Cooking time: 5 minutes
Servings: 18

Ingredients:

- 1 cup vegan chocolate chips
- ½ cup soy milk

Directions:

1. Line an 8-inch portion skillet with wax paper. Set aside. Clear some space in your refrigerator for this dish as you will need it later.

2. Melt chocolate chips in a double boiler or add chocolate and almond spread

158

to a medium, microwave-safe bowl. Melt it in the microwave in 20-second increments until chocolate melts. In between each 20-second burst, stir the chocolate until it is smooth.

3. Empty the melted chocolate mixture into the lined skillet. Tap the sides of the skillet to make sure the mixture spreads into an even layer. Alternatively, use a spoon to make swirls on top.

4. Move skillet to the refrigerator until it is firm. Remove the skillet from the refrigerator and cut fudge into 18 squares.

245.Chocolate Chip Cookies

Preparation time: 20 minutes
Cooking time: 0 minutes
Servings: 20

Ingredients:

- 1½ cups roasted, salted cashews
- 8 oz pitted Medjool dates
- 3 tbsp coconut oil
- 2 tsp vanilla extract
- 2 cups old-fashioned oats
- 1 cup semi-sweet or dark chocolate chips

Directions:

1. Line a baking sheet with parchment paper.

2. In the bowl of a food processor, add the cashews, dates, coconut oil, vanilla, and oats.

3. Pulse until combined, and all lumps are broken up.

4. On the off chance that the batter appears to be dry, add 1 more tbsp of coconut oil and a sprinkle of water. Mix in the chocolate chips.

5. Divide the mixture into 18 to 20 tbsp-size balls and place them on the prepared baking sheet. Using the palm of your hand, delicately press down each ball into flat circles. Move the sheet to the refrigerator for 10 to 15 minutes or until cookies are firm.

6. Serve and enjoy.

246.Oatmeal & Peanut Butter Bar

Preparation time: 4 minutes
Cooking time: 6 minutes
Servings: 8

Ingredients

- 1½ cups date, pit removed
- ½ cup peanut butter
- ½ cup old-fashioned rolled oats

Directions:

1. Grease and line an 8" x 8" baking tin with parchment and pop to one side.

2. Grab your food processor, add the dates and whizz until chopped.

3. Add the peanut butter and the oats and pulse.

4. Scoop into the baking tin then pop into the fridge or freezer until set and serve.

247.Chocolate Chip Banana Pancake

Preparation time: 5 minutes
Cooking time: 10 minutes
Servings: 6

Ingredients

- 1 large ripe banana, mashed
- 2 tablespoons coconut sugar
- 3 tablespoons coconut oil, melted
- 1 cup coconut milk

- 1 ½ cups whole wheat flour
- 1 teaspoon baking soda
- ½ cup vegan chocolate chips
- Olive oil, for frying

Directions:

1. Grab a large bowl and add the banana, sugar, oil and milk. Stir well.
2. Add the flour and baking soda and stir again until combined.
3. Add the chocolate chips and fold through then pop to one side.
4. Place a skillet over a medium heat and add a drop of oil.
5. Pour ¼ of the batter into the pan and move the pan to cover.
6. Cook for 3 minutes then flip and cook on the other side.
7. Repeat with the remaining pancakes then serve and enjoy.

248.Mixed Seed Crackers

Preparation time: 20 minutes
Cooking time: 40 minutes
Servings: 30

Ingredients:

- 1 c. boiling water
- ¼ c. coconut oil, melted
- 1 t. salt
- 1 tbsp. psyllium husk powder
- 1/3 c. of the following:
- sesame seeds
- flaxseed
- pumpkin seeds, unsalted
- sunflower seeds, unsalted
- almond flour

Directions:

1. Set the oven to 300 setting.
2. With a fork, combine the almond flour, seeds, psyllium, and salt.
3. Cautiously pour the boiling water and oil to the bowl, using the fork to combine.
4. The mixture should form a gel-like consistency.
5. Line a cookie sheet using a non-stick paper or a similar alternative, and transfer the mixture to the cookie sheet.
6. Using the second sheet of parchment, place it on top of the mixture, and with a rolling pin, roll out the mixture to an even and flat consistency.
7. Remove the top parchment paper and bake in the oven for 40 minutes, checking frequently to ensure the seeds do not burn.
8. After 40 minutes, or when the seeds are browning, turn off the oven but leave the crackers inside for further cooking.
9. Once cool break into pieces and enjoy

249.Crispy Squash Chips

Preparation time: 10 minutes
Cooking time: 20 minutes
Servings: 2

Ingredients:

- 1 t. cayenne pepper
- 1 t. cumin
- 1 t. paprika
- 1 tbsp. avocado oil
- 1 medium butternut squash, skinny neck
- Sea salt to taste

Directions:

1. Set the oven to 375 heat setting.

2. Prepare the butternut squash by removing the top.

3. Using a mandolin, cut the squash into even slices; it is not necessary to skin the squash.

4. In a big mixing bowl, place your slices of squash and cover with oil, using your hands to mix them well. Ensure all slices are oiled.

5. Line a cookie sheet with parchment paper and spread out your slices, so they do not overlap.

6. In a little bowl, mix together cayenne pepper, paprika, and cumin then sprinkle the chips over the top.

7. Season with sea salt to taste

8. Once cool, enjoy alone or with your favorite dip.

250.Paprika Nuts

Preparation time: 15 minutes
Cooking time: 15 minutes
Servings: 8

Ingredients:

- 1 ½ t. smoked paprika
- 1 t. salt
- 2 tbsp. garlic-infused olive oil
- 1 c. of the following:
- cashews
- almonds
- pecans
- walnuts

Directions:

1. Adjust the racks in the oven so that there is one rack in the middle.

2. Set the oven to 325 before you start preparing the ingredients.

3. In a big mixing bowl, toss the nuts.

4. Pour olive oil over the nuts and toss to coat all the nuts.

5. Sprinkle the salt and paprika over the nuts and mix well. If you want more paprika flavor, then add additional paprika.

6. Line a big cookie sheet with parchment and spread the nuts out in one layer.

7. Bake for approximately 15 minutes, then remove from oven and let cool.

8. Enjoy.

251.Basil Zoodles and Olives

Preparation time: 30 minutes
Cooking time: 4 hours
Servings: 6

Ingredients:

- 1 can black olives pitted
- 1 little container cherry tomatoes, halved
- 4 medium-size zucchini
- Sauce:
- ½ c basil leaves, chopped
- ½ t. pink Himalayan salt
- 2 t. nutritional yeast
- 1 tbsp. lemon juice
- ½ c. water
- ¼ c. of the following:
- sunflower seeds, soaked
- cashew nuts, soaked

Directions:

1. Begin by preparing the sunflower

seeds and cashews. Place each in a little bowl and cover with water. Allow to soak for 4 hours then drain and rinse well.

2. Next, place the seeds and cashews into a blender and mix until completely blended. Then add in basil, salt, nutritional yeast, lemon juice, and water. Blend until a smooth sauce is formed.

3. Using a spiralizer, make the zoodles from the zucchini.

4. Place the zoodles in a big serving bowl and then pour the sauce over the top. Stir to combine.

5. Top with cherry tomatoes and olives.

6. Serve and enjoy.

252. Roasted Beetroot Noodles

Preparation time: 15 minutes
Cooking time: 20 minutes
Servings: 4

Ingredients:

- 1 t. orange zest
- 2 tbsp. of the following:
- parsley, chopped
- balsamic vinegar
- olive oil
- 2 big beets, peeled and spiraled

Directions:

1. Set the oven to 425 high-heat setting.

2. In a big bowl, combine the beet noodles, olive oil, and vinegar. Toss until well-combined. Season with salt and pepper to your liking.

3. Line a big cookie sheet with parchment paper, and spread the noodles out into a single layer. Roast the noodles for 20 minutes.

4. Place into bowls and zest with orange and sprinkle parsley. Gently toss and serve.

253. Turnip Fries

Preparation time: 25 minutes
Cooking time: 20 minutes
Servings:

Ingredients:

- 1 t. of the following:
- onion powder
- paprika
- garlic salt
- 1 tbsp. vegetable oil
- 3 pounds turnips

Directions:

1. Set the oven to 425 heat setting.

2. Prepare a lightly greased aluminum foil-lined cookie sheet

3. Using a hand peeler, peel the turnips. With a Mandolin, cut the turnips into French fry sticks. Then place in a big bowl.

4. Toss the turnips with oil to coat then season with onion powder, paprika, and garlic and coat again.

5. Spread evenly across the cookie sheet.

6. Bake for 20 minutes or until the outside is crisp.

7. Serve with your favorite sauce or enjoy alone.

254. Lime and Chili Carrots Noodles

Preparation time: 10 minutes
Cooking time: 0 minutes
Servings: 4

Ingredients:

- ½ t. of the following:
- black pepper
- salt
- 2 tbsp. coconut oil
- ¼ c. coriander, finely chopped
- 2 Jalapeno chili's
- 1 tbsp. lime juice
- 2 carrots, peeled and spiralized

Directions:

1. In a little bowl, combine jalapeno, lime juice, and coconut oil to form a sauce.

2. In a big bowl, place the carrot noodles and pour dressing over the top.

3. Toss to ensure the dressing fully coats the noodles.

4. Season with salt and pepper to your liking.

5. Serve and enjoy.

255. Pesto Zucchini Noodles

Preparation time: 15 minutes
Cooking time: 0 minutes

Ingredients:

- 4 little zucchini ends trimmed
- Cherry tomatoes
- 2 t. fresh lemon juice
- 1/3 c olive oil (best if extra-virgin)
- 2 cups packed basil leaves
- 2 c. garlic
- Salt and pepper to taste

Directions:

1. Spiral zucchini into noodles and set to the side.

2. In a food processor, combine the basil and garlic and chop. Slowly add olive oil while chopping. Then pulse blend it until thoroughly mixed.

3. In a big bowl, place the noodles and pour pesto sauce over the top. Toss to combine.

4. Garnish with tomatoes and serve and enjoy.

256. Cabbage Slaw

Preparation time: 2 hours 5 minutes
Cooking time: 0 minutes
Servings: 6

Ingredients:

- 1/8 t. celery seed
- ¼ t. salt
- 2 tbsp. of the following:
- apple cider vinegar
- sweetener of your choice
- ½ c. vegan mayo
- 4 c. coleslaw mix with red cabbage and carrots

Directions:

1. In a big mixing bowl, whisk together the celery seed, salt, apple cider vinegar, sweetener, and vegan mayo.

2. Add the coleslaw and stir until appropriately combined.

3. Refrigerate while covered for a minimum of 2 hours or overnight if you're not in a hurry.

4. Garnish with tomatoes and serve and enjoy.

257. Zucchini Chips

Preparation time: 1 hour 40 minutes
Cooking time: 60 minutes
Servings: 4

Ingredients:

- 2 tbsp. olive oil (best if extra virgin)
- 1 big zucchini
- ½ t. of the following:
- black pepper, ground
- salt

Directions:

1. Bring the oven to 400 heat setting.
2. Using a mandolin, slice the zucchini into 1/8th-inch slices.
3. Once sliced, use a paper towel to remove the excess moisture from the zucchini by blotting the tops.
4. Prepare two cookie sheets with parchment paper, and spread the zucchini out into a single layer.
5. Whisk well the olive oil and seasonings. With this mixture, brush each zucchini.
6. Bake this for 60 minutes then flip.
7. Check every 20 minutes, and once the zucchini is crispy, remove from the oven and serve.

258. Peanut Tofu Wrap

Preparation time: 25 minutes
Cooking time: 5 minutes
Servings: 4

Ingredients:

- ¼ c. cilantro, finely chopped
- 1 c. of the following:
- Asian pear
- English cucumber
- 1 ½ t. lime zest
- 1 tbsp. of the following:
- rice vinegar
- canola oil
- 5 tbsp. peanut sauce
- 14 oz. tofu, extra firm
- 8 cabbage leaves

Directions:

1. Prepare cabbage leaves by washing and drying. Be sure to remove any stems or ribs.
2. Place the tofu on a paper towel-lined plate and blot to remove the extra moisture.
3. Set a big nonstick skillet over medium-high heat and place the oil. Once the oil is warm, add the tofu and crumble it to cook, stirring often. Wait for approximately 5 minutes or until the tofu turns golden brown. Remove from the heat and set to the side.
4. Mix well using a spatula the liquid ingredients, except the oil, and add the lime zest.
5. Add the sauce to the skillet and combine.
6. Place the cabbage leaves on the plates and spoon the tofu mixture into the center, topping it with cilantro, cucumber, and pear.

259. Cinnamon Granola

Preparation time: 5 minutes
Cooking time: 25 minutes
Servings: 4

Ingredients:

- 1 ½ t. cinnamon, ground
- 4 tbsp. maple syrup
- 1/5 oz. nuts
- 1 tbsp. chia seeds
- 5 tbsp. of the following:

- coconut flakes, unsweetened
- flaxseed meal

Directions:

1. Bring the oven to 350 heat setting.
2. In a medium mixing bowl, combine the flaxseed, coconut, chia seed, nuts, and maple syrup. Mix well until combined.
3. Line a cookie sheet with parchment and spread the mixture in a single layer on the cookie sheet.
4. Across the top, sprinkle the cinnamon.
5. Place the cookie sheet in the oven, and wait for 20 minutes, approximately.
6. Once done, take it out and allow the granola to cool while still on the sheet.
7. Once cool, crumble to your desired liking and enjoy.

260. Chocolate Granola

Preparation time: 20 minutes
Cooking time: 60 minutes
Servings: 12

Ingredients:

- ¼ t. sea salt
- ¼ c. of the following:
- hot water
- cocoa powder
- 1/3 c. of the following:
- coconut oil
- maple syrup, sugar-free
- ½ c. of the following:
- almond butter
- almond flour
- cashews, chopped
- 1 c. mixed seeds (flaxseed, sesame, sunflower, pumpkin)
- 2 c. coconut, flaked
- 2/3 c. almonds, flaked

Directions:

1. Bring the oven to 300 heat setting.
2. In a little bowl, mix cocoa and hot water to form a thick paste.
3. Next, add to the little bowl the coconut oil, maple syrup, nut butter, and salt; mix until combined thoroughly.
4. In a big bowl, mix the almond meal, coconut flakes, seeds, and nuts.
5. Transfer the chocolate mixture to the big bowl and combine well.
6. Using a parchment-lined cookie sheet, spread out the granola mixture.
7. Bake for 40 minutes or until firm.
8. Allow to completely cool on the parchment.
9. Once cool, crumble to your desired liking and enjoy.

261. Radish Chips

Preparation time: 30 minutes
Cooking time: 1 hour 10 minutes
Servings: 4

Ingredients:

- 2 tbsp. olive oil (best if extra virgin)
- 16 oz. radishes
- ½ t. of the following:
- Black pepper, ground
- Salt

Directions:

1. Bring the oven to 400 heat setting.
2. Using a mandolin, slice the radishes

into 1/8th-inch slices.

3. Once sliced, use a paper towel to remove the excess moisture from the radishes by blotting the tops.

4. Prepare two cookie sheets with parchment paper, and spread the zucchini out into a single layer.

5. Add the seasonings in a bowl, with the olive oil. Whisk well and then brush each radish with this mixture, coating evenly and generously.

6. Bake for 10 minutes and then flip

7. Check every 5 minutes; once the radish is crispy, remove from the oven and serve.

262.Asparagus Fries

Preparation time: 30 minutes
Cooking time: 1 hour 5 minutes
Servings: 4

Ingredients:

- 2 tbsp. nutritional yeast
- 1 c. almond meal
- 1 t. of the following:
- maple syrup
- smoked paprika
- Himalayan pink salt
- ½ t. black pepper, ground
- 1 t. extra virgin olive oil
- 1 bunch asparagus

Directions:

1. Set the oven to 400.

2. Prepare the asparagus by washing and cutting into equal halves.

3. In a big bowl, place the asparagus, add olive oil to the top, and toss to coat.

4. Add to the bowl the syrup, paprika, pepper, and salt and toss to coat.

5. In a medium, shallow bowl, mix the almond meal and nutritional yeast.

6. Line a cookie sheet with parchment paper and set to the side

7. Individually add each asparagus piece to the bowl, coating with your crumb mixture.

8. Place the asparagus on a lined cookie sheet; be sure not to overlap them.

9. Bake for 20 minutes or until brown.

10. Remove from the oven and serve.

263.Nori Snack Rolls

Preparation time: 5 minutes
Cooking time: 10 minutes
Servings: 4

Ingredients

- 2 tablespoons almond, cashew, peanut, or other nut butter
- 2 tablespoons tamari, or soy sauce
- 4 standard nori sheets
- 1 mushroom, sliced
- 1 tablespoon pickled ginger
- ½ cup grated carrots

Directions

1. Preparing the Ingredients.

2. Preheat the oven to 350°F.

3. Mix together the nut butter and tamari until smooth and very thick. Lay out a nori sheet, rough side up, the long way.

4. Spread a thin line of the tamari mixture on the far end of the nori sheet, from side to side. Lay the mushroom slices, ginger, and carrots in a line at the other end (the end closest to you).

5. Fold the vegetables inside the nori, rolling toward the tahini mixture, which will seal the roll. Repeat to make 4 rolls.

6. Put on a baking sheet and bake for 8 to 10 minutes, or until the rolls are slightly browned and crispy at the ends. Let the rolls cool for a few minutes, then slice each roll into 3 smaller pieces.

264.Risotto Bites

Preparation time: 15 minutes
Cooking time: 20 minutes
Servings: 12

Ingredients

- ½ cup panko bread crumbs
- 1 teaspoon paprika
- 1 teaspoon chipotle powder or ground cayenne pepper
- 1½ cups cold Green Pea Risotto
- Nonstick cooking spray

Directions

1. Preparing the Ingredients.
2. Preheat the oven to 425ºF.
3. Line a baking sheet with parchment paper.
4. On a large plate, combine the panko, paprika, and chipotle powder. Set aside.
5. Roll 2 tablespoons of the risotto into a ball.
6. Gently roll in the bread crumbs, and place on the prepared baking sheet. Repeat to make a total of 12 balls.
7. Spritz the tops of the risotto bites with nonstick cooking spray and bake for 15 to 20 minutes, until they begin to brown. Cool completely before storing

in a large airtight container in a single layer (add a piece of parchment paper for a second layer) or in a plastic freezer bag.

265.Jicama and Guacamole

Preparation time: 15 minutes
Cooking time: 0 minutes
Servings: 4

Ingredients

- juice of 1 lime, or 1 tablespoon prepared lime juice
- 2 hass avocados, peeled, pits removed, and cut into cubes
- ½ teaspoon sea salt
- ½ red onion, minced
- 1 garlic clove, minced
- ¼ cup chopped cilantro (optional)
- 1 jicama bulb, peeled and cut into matchsticks

Directions

1. Preparing the Ingredients.
2. In a medium bowl, squeeze the lime juice over the top of the avocado and sprinkle with salt.
3. Lightly mash the avocado with a fork. Stir in the onion, garlic, and cilantro, if using.
4. Serve with slices of jicama to dip in guacamole.
5. To store, place plastic wrap over the bowl of guacamole and refrigerate. The guacamole will keep for about 2 days.

266.Curried Tofu "Egg Salad" Pitas

Preparation time: 15 minutes
Cooking time: 0 minutes
Servings: 4

Ingredients

- 1 pound extra-firm tofu, drained and patted dry
- 1/2 cup vegan mayonnaise, homemade or store-bought
- 1/4 cup chopped mango chutney, homemade or store-bought
- 2 teaspoons Dijon mustard
- 1 tablespoon hot or mild curry powder
- 1 teaspoon salt
- 1/8 teaspoon ground cayenne
- ¾ cup shredded carrots
- 2 celery ribs, minced
- 1/4 cup minced red onion
- 8 small Boston or other soft lettuce leaves
- 4 (7-inch) whole wheat pita breads, halved

Directions

1. Crumble the tofu and place it in a large bowl. Add the mayonnaise, chutney, mustard, curry powder, salt, and cayenne, and stir well until thoroughly mixed.

2. Add the carrots, celery, and onion and stir to combine. Refrigerate for 30 minutes to allow the flavors to blend.

3. Tuck a lettuce leaf inside each pita pocket, spoon some tofu mixture on top of the lettuce, and serve.

267.Garden Patch Sandwiches On Multigrain Bread

Preparation time: 15 minutes
Cooking time: 0 minutes
Servings: 4

Ingredients

- 1pound extra-firm tofu, drained and patted dry
- 1 medium red bell pepper, finely chopped
- 1 celery rib, finely chopped
- 3 green onions, minced
- 1/4 cup shelled sunflower seeds
- 1/2 cup vegan mayonnaise, homemade or store-bought
- 1/2 teaspoon salt
- 1/2 teaspoon celery salt
- 1/4 teaspoon freshly ground black pepper
- 8 slices whole grain bread
- 4 (1/4-inch) slices ripe tomato
- 4 lettuce leaves

Directions

1. Crumble the tofu and place it in a large bowl. Add the bell pepper, celery, green onions, and sunflower seeds. Stir in the mayonnaise, salt, celery salt, and pepper and mix until well combined.

2. Toast the bread, if desired. Spread the mixture evenly onto 4 slices of the bread. Top each with a tomato slice, lettuce leaf, and the remaining bread. Cut the sandwiches diagonally in half and serve.

268.Garden Salad Wraps

Preparation time: 15 minutes
Cooking time: 10 minutes
Servings: 4

Ingredients

- 6 tablespoons olive oil
- 1 pound extra-firm tofu, drained, patted dry, and cut into 1/2-inch

strips

- 1 tablespoon soy sauce
- 1/4 cup apple cider vinegar
- 1 teaspoon yellow or spicy brown mustard
- 1/2 teaspoon salt
- 1/4 teaspoon freshly ground black pepper
- 3 cups shredded romaine lettuce
- 3 ripe Roma tomatoes, finely chopped
- 1 large carrot, shredded
- 1 medium English cucumber, peeled and chopped
- 1/3 cup minced red onion
- 1/4 cup sliced pitted green olives
- 4 (10-inch) whole-grain flour tortillas or lavash flatbread

Directions

1. In a large skillet, heat 2 tablespoons of the oil over medium heat. Add the tofu and cook until golden brown, about 10 minutes. Sprinkle with soy sauce and set aside to cool.

2. In a small bowl, combine the vinegar, mustard, salt, and pepper with the remaining 4 tablespoons oil, stirring to blend well. Set aside.

3. In a large bowl, combine the lettuce, tomatoes, carrot, cucumber, onion, and olives. Pour on the dressing and toss to coat.

4. To assemble wraps, place 1 tortilla on a work surface and spread with about one-quarter of the salad. Place a few strips of tofu on the tortilla and roll up tightly. Slice in half

269.Black Sesame Wonton Chips

Preparation time: 5 minutes
Cooking time: 5 minutes
Servings: 24 chips

Ingredients

- 12 Vegan Wonton Wrappers
- Toasted sesame oil
- 1/3 cup black sesame seeds
- Salt

Directions

1. Preheat the oven to 450°F. Lightly oil a baking sheet and set aside. Cut the wonton wrappers in half crosswise, brush them with sesame oil, and arrange them in a single layer on the prepared baking sheet.

2. Sprinkle wonton wrappers with the sesame seeds and salt to taste, and bake until crisp and golden brown, 5 to 7 minutes. Cool completely before serving. These are best eaten on the day they are made but, once cooled, they can be covered and stored at room temperature for 1 to 2 days.

270.Marinated Mushroom Wraps

Preparation time: 15 minutes
Cooking time: 0 minutes
Servings: 2

Ingredients

- 3 tablespoons soy sauce
- 3 tablespoons fresh lemon juice
- 11/2 tablespoons toasted sesame oil
- 2 portobello mushroom caps, cut into 1/4-inch strips
- 1 ripe Hass avocado, pitted and peeled
- 2 (10-inch) whole-grain flour tortillas
- 2 cups fresh baby spinach leaves
- 1 medium red bell pepper, cut into

1/4-inch strips

- 1 ripe tomato, chopped
- Salt and freshly ground black pepper

Directions

1. In a medium bowl, combine the soy sauce, 2 tablespoons of the lemon juice, and the oil. Add the portobello strips, toss to combine, and marinate for 1 hour or overnight. Drain the mushrooms and set aside.

2. Mash the avocado with the remaining 1 tablespoon of lemon juice.

3. To assemble wraps, place 1 tortilla on a work surface and spread with some of the mashed avocado. Top with a layer of baby spinach leaves. In the lower third of each tortilla, arrange strips of the soaked mushrooms and some of the bell pepper strips. Sprinkle with the tomato and salt and black pepper to taste. Roll up tightly and cut in half diagonally. Repeat with the remaining Ingredients and serve.

271Tamari Toasted Almonds

Preparation time: 2 minutes
Cooking time: 8 minutes

Ingredients

- ½ cup raw almonds, or sunflower seeds
- 2 tablespoons tamari, or soy sauce
- 1 teaspoon toasted sesame oil

Directions

1. Preparing the Ingredients.

2. Heat a dry skillet to medium-high heat, then add the almonds, stirring very frequently to keep them from burning. Once the almonds are toasted, 7 to 8 minutes for almonds, or 3 to 4 minutes for sunflower seeds,

pour the tamari and sesame oil into the hot skillet and stir to coat.

3. You can turn off the heat, and as the almonds cool the tamari mixture will stick to and dry on the nuts.

4. Per Serving (1 tablespoon) Calories: 89; Total fat: 8g; Carbs: 3g; Fiber: 2g; Protein: 4g

272.Avocado And Tempeh Bacon Wraps

Preparation time: 10 minutes
Cooking time: 8 minutes
Servings: 4

Ingredients

- 2 tablespoons olive oil
- 8 ounces tempeh bacon, homemade or store-bought
- 4 (10-inch) soft flour tortillas or lavash flat bread
- 1/4 cup vegan mayonnaise, homemade or store-bought
- 4 large lettuce leaves
- 2 ripe Hass avocados, pitted, peeled, and cut into 1/4-inch slices
- 1 large ripe tomato, cut into 1/4-inch slices

Directions

1. In a large skillet, heat the oil over medium heat. Add the tempeh bacon and cook until browned on both sides, about 8 minutes. Remove from the heat and set aside.

2. Place 1 tortilla on a work surface. Spread with some of the mayonnaise and one-fourth of the lettuce and tomatoes.

3. Pit, peel, and thinly slice the avocado and place the slices on top of the

tomato. Add the reserved tempeh bacon and roll up tightly. Repeat with remaining Ingredients and serve.

273.Kale Chips

Preparation time: 5 minutes
Cooking time: 25 minutes
Servings: 2

Ingredients

- 1 large bunch kale
- 1 tablespoon extra-virgin olive oil
- ½ teaspoon chipotle powder
- ½ teaspoon smoked paprika
- ¼ teaspoon salt

Directions

1. Preparing the Ingredients.
2. Preheat the oven to 275ºF.
3. Line a large baking sheet with parchment paper. In a large bowl, stem the kale and tear it into bite-size pieces. Add the olive oil, chipotle powder, smoked paprika, and salt.
4. Toss the kale with tongs or your hands, coating each piece well.
5. Spread the kale over the parchment paper in a single layer.
6. Bake for 25 minutes, turning halfway through, until crisp.
7. Cool for 10 to 15 minutes before dividing and storing in 2 airtight containers.

274.Tempeh-Pimiento Cheeze Ball

Preparation time: 5 minutes
Cooking time: 30 minutes
Servings: 8

Ingredients

- 8 ounces tempeh, cut into 1/2-inch pieces
- 1 (2-ounce) jar chopped pimientos, drained
- 1/4 cup nutritional yeast
- 1/4 cup vegan mayonnaise, homemade or store-bought
- 2 tablespoons soy sauce
- ¾ cup chopped pecans

Directions

1. In a medium saucepan of simmering water, cook the tempeh for 30 minutes. Set aside to cool. In a food processor, combine the cooled tempeh, pimientos, nutritional yeast, mayo, and soy sauce. Process until smooth.
2. Transfer the tempeh mixture to a bowl and refrigerate until firm and chilled, at least 2 hours or overnight.
3. In a dry skillet, toast the pecans over medium heat until lightly toasted, about 5 minutes. Set aside to cool.
4. Shape the tempeh mixture into a ball, and roll it in the pecans, pressing the nuts slightly into the tempeh mixture so they stick. Refrigerate for at least 1 hour before serving. If not using right away, cover and keep refrigerated until needed. Properly stored, it will keep for 2 to 3 days.

275.Peppers and Hummus

Preparation time: 15 minutes
Cooking time: 0 minutes4
Servings:

Ingredients

- one 15-ounce can chickpeas, drained and rinsed
- juice of 1 lemon, or 1 tablespoon

prepared lemon juice

- ¼ cup tahini
- 3 tablespoons olive oil
- ½ teaspoon ground cumin
- 1 tablespoon water
- ¼ teaspoon paprika
- 1 red bell pepper, sliced
- 1 green bell pepper, sliced
- 1 orange bell pepper, sliced

Directions

1. Preparing the Ingredients.

2. In a food processor, combine chickpeas, lemon juice, tahini, 2 tablespoons of the olive oil, the cumin, and water.

3. Process on high speed until blended, about 30 seconds. Scoop the hummus into a bowl and drizzle with the remaining tablespoon of olive oil. Sprinkle with paprika and serve with sliced bell peppers.

276.Deconstructed Hummus Pitas

Preparation time: 15 minutes
Cooking time: 0 minutes
Servings: 4

Ingredients

- 1 garlic clove, crushed
- ¾ cup tahini (sesame paste)
- 2 tablespoons fresh lemon juice
- 1 teaspoon salt
- 1/8 teaspoon ground cayenne
- 1/4 cup water
- 11/2 cups cooked or 1 (15.5-ounce) can chickpeas, rinsed and drained
- 2 medium carrots, grated (about 1

cup)

- 4 (7-inch) pita breads, preferably whole wheat, halved
- 1 large ripe tomato, cut into 1/4-inch slices
- 2 cups fresh baby spinach

Directions

1. In a blender or food processor, mince the garlic. Add the tahini, lemon juice, salt, cayenne, and water. Process until smooth.

2. Place the chickpeas in a bowl and crush slightly with a fork. Add the carrots and the reserved tahini sauce and toss to combine. Set aside.

3. Spoon 2 or 3 tablespoons of the chickpea mixture into each pita half. Tuck a tomato slice and a few spinach leaves into each pocket and serve.

277.Savory Roasted Chickpeas

Preparation time: 5 minutes
Cooking time: 25 minutes
Servings: 1

Ingredients

- 1 (14-ounce) can chickpeas, rinsed and drained, or 1½ cups cooked
- 2 tablespoons tamari, or soy sauce
- 1 tablespoon nutritional yeast
- 1 teaspoon smoked paprika, or regular paprika
- 1 teaspoon onion powder
- ½ teaspoon garlic powder

Directions

1. Preparing the Ingredients.

2. Preheat the oven to 400°F.

3. Toss the chickpeas with all the other

ingredients, and spread them out on a baking sheet. Bake for 20 to 25 minutes, tossing halfway through.

4. Bake these at a lower temperature, until fully dried and crispy, if you want to keep them longer.

5. You can easily double the batch, and if you dry them out they will keep about a week in an airtight container.

278.Mango And Banana Shake

Preparation time: 10 minutes
Cooking time: 0 minutes
Servings: 2

Ingredients

- 1 banana, sliced and frozen
- 1 cup frozen mango chunks
- 1 cup almond milk
- 1 tbsp. maple syrup
- 1 tsp lime juice
- 2-4 raspberries for topping
- Mango slice for topping

Directions

1. In blender, pulse banana, mango with milk, maple syrup, lime juice until smooth but still thick
2. Add more liquid if needed.
3. Pour shake into 2 bowls.
4. Top with berries and mango slice.
5. Enjoy!

279.Avocado Toast With Flaxseeds

Preparation time: 5 minutes
Cooking time: 0 minutes
Servings: 3

Ingredients

- 3 slice of whole grain bread

- 1 large avocado, ripe
- ¼ cup chopped parsley
- 1 tbsp. Flax seeds
- 1 tbsp. Sesame seeds
- 1 tbsp. Lime juice

Directions

1. First, toast your piece of bread.
2. Remove the avocado seed.
3. Slice half avocado and mash half avocado with fork in bowl.
4. Spread mashed avocado on 2 toasted bread.
5. Place avocado slice on 1 toast.
6. Top with flax seeds and sesame seeds.
7. Drizzle lime juice and chopped parsley on top.
8. Serve and enjoy!

280.Avocado Hummus

Preparation time: 10 minutes
Cooking time: 0 minutes
Servings: 4

Ingredients

- 2 ripe avocados
- ½ cup coconut cream
- ¼ cup sesame paste
- ½ lemon juice
- 1 tsp. Clove, pressed
- ½ tsp ground cumin
- ½ tsp salt
- ¼ tsp ground black pepper

Directions

1. Cut the avocado lengthways and remove seed from the fruit.

2. Put all ingredients in a blender or food processor and mix until thoroughly smooth.

3. Add more cream, lemon juice or water if you want to have a looser texture.

4. Adjust seasonings as needed.

5. Serve with naan and enjoy.

281.Plant Based Crispy Falafel

Preparation time: 20 minutes
Cooking time: 30 minutes
Servings: 8

Ingredients

- 1 tbsp. Extra-virgin olive oil
- 1 cup dried chickpeas soaked for 24 hours in the refrigerator
- 1 cup cauliflower, chopped
- ½ cup red onion, chopped
- ½ cup packed fresh parsley
- 2 cloves garlic, quartered
- 1 tsp. Sea salt
- ½ tsp. Ground black pepper
- ½ tsp. Ground cumin
- ¼ tsp. Ground cinnamon

Directions

1. Preheat oven to 375° F.

2. In a food processor, mix chickpeas, cauliflower, onion, parsley, garlic, salt, pepper, cumin seeds, cinnamon, and olive oil until mixture is smooth.

3. Take 2 tbsps. of mixture and make the falafel into small patties.

4. Keep falafel on greased baking tray.

5. Bake falafel for about 25 to 30 minutes in preheated oven until golden brown from both sides.

6. Once cooked remove from oven.

7. Serve hot fresh vegetable salad and enjoy!

282.Waffles With Almond Flour

Preparation time: 15 minutes
Cooking time: 15 minutes
Servings: 4

Ingredients

- 1 Cup Almond Milk
- 2 Tbsps. Chia Seeds
- 2 Tsp Lemon Juice
- 4 Tbsps. Coconut Oil
- 1/2 Cup Almond Flour
- 2 Tbsps. Maple Syrup
- Cooking Spray Or Cooking Oil

Directions

1. Mix coconut milk with lemon juice in a mixing bowl.

2. Leave it for 5-8 minutes on room temperature to turn it into butter milk.

3. Once coconut milk is turned into butter milk, add chai seeds into milk and whisk together.

4. Add other ingredients in milk mixture and mix well.

5. Preheat a waffle iron and spray it with coconut oil spray.

6. Pour 2 tbsp. of waffle mixture into the waffle machine and cook until golden.

7. Top with some berries and serve hot.

8. Enjoy with black coffee!

283.Mint & Avocado Smoothie

Preparation time: 10 minutes
Cooking time: 0 minutes

Servings: 2

Ingredients

- 1 Cup Coconut Water
- 1/2 Lemon Juice
- ½ Cup Cucumber
- 1 Cup Mint. Fresh
- 1/2 Medium Size Avocado
- I/2 Tsp Maple Syrup
- 1 Cup Ice

Directions

1. Place all ingredients into a blender, cover lid and blend until smooth.
2. Blend on high speed until smoothie has fluffy texture.
3. Pour smoothie in glass and top with mint leaves.
4. Serve and enjoy!

284. Date & Seed Bites

Preparation time: 15 minutes
Cooking time: 0 minutes
Servings: 10

Ingredients

1. 1 cup cashew butter
2. 6 Medjool dates, pitted
3. 2/3 cup hemp seeds
4. ¼ cup chia seeds

5. ¼ cup unsweetened vegan protein powder
6. ¾ cup unsweetened coconut, shredded

Directions:

1. In a food processor, place all the ingredients and pulse until well combined.
2. With your hands, make equal-sized balls from mixture.
3. In a shallow dish, place the coconut.
4. Roll the balls in the coconut evenly.
5. Refrigerate the balls till serving.
6. Arrange the balls onto a parchment paper-lined baking sheet in a single layer.
7. Refrigerate to set for about 30 minutes before serving.

285. Chocolatey Oat Bites

Preparation time: 15 minutes
Cooking time: 0 minutes
Servings: 6

Ingredients

- 2/3 cup creamy peanut butter
- 1 cup old-fashioned oats
- ½ cups unsweetened vegan chocolate chips
- ½ cups ground flaxseeds

- 2 tablespoons maple syrup

Directions:

1. In a bowl, place all the ingredients and mix until well combined.

2. Refrigerate for about 20–30 minutes.

3. With your hands, make equal-sized balls from mixture.

4. Arrange the balls onto a parchment paper-lined baking sheet in a single layer.

5. Refrigerate to set for about 15 minutes before serving.

286. Brownie Bites

Preparation time: 15 minutes
Cooking time: 0 minutes
Servings: 8

Ingredients

- ¾ cup blanched almond flour
- ¾ cup cacao powder
- 2 tablespoons ground flaxseed
- ½ cup unsweetened vegan mini chocolate chips
- ¾ cup creamy almond butter, melted
- ¼ cup pure maple syrup
- 1 teaspoon pure vanilla extract

Directions:

1. In a large bowl, mix together the almond flour, cocoa powder, flaxseed,

and chocolate chips.

2. Add the almond butter, maple syrup, and vanilla extract, and gently stir to combine.

3. Using a sturdy spatula, stir and fold together until well incorporated.

4. With your hands, make equal-sized balls from mixture.

5. Arrange the balls onto a parchment paper-lined baking sheet in a single layer.

6. Refrigerate to set for about 15 minutes before serving.

287. Fruity Bites

Preparation time: 15 minutes
Cooking time: 0 minutes
Servings: 6

Ingredients

- 1 ripe banana, peeled
- ¼ cup maple syrup
- ¼ cup sunflower seed butter, melted
- 1½ cups quick oats
- ¾ cup rolled oats
- 1/3 cup unsweetened vegan protein powder
- 2 teaspoons ground flaxseed
- 1 teaspoon vanilla extract
- 1/3 cup dried unsweetened

cranberries

Directions:

1. In a large bowl, add the banana and with a fork, mash it.

2. Add the maple syrup and sunflower seed butter and mix until smooth.

3. Add the oats, protein powder, flaxseed, and vanilla extract and mix until well combined.

4. Gently, fold in the cranberries.

5. With your hands, make equal-sized balls from mixture.

6. Arrange the balls onto a parchment paper-lined baking sheet in a single layer.

7. Refrigerate to set for about 15 minutes before serving.

288.Energy Bars

Preparation time: 15 minutes
Cooking time: 0 minutes
Servings: 8

Ingredients

- 1½ cups rolled oats
- ½ cup almonds, chopped roughly
- ½ cup cashews, chopped roughly
- ½ cup mini unsweetened vegan chocolate chips
- 1/3 cup pumpkin seeds
- ¼ cup sesame seeds
- ¼ cup sunflower seeds
- ¼ cup flaxseed meal
- 2 tablespoons chia seeds
- 1 teaspoon ground cinnamon
- ½ cup maple syrup
- 1 cup almond butter, softened

Directions:

1. Line an 8x8-inch baking dish with a large lightly greased parchment paper.

2. In a large bowl, add oats, nuts, chocolate chips, seeds, and cinnamon, and mix well.

3. Add in the maple syrup and stir to combine.

4. Add the almond butter and mix until well combined.

5. Place oat mixture into prepared baking dish evenly and with the back of a spatula, smooth the top surface, by pressing in the bottom.

6. Refrigerate for about 6–8 hours, or until set completely.

7. Remove from refrigerator and with a sharp knife, cut into desired sized bars.

289.Vegetable Mushroom Side Dish

Preparation time: 25 minutes
Cooking time: 60 minutes
Servings: 4

Ingredients

- 2 tbsp plant butter
- 1 large onion, diced
- 1 cup celery, diced

- ½ cup carrots, diced
- ½ tsp dried marjoram
- 1 tsp dried basil
- 2 cups chopped cremini mushrooms
- 1 cup vegetable broth
- ¼ cup chopped fresh parsley
- 1 medium whole-grain bread loaf, cubed

Directions

1. Melt the butter in large skillet and sauté the onion, celery, mushrooms, and carrots until softened, 5 minutes.

2. Mix in the marjoram, basil, and season with salt and black pepper.

3. Pour in the vegetable broth and mix in the parsley and bread. Cook until the broth reduces by half, 10 minutes.

4. Pour the mixture into a baking dish and cover with foil. Bake in the oven at 375 F for 30 minutes.

5. Uncover and bake further for 30 minutes or until golden brown on top and the liquid absorbs.

6. Remove the dish from the oven and serve the stuffing.

290. Summer Vegetable Mix

Preparation time: 5 minutes
Cooking time: 30 minutes
Servings: 4

Ingredients

- 2 medium zucchinis, chopped
- 2 medium yellow squash, chopped
- 1 medium red onion, cut into 1-inch wedges
- 1 medium red bell pepper, deseeded and cut into 1-inch dices

- 1 cup cherry tomatoes, halved
- 4 tbsp olive oil
- Salt and black pepper to taste
- 3 garlic cloves, minced
- 2/3 cup whole-wheat breadcrumbs
- 1 lemon, zested
- ¼ cup chopped fresh basil

Directions

1. Preheat the oven to 450 F and lightly grease a large baking sheet with cooking spray.

2. In a medium bowl, add the zucchini, yellow squash, red onion, bell pepper, tomatoes, olive oil, salt, black pepper, and garlic. Toss well and spread the mixture on the baking sheet.

3. Roast in the oven for 25 to 30 minutes or until the vegetables are tender, while stirring every 5 minutes.

4. Meanwhile, heat the olive oil in a medium skillet and sauté the garlic until fragrant. Mix in the breadcrumbs, lemon zest, and basil. Cook for 2 to 3 minutes.

5. Remove the vegetables from the oven and toss in the breadcrumb's mixture.

6. Serve warm.

291. Seitan Bell Pepper Balls

Preparation time: 5 minutes
Cooking time: 25 minutes
Servings: 4

Ingredients

- 1 tbsp flax seed powder + 3 tbsp water
- 1 lb seitan, crumbled
- ¼ cup chopped mixed bell peppers
- Salt and black pepper to taste

- 1 tbsp almond flour
- 1 tsp garlic powder
- 1 tsp onion powder
- 1 tsp tofu mayonnaise
- Olive oil for brushing

Directions

1. Preheat the oven to 400 F and line a baking sheet with parchment paper.

2. In a medium bowl, mix the flax seed powder with water and allow thickening for 5 minutes.

3. Add the seitan, bell peppers, salt, black pepper, almond flour, garlic powder, onion powder, and tofu mayonnaise. Mix well and form 1-inch balls from the mixture.

4. Arrange on the baking sheet, brush with cooking spray and bake in the oven for 15 to 20 minutes or until brown and compacted.

5. Remove from the oven and serve.

292.Quinoa Stuffed Tomatoes

Preparation time: 20 minutes
Cooking time: 30 minutes
Servings: 4

Ingredients

- 8 medium sized tomatoes
- ¾ cup quinoa, rinsed and drained
- 1 ½ cups water
- 1 tbsp olive oil
- 1 small onion, diced
- 3 garlic cloves, minced
- Salt and black pepper to taste
- 1 cup chopped spinach
- 1 (7 oz) can chickpeas, drained and rinsed

- ½ cup chopped fresh basil

Directions

1. Preheat the oven to 400 F.

2. Cut off the heads of tomatoes and use a paring knife to scoop the inner pulp of the tomatoes. Season with some olive oil, salt, and black pepper.

3. Add the quinoa and water to a medium pot, season with salt and cook until the quinoa is tender and the water absorbs, 10 to 15 minutes. Fluff and set aside.

4. Heat the remaining olive oil in a medium skillet and sauté the onion and garlic until softened and fragrant, 30 seconds.

5. Mix in the spinach and cook until wilted, 2 minutes. Stir in the basil, chickpeas, and quinoa; allow warming from 2 minutes.

6. Spoon the mixture into the tomatoes, place the tomatoes into the baking dish and bake in the oven for 20 minutes or until the tomatoes soften. Remove the tomatoes from the oven and dish the food. Serve warm.

293.Walnut & Chocolate Bars

Preparation time: 60 minutes
Cooking time: 0 minutes
Servings: 4

Ingredients

- 1 cup walnuts
- 3 tbsp sunflower seeds
- 2 tbsp unsweetened chocolate chips
- 1 tbsp unsweetened cocoa powder
- 1 ½ tsp vanilla extract
- ¼ tsp cinnamon powder
- 2 tbsp melted coconut oil

179

- 2 tbsp toasted almond meal
- 2 tsp pure maple syrup

Directions

1. In a food processor, add the walnuts, sunflower seeds, chocolate chips, cocoa powder, vanilla extract, cinnamon powder, coconut oil, almond meal, maple syrup, and blitz a few times until coarsely combined.

2. Line a flat baking sheet with plastic wrap, pour the mixture onto the sheet, and place another plastic wrap on top. Use a rolling pin to flatten the batter and then remove the top plastic wrap.

3. Freeze the snack until firm, 1 hour.

4. Remove from the freezer, cut into 1 ½-inch bars and enjoy immediately.

294.Avocado Sandwich

Preparation Time: 5 Minutes
Cooking Time: 5 Minutes
Serving: 2

Ingredients:

- 8 whole-wheat bread slices
- ½ oz. vegan butter
- 2 oz. little gem lettuce, cleaned and patted dry

- 1 oz. tofu cheese, sliced
- 1 avocado, pitted, peeled, and sliced
- 1 small cucumber, sliced into 4 rings
- Freshly chopped parsley to garnish

Directions:

1. Arrange the 4 bread slices on a flat surface and smear the vegan butter on one end each.

2. Place a lettuce leaf on each and arrange some tofu cheese on top. Top with the avocado and cucumber slices.

3. Garnish the sandwiches with a little parsley, cover with the remaining bread slices, and serve immediately.

295.Sweet Potato Toast

Preparation Time: 5 Minutes
Cooking Time: 10 Minutes
Serving: 1

Ingredients:

- ½ of 1 Avocado, ripe
- 2 tbsp. Sun-dried Tomatoes
- 1 Sweet Potato, sliced into ¼-inch thick slices
- ½ cup Chickpeas
- Salt & Pepper, as needed
- 1 tsp. Lemon Juice
- Pinch of Red Pepper
- 2 tbsp. Vegan Cheese

Directions:

1. Start by slicing the sweet potato into five ¼ inch wide slices.

2. Next, toast the sweet potato in the toaster for 9 to 11 minutes.

3. Then, place the chickpeas in a medium-sized bowl and mash with the avocado.

4. Stir in the crushed red pepper, lemon juice, pepper, and salt.

5. Stir until everything comes together.

6. Finally, place the mixture on to the top of the sweet potato toast.

7. Top with cheese and sun-dried tomatoes.

296.Hummus Toast

Preparation Time: 5 Minutes
Cooking Time: 5 Minutes
Serving: 1

297.Ingredients:

- o tbsp. Hemp Seeds
- 1 tbsp. Sunflower Seeds, roasted & unsalted
- o Vegan Bread Slices
- ¼ cup Hummus
- For the hummus:
- 15 oz. Chickpeas
- ¾ tsp. Salt
- o tbsp. Lime Juice, fresh
- 2 tbsp. Extra Virgin Olive Oil
- 2 Garlic cloves
- ½ cup Tahini

Directions:

1. To begin with, toast the bread for 1 to 1 ½ minutes or until lightly toasted.

2. Meanwhile, to make the hummus place the undrained chickpeas and garlic cloves in a medium bowl.

3. Microwave for 2 to 3 minutes on a high heat.

4. After that, put the lime juice, tahini, and salt along with the cooked chickpeas into a food processor.

5. Blend for 2 to 3 minutes or until smooth.

6. While blending, spoon in the olive oil gradually. Combine. Taste the mixture for seasoning. If needed, add more salt and pepper.

7. Next, top the toast with the hummus, hemp and sunflower seeds.

8. Serve and enjoy.

298.Tacos

Preparation Time: 10 Minutes
Cooking Time: 30 Minutes
Serving: 4

Ingredients:

- 6 Taco Shells
- For the slaw:
- 1 cup Red Cabbage, shredded
- 3 Scallions, chopped
- 1 cup Green Cabbage, shredded
- 1 cup Carrots, sliced
- For the dressing:
- 1 tbsp. Sriracha
- ¼ cup Apple Cider Vinegar
- ¼ tsp. Salt
- 2 tbsp. Sesame Oil
- 1 tbsp. Dijon Mustard
- 1 tbsp. Lime Juice
- ½ tbsp. Tamari
- 1 tbsp. Maple Syrup
- ¼ tsp. Salt

Directions:

1. To start with, make the dressing, whisk all the ingredients in a small bowl until mixed well.
2. Next, combine the slaw ingredients in another bowl and toss well.
3. Finally, take a taco shell and place the slaw in it.
4. Serve and enjoy.

299.Breakfast Burritos

Preparation Time: 5 Minutes
Cooking Time: 10 Minutes
Serving: 4

Ingredients:

- 2 (15 oz) cans black beans, drained and rinsed
- ½ cup water
- 4 whole wheat tortillas
- 8 leaves romaine lettuce
- 2 tomatoes, sliced
- 2 avocados, peeled, pitted, and sliced
- 1 ½ cups salsa
- Seasonings:
- 1 tbsp garlic powder
- 1 tbsp onion powder
- 1 tbsp chili powder
- 1 tsp dried cumin
- 1 tsp dried oregano

Directions:

1. In a medium-sized pot, add the beans, water, and seasonings. Allow boiling over medium heat and then simmer for 10 minutes. Drain the beans after.
2. Onto the whole wheat tortillas, add one or two leaves of romaine lettuce, tomatoes, and avocado.

3. Add the black beans on top and then, the salsa.

4. Serve the burritos immediately.

300.Kale Chips

Preparation Time: 10 Minutes
Cooking Time: 1 Hour 30 Minutes
Serving: 10

Ingredients:

- ½ tsp. Smoked Paprika
- 2 bunches of Curly Kale
- 1 tsp. Garlic Powder
- ½ cup Nutritional Yeast
- 2 cups Cashew, soaked for 2 hours
- 1 tsp. Salt
- ½ cup Nutritional Yeast

Directions:

1. To make these tasty, healthy chips place the kale in a large mixing bowl.

2. Now, combine all the remaining ingredients in the high-speed blender and blend for 1 minute or until smooth.

3. Next, pour this dressing over the kale chips and mix well with your hands.

4. Then, preheat your oven to 225 ° F or 107 °C.

5. Once heated, arrange the kale leaves on a large baking sheet leaving ample space between them.

6. Bake the leaves for 80 to 90 minutes flipping them once in between.

7. Finally, allow them to cool completely and then store them in an air-tight container.

301.Coconut Smoothie

Preparation Time: 5 Minutes
Cooking Time: 5 Minutes
Serving: 1

Ingredients:

- 1 cup Coconut Milk
- 1 cup Pineapple, frozen
- ½ Ginger Piece
- ½ cup Kale, stems discarded
- 1 tsp. Chia Seeds
- 1/3 cup Mint Leaves
- ½ cup Spinach Leaves
- 1 Lime, peel & rind removed

Directions:

1. To start, place all the ingredients into a high-speed blender and blend for a minute or two or until you get a smooth drink.

2. Serve immediately and enjoy.

302.Spicy Roasted Chickpeas

Preparation Time: 10 Minutes
Cooking Time: 25 Minutes
Serving: 6

Ingredients:

- ½ tsp. Cumin
- 2 × 15 oz. Chickpeas
- ¼ tsp. Cayenne Pepper
- ¼ cup Olive Oil
- ½ tsp. Onion Powder
- 1 tsp. Sea Salt
- ¾ tsp. Garlic Powder
- ½ tsp. Chili Powder
- ¾ tsp. Paprika
- Sea Salt, as needed

Directions:

- Preheat the oven to 425 ° F.
- After that, put the chickpeas in a strainer lined with a paper towel and allow to dry for 10 to 15 minutes.
- Then, transfer the chickpeas onto a baking paper-lined baking sheet and then spoon some olive oil over it.
- Coat the chickpeas with the oil. Sprinkle a dash of salt over it.
- Now, put the baking sheet in the oven and bake for 23 to 25 minutes tossing them every 5 minutes or until they are golden brown.

- Once they have become crispy, remove the sheet from the oven.
- Next, mix all the remaining seasoning ingredients in another bowl until combined well.
- Finally, stir the chickpeas into this mixture and toss well.
- Serve immediately.

303.Desserts

Apple Crumble
Preparation time: 20 minutes25 minutes
Cooking time:
Servings: 6

Ingredients

- For the filling
- 4 to 5 apples, cored and chopped (about 6 cups)
- ½ cup unsweetened applesauce, or ¼ cup water
- 2 to 3 tablespoons unrefined sugar (coconut, date, sucanat, maple syrup)
- 1 teaspoon ground cinnamon
- Pinch sea salt
- For the crumble
- 2 tablespoons almond butter, or cashew or sunflower seed butter
- 2 tablespoons maple syrup
- 1½ cups rolled oats
- ½ cup walnuts, finely chopped
- ½ teaspoon ground cinnamon
- 2 to 3 tablespoons unrefined granular sugar (coconut, date, sucanat)

Directions

1. Preparing the Ingredients.
2. Preheat the oven to 350°F. Put the apples and applesauce in an 8-inch-

square baking dish, and sprinkle with the sugar, cinnamon, and salt. Toss to combine.

3. In a medium bowl, mix together the nut butter and maple syrup until smooth and creamy. Add the oats, walnuts, cinnamon, and sugar and stir to coat, using your hands if necessary. (If you have a small food processor, pulse the oats and walnuts together before adding them to the mix.)

4. Sprinkle the topping over the apples, and put the dish in the oven.

5. Bake for 20 to 25 minutes, or until the fruit is soft and the topping is lightly browned.

304. Cashew-Chocolate Truffles

Preparation time: 15 minutes
Cooking time: 0 minutes
Servings: 12

Ingredients

- 1 cup raw cashews, soaked in water overnight
- ¾ cup pitted dates
- 2 tablespoons coconut oil
- 1 cup unsweetened shredded coconut, divided
- 1 to 2 tablespoons cocoa powder, to taste

Directions

1. Preparing the Ingredients.

2. In a food processor, combine the cashews, dates, coconut oil, ½ cup of shredded coconut, and cocoa powder. Pulse until fully incorporated; it will resemble chunky cookie dough. Spread the remaining ½ cup of shredded coconut on a plate.

3. Form the mixture into tablespoon-size

balls and roll on the plate to cover with the shredded coconut. Transfer to a parchment paper–lined plate or baking sheet. Repeat to make 12 truffles.

4. Place the truffles in the refrigerator for 1 hour to set. Transfer the truffles to a storage container or freezer-safe bag and seal.

305. Banana Chocolate Cupcakes

Preparation time: 20 minutes
Cooking time: 20 minutes
Servings: 12

Ingredients

- 3 medium bananas
- 1 cup non-dairy milk
- 2 tablespoons almond butter
- 1 teaspoon apple cider vinegar
- 1 teaspoon pure vanilla extract
- 1¼ cups whole-grain flour
- ½ cup rolled oats
- ¼ cup coconut sugar (optional)
- 1 teaspoon baking powder
- ½ teaspoon baking soda
- ½ cup unsweetened cocoa powder
- ¼ cup chia seeds, or sesame seeds
- Pinch sea salt
- ¼ cup dark chocolate chips, dried cranberries, or raisins (optional)

Directions

1. Preparing the Ingredients.

2. Preheat the oven to 350°F. Lightly grease the cups of two 6-cup muffin tins or line with paper muffin cups.

3. Put the bananas, milk, almond butter, vinegar, and vanilla in a blender and

purée until smooth. Or stir together in a large bowl until smooth and creamy.

4. Put the flour, oats, sugar (if using), baking powder, baking soda, cocoa powder, chia seeds, salt, and chocolate chips in another large bowl, and stir to combine. Mix together the wet and dry ingredients, stirring as little as possible. Spoon into muffin cups, and bake for 20 to 25 minutes. Take the cupcakes out of the oven and let them cool fully before taking out of the muffin tins, since they'll be very moist.

306.Minty Fruit Salad

Preparation time: 15 minutes
Cooking time: 5 minutes
Servings: 4

Ingredients

- ¼ cup lemon juice (about 2 small lemons)
- 4 teaspoons maple syrup or agave syrup
- 2 cups chopped pineapple
- 2 cups chopped strawberries
- 2 cups raspberries
- 1 cup blueberries
- 8 fresh mint leaves

Directions

1. Preparing the Ingredients.
2. Beginning with 1 mason jar, add the ingredients in this order:
3. 1 tablespoon of lemon juice, 1 teaspoon of maple syrup, ½ cup of pineapple, ½ cup of strawberries, ½ cup of raspberries, ¼ cup of blueberries, and 2 mint leaves.
4. Repeat to fill 3 more jars. Close the jars tightly with lids.

5. Place the airtight jars in the refrigerator for up to 3 days.

307.Mango Coconut Cream Pie

Preparation time: 20 minutes
Cooking time: 30 minutes
Servings: 8

Ingredients

- For the crust
- ½ cup rolled oats
- 1 cup cashews
- 1 cup soft pitted dates
- For the filling
- 1 cup canned coconut milk
- ½ cup water
- 2 large mangos, peeled and chopped, or about 2 cups frozen chunks
- ½ cup unsweetened shredded coconut

Directions

1. Preparing the Ingredients.
2. Put all the crust ingredients in a food processor and pulse until it holds together. If you don't have a food processor, chop everything as finely as possible and use ½ cup cashew or almond butter in place of half the cashews. Press the mixture down firmly into an 8-inch pie or springform pan.
3. Put the all filling ingredients in a blender and purée until smooth (about 1 minute). It should be very thick, so you may have to stop and stir until it's smooth.
4. Pour the filling into the crust, use a rubber spatula to smooth the top, and put the pie in the freezer until set, about 30 minutes. Once frozen, it

should be set out for about 15 minutes to soften before serving.

5. Top with a batch of Coconut Whipped Cream scooped on top of the pie once it's set. Finish it off with a sprinkling of toasted shredded coconut.

308.Cherry-Vanilla Rice Pudding (Pressure cooker)

Preparation time: 5 minutes
Cooking time: 30 minutes
Servings: 4-6

Ingredients

- 1 cup short-grain brown rice
- 1¾ cups nondairy milk, plus more as needed
- 1½ cups water
- 4 tablespoons unrefined sugar or pure maple syrup (use 2 tablespoons if you use a sweetened milk), plus more as needed
- 1 teaspoon vanilla extract (use ½ teaspoon if you use vanilla milk)
- Pinch salt
- ¼ cup dried cherries or ½ cup fresh or frozen pitted cherries

Directions

1. Preparing the Ingredients. In your electric pressure cooker's cooking pot, combine the rice, milk, water, sugar, vanilla, and salt.

2. High pressure for 30 minutes. Close and lock the lid, and select High Pressure for 30 minutes.

3. Pressure Release. Once the cook time is complete, let the pressure release naturally, about 20 minutes. Unlock and remove the lid. Stir in the cherries and put the lid back on loosely for about 10 minutes. Serve, adding more

milk or sugar, as desired.

309.Lime in the Coconut Chia Pudding

Preparation time: 10 minutes
Cooking time: 20 minutes
Servings: 4

Ingredients

- Zest and juice of 1 lime
- 1 (14-ounce) can coconut milk
- 1 to 2 dates, or 1 tablespoon coconut or other unrefined sugar, or 1 tablespoon maple syrup, or 10 to 15 drops pure liquid stevia
- 2 tablespoons chia seeds, whole or ground
- 2 teaspoons matcha green tea powder (optional)

Directions

1. Preparing the Ingredients.

2. Blend all the ingredients in a blender until smooth. Chill in the fridge for about 20 minutes, then serve topped with one or more of the topping ideas.

3. Try blueberries, blackberries, sliced strawberries, Coconut Whipped Cream, or toasted unsweetened coconut.

310.Mint Chocolate Chip Sorbet

Preparation time: 5 minutes
Cooking time: 0 minute
Servings: 1

Ingredients

- 1 frozen banana
- 1 tablespoon almond butter, or peanut butter, or other nut or seed butter

- 2 tablespoons fresh mint, minced

- ¼ cup or less non-dairy milk (only if needed)

- 2 to 3 tablespoons non-dairy chocolate chips, or cocoa nibs

- 2 to 3 tablespoons goji berries (optional)

Directions

1. Preparing the Ingredients.

2. Put the banana, almond butter, and mint in a food processor or blender and purée until smooth.

3. Add the non-dairy milk if needed to keep blending (but only if needed, as this will make the texture less solid). Pulse the chocolate chips and goji berries (if using) into the mix so they're roughly chopped up.

311.Peach-Mango Crumble (Pressure cooker)

Preparation time: 10 minutes
Cooking time: 6 minutes
Servings: 4-6

Ingredients

- 3 cups chopped fresh or frozen peaches

- 3 cups chopped fresh or frozen mangos

- 4 tablespoons unrefined sugar or pure maple syrup, divided

- 1 cup gluten-free rolled oats

- ½ cup shredded coconut, sweetened or unsweetened

- 2 tablespoons coconut oil or vegan margarine

Directions

1. Preparing the Ingredients. In a 6- to 7-inch round baking dish, toss together the peaches, mangos, and 2 tablespoons of sugar. In a food processor, combine the oats, coconut, coconut oil, and remaining 2 tablespoons of sugar. Pulse until combined. (If you use maple syrup, you'll need less coconut oil. Start with just the syrup and add oil if the mixture isn't sticking together.) Sprinkle the oat mixture over the fruit mixture.

2. Cover the dish with aluminum foil. Put a trivet in the bottom of your electric pressure cooker's cooking pot and pour in a cup or two of water. Using a foil sling or silicone helper handles, lower the pan onto the trivet.

3. High pressure for 6 minutes. Close and lock the lid, and select High Pressure for 6 minutes.

4. Pressure Release. Once the cook time is complete, quick release the pressure. Unlock and remove the lid.

5. Let cool for a few minutes before carefully lifting out the dish with oven mitts or tongs. Scoop out portions to serve.

312.Zesty Orange-Cranberry Energy Bites

Preparation time: 10 minutes
Cooking time: 15 minutes
Servings: 12

Ingredients

- 2 tablespoons almond butter, or cashew or sunflower seed butter

- 2 tablespoons maple syrup, or brown rice syrup

- ¾ cup cooked quinoa

- ¼ cup sesame seeds, toasted

- 1 tablespoon chia seeds

- ½ teaspoon almond extract, or vanilla extract
- Zest of 1 orange
- 1 tablespoon dried cranberries
- ¼ cup ground almonds

Directions

1. Preparing the Ingredients.

2. In a medium bowl, mix together the nut or seed butter and syrup until smooth and creamy. Stir in the rest of the ingredients, and mix to make sure the consistency is holding together in a ball. Form the mix into 12 balls.

3. Place them on a baking sheet lined with parchment or waxed paper and put in the fridge to set for about 15 minutes.

4. If your balls aren't holding together, it's likely because of the moisture content of your cooked quinoa. Add more nut or seed butter mixed with syrup until it all sticks together.

313. Almond-Date Energy Bites

Preparation time: 5 minutes
Cooking time: 15 minutes
Servings: 24
Ingredients
- 1 cup dates, pitted
- 1 cup unsweetened shredded coconut
- ¼ cup chia seeds
- ¾ cup ground almonds
- ¼ cup cocoa nibs, or non-dairy chocolate chips

Directions

Directions:

1. Purée everything in a food processor until crumbly and sticking together, pushing down the sides whenever

necessary to keep it blending. If you don't have a food processor, you can mash soft Medjool dates. But if you're using harder baking dates, you'll have to soak them and then try to purée them in a blender.

2. Form the mix into 24 balls and place them on a baking sheet lined with parchment or waxed paper. Put in the fridge to set for about 15 minutes. Use the softest dates you can find. Medjool dates are the best for this purpose. The hard dates you see in the baking aisle of your supermarket are going to take a long time to blend up. If you use those, try soaking them in water for at least an hour before you start, and then draining.

314. Pumpkin Pie Cups (Pressure cooker)

Preparation time: 5 minutes
Cooking time: 6 minutes
Servings: 4-6

Ingredients

- 1 cup canned pumpkin purée
- 1 cup nondairy milk
- 6 tablespoons unrefined sugar or pure maple syrup (less if using sweetened milk), plus more for sprinkling
- ¼ cup spelt flour or whole-grain flour
- ½ teaspoon pumpkin pie spice
- Pinch salt

Directions

1. Preparing the Ingredients. In a medium bowl, stir together the pumpkin, milk, sugar, flour, pumpkin pie spice, and salt. Pour the mixture into 4 heat-proof ramekins. Sprinkle a bit more sugar on the top of each, if you like. Put a trivet in the bottom of

your electric pressure cooker's cooking pot and pour in a cup or two of water. Place the ramekins onto the trivet, stacking them if needed (3 on the bottom, 1 on top).

2. High pressure for 6 minutes. Close and lock the lid, and select High Pressure for 6 minutes.

3. Pressure Release. Once the cook time is complete, quick release the pressure. Unlock and remove the lid. Let cool for a few minutes before carefully lifting out the ramekins with oven mitts or tongs. Let cool for at least 10 minutes before serving.

315.Coconut and Almond Truffles

Preparation time: 15 minutes
Cooking time: 0 minutes
Servings: 8

Ingredients

- 1 cup pitted dates
- 1 cup almonds
- ½ cup sweetened cocoa powder, plus extra for coating
- ½ cup unsweetened shredded coconut
- ¼ cup pure maple syrup
- 1 teaspoon vanilla extract
- 1 teaspoon almond extract
- ¼ teaspoon sea salt

Directions

1. Preparing the Ingredients.

2. In the bowl of a food processor, combine all the ingredients and process until smooth. Chill the mixture for about 1 hour.

3. Roll the mixture into balls and then roll the balls in cocoa powder to coat.

4. Serve immediately or keep chilled until ready to serve.

316.Fudgy Brownies(Pressure cooker)

Preparation time: 10 minutes
Cooking time: 5 minutes
Servings: 4-6

Ingredients

- 3 ounces dairy-free dark chocolate
- 1 tablespoon coconut oil or vegan margarine
- ½ cup applesauce
- 2 tablespoons unrefined sugar
- ⅓ cup whole-grain flour
- ½ teaspoon baking powder
- Pinch salt

Directions

1. Preparing the Ingredients. Put a trivet in your electric pressure cooker's cooking pot and pour in a cup or two of two of water. Select Sauté or Simmer. In a large heat-proof glass or ceramic bowl, combine the chocolate and coconut oil. Place the bowl over the top of your pressure cooker, as you would a double boiler. Stir occasionally until the chocolate is melted, then turn off the pressure cooker. Stir the applesauce and sugar into the chocolate mixture. Add the flour, baking powder, and salt and stir just until combined. Pour the batter into 3 heat-proof ramekins. Put them in a heat-proof dish and cover with aluminum foil. Using a foil sling or silicone helper handles, lower the dish onto the trivet. (Alternately, cover each ramekin with foil and place them directly on the trivet, without the dish.)

2. High pressure for 6 minutes. Close and lock the lid, and select High Pressure for 5 minutes.

3. Pressure Release. Once the cook time is complete, quick release the pressure. Unlock and remove the lid.

4. Let cool for a few minutes before carefully lifting out the dish, or ramekins, with oven mitts or tongs. Let cool for a few minutes more before serving.

5. Top with fresh raspberries and an extra drizzle of melted chocolate.

317.Chocolate Macaroons

Preparation time: 10 minutes
Cooking time: 15 minutes
Servings: 8

Ingredients

- 1 cup unsweetened shredded coconut
- 2 tablespoons cocoa powder
- ⅔ cup coconut milk
- ¼ cup agave
- pinch of sea salt

Directions

1. Preparing the Ingredients.

2. Preheat the oven to 350°F. Line a baking sheet with parchment paper. In a medium saucepan, cook all the ingredients over -medium-high heat until a firm dough is formed. Scoop the dough into balls and place on the baking sheet.

3. Bake for 15 minutes, remove from the oven, and let cool on the baking sheet.

4. Serve cooled macaroons or store in a tightly sealed container for up to

318.Chocolate Pudding

Preparation time: 5 minutes
Cooking time: 0 minutes
Servings: 1

Ingredients

- 1 banana
- 2 to 4 tablespoons nondairy milk
- 2 tablespoons unsweetened cocoa powder
- 2 tablespoons sugar (optional)
- ½ ripe avocado or 1 cup silken tofu (optional)

Directions

1. Preparing the Ingredients.

2. In a small blender, combine the banana, milk, cocoa powder, sugar (if using), and avocado (if using). Purée until smooth. Alternatively, in a small bowl, mash the banana very well, and stir in the remaining ingredients.

319.Lime and Watermelon Granita

Preparation time: 15 minutes
Cooking time: 0 minutes
Servings: 4

Ingredients

- 8 cups seedless -watermelon chunks
- juice of 2 limes, or 2 tablespoons prepared lime juice
- ½ cup. brown sugar
- strips of lime zest, for garnish

Directions

1. Preparing the Ingredients.

2. In a blender or food processor, combine the watermelon, lime juice, and sugar and process until smooth. You may have to do this in two batches. After processing, stir well to

combine both batches.

3. Pour the mixture into a 9-by-13-inch glass dish. Freeze for 2 to 3 hours. Remove from the freezer and use a fork to scrape the top layer of ice. Leave the shaved ice on top and return to the freezer.

4. In another hour, remove from the freezer and repeat. Do this a few more times until all the ice is scraped up. Serve frozen, garnished with strips of lime zest.

320.Coconut-Banana Pudding

Preparation time: 4 minutes
Cooking time: 5 minutes
Servings: 4

Ingredients

- 3 bananas, divided
- 1 (13.5-ounce) can full-fat coconut milk
- ¼ cup organic cane sugar
- 1 tablespoon cornstarch
- 1 teaspoon vanilla extract
- 2 pinches sea salt
- 6 drops natural yellow food coloring (optional)
- Ground cinnamon, for garnish

Directions

1. Preparing the Ingredients.
2. Combine 1 banana, the coconut milk, sugar, cornstarch, vanilla, and salt in a blender. Blend until smooth and creamy. If you're using the food coloring, add it to the blender now and blend until the color is evenly dispersed.
3. Transfer to a saucepot and bring to a boil over medium-high heat.

Immediately reduce to a simmer and whisk for 3 minutes, or until the mixture thickens to a thin pudding and sticks to a spoon.

4. Transfer the mixture to a container and allow to cool for 1 hour. Cover and refrigerate overnight to set. When you're ready to serve, slice the remaining 2 bananas and build individual servings as follows: pudding, banana slices, pudding, and so on until a single-serving dish is filled to the desired level. Sprinkle with ground cinnamon.

321.Spiced Apple Chia Pudding

Preparation time: 5 minutes
Cooking time: 0 minutes
Servings: 1

Ingredients

- ½ cup unsweetened applesauce
- ¼ cup nondairy milk or canned coconut milk
- 1 tablespoon chia seeds
- 1½ teaspoons sugar
- Pinch ground cinnamon or pumpkin pie spice

Directions

1. Preparing the Ingredients.
2. In a small bowl, stir together the applesauce, milk, chia seeds, sugar, and cinnamon. Enjoy as is, or let sit for 30 minutes so the chia seeds soften and expand.

322.Caramelized Pears with Balsamic Glaze

Preparation time: 5 minutes
Cooking time: 15 minutes
Servings: 4

Ingredients

- 1 cup balsamic vinegar
- ¼ cup plus 3 tablespoons brown sugar
- ¼ teaspoon grated nutmeg
- pinch of sea salt
- ¼ cup coconut oil
- 4 pears, cored and cut into slices

Directions

1. Preparing the Ingredients.

2. In a medium saucepan, heat the balsamic vinegar, ¼ cup of the brown sugar, the nutmeg, and salt over medium-high heat, stirring to thoroughly incorporate the sugar. Allow to simmer, stirring occasionally, until the glaze reduces by half, 10 to 15 minutes.

3. Meanwhile, heat the coconut oil in a large sauté pan over medium-high heat until it shimmers. Add the pears to the pan in a single layer. Cook until they turn golden, about 5 minutes. Add the remaining 3 tablespoons brown sugar and continue to cook, stirring occasionally, until the pears caramelize, about 5 minutes more.

4. Place the pears on a plate. Drizzle with balsamic glaze and serve.

323.Salted Coconut-Almond Fudge

Preparation time: 5 minutes
Cooking time: 0 minutes
Servings: 12

Ingredients

- ¾ cup creamy almond butter
- ½ cup maple syrup
- ⅓ cup coconut oil, softened or melted
- 6 tablespoons fair-trade unsweetened

cocoa powder

- 1 teaspoon coarse or flaked sea salt

Directions

1. Preparing the Ingredients.

2. Line a loaf pan with a double layer of plastic wrap. Place one layer horizontally in the pan with a generous amount of overhang, and the second layer vertically with a generous amount of overhang.

3. In a medium bowl, gently mix together the almond butter, maple syrup, and coconut oil until well combined and smooth. Add the cocoa powder and gently stir it into the mixture until well combined and creamy.

4. Pour the mixture into the prepared pan and sprinkle with the sea salt. Bring the overflowing edges of the plastic wrap over the top of the fudge to completely cover it. Place the pan in the freezer for at least 1 hour or overnight, until the fudge is firm.

5. Remove the pan from the freezer and lift the fudge out of the pan using the plastic-wrap overhangs to pull it out. Transfer to a cutting board and cut into 1-inch pieces.

234.Caramelized Bananas

Preparation time: 5 minutes
Cooking time: 10 minutes
Servings: 2

Ingredients

- 2 tablespoons vegan margarine or coconut oil
- 2 bananas, peeled, halved crosswise and then lengthwise
- 2 tablespoons dark brown sugar, demerara sugar, or coconut sugar

- 2 tablespoons spiced apple cider
- Chopped walnuts, for topping

Directions

1. Preparing the Ingredients.

2. Melt the margarine in a nonstick skillet over medium heat. Add the bananas, and cook for 2 minutes. Flip, and cook for 2 minutes more.

3. Sprinkle the sugar and cider into the oil around the bananas, and cook for 2 to 3 minutes, until the sauce thickens and caramelizes around the bananas. Carefully scoop the bananas into small bowls, and drizzle with any remaining liquid in the skillet. Sprinkle with walnuts.

325.Mixed Berries and Cream

Preparation time: 10 minutes
Cooking time: 0 minutes
Servings: 4

Ingredients

- two 15-ounce cans full-fat coconut milk
- 3 tablespoons agave
- ½ teaspoon vanilla extract
- 1 pint fresh blueberries
- 1 pint fresh raspberries
- 1 pint fresh strawberries, sliced

Directions

1. Preparing the Ingredients.

2. Refrigerate the coconut milk overnight. When you open the can, the liquid will have separated from the solids. Spoon out the solids and reserve the liquid for another purpose.

3. In a medium bowl, whisk the agave

and vanilla extract into the coconut solids. Divide the berries among four bowls. Top with the coconut cream. Serve immediately.

326."Rugged" Coconut Balls

Preparation time: 15 minutes
Cooking time: 0 minute
Servings: 8

Ingredients

- 1/3 cup coconut oil melted
- 1/3 cup coconut butter softened
- 2 oz coconut, finely shredded, unsweetened
- 4 Tbsp coconut palm sugar
- 1/2 cup shredded coconut

Directions:

1. Combine all ingredients in a blender.

2. Blend until soft and well combined.

3. Form small balls from the mixture and roll in shredded coconut.

4. Place on a sheet lined with parchment paper and refrigerate overnight.

5. Keep coconut balls into sealed container in fridge up to one week.

327.Almond - Choco Cake

Preparation time: 45 minutes
Cooking time: 32 minutes
Servings: 8

Ingredients

- 1 1/2 cups of almond flour
- 1/3 cup almonds finely chopped
- 1/4 cup of cocoa powder unsweetened
- Pinch of salt
- 1/2 tsp baking soda
- 2 Tbsp almond milk
- 1/2 cup Coconut oil melted
- 2 tsp pure vanilla extract
- 1/3 cup brown sugar (packed)

Directions:

1. Preheat oven to 350 F.
2. Line 9" cake pan with parchment paper, and grease with a little melted coconut oil; set aside.
3. Stir the almond flour, chopped almonds, cocoa powder, salt, and baking soda in a bowl.
4. In a separate bowl, stir the remaining ingredients.
5. Combine the almond flour mixture with the almond milk mixture and stir well.
6. Place batter in a prepared cake pan.
7. Bake for 30 to 32 minutes.
8. Remove from the oven, allow it to cool completely.
9. Store the cake-slices a freezer, tightly

wrapped in a double layer of plastic wrap and a layer of foil. It will keep on this way for up to a month.

328.Banana-Almond Cake

Preparation time: 15 minutes
Cooking time: 45 minutes
Servings: 8

Ingredients

- 4 ripe bananas in chunks
- 3 Tbsš honey or maple syrup
- 1 tsp pure vanilla extract
- 1/2 cup almond milk
- 3/4 cup of self-raising flour
- 1 tsp cinnamon
- 1 tsp baking powder
- 1 pinch of salt
- 1/3 cup of almonds finely chopped
- Almond slices for decoration

Directions:

1. Preheat the oven to 400 F (air mode).
2. Oil a cake mold; set aside.
3. Add bananas into a bowl and mash with the fork.
4. Add honey, vanilla, almond, and stir well.
5. In a separate bowl, stir flour, cinnamon, baking powder, salt, the almonds broken, and mix with a

spoon.

6. Combine the flour mixture with the banana mixture, and stir until all ingredients combined well.

7. Transfer the mixture to prepared cake mold and sprinkle with sliced almonds.

8. Bake for 40-45 minutes or until the toothpick inserted comes out clean.

9. Remove from the oven, and allow the cake to cool completely.

10. Cut cake into slices, place in tin foil, or an airtight container, and keep refrigerated up to one week.

329.Banana-Coconut Ice Cream

Preparation time: 15 minutes
Cooking time: 0 minutes
Servings: 6

Ingredients

- 1 cup coconut cream
- 1/2 cup Inverted sugar
- 2 large frozen bananas (chunks)
- 3 Tbsp honey extracted
- 1/4 tsp cinnamon powder

Directions:

1. In a bowl, whip the coconut cream with the inverted sugar.

2. In a separate bowl, beat the banana with honey and cinnamon.

3. Incorporate the coconut whipped cream and banana mixture; stir well.

4. Cover the bowl and let cool in the refrigerator over the night.

5. Stir the mixture 3 to 4 times to avoid crystallization.

6. Keep frozen 1 to 2 months.

330.Coconut Butter Clouds Cookies

Preparation time: 15 minutes
Cooking time: 10 minutes
Servings: 8

Ingredients

- 1/2 cup coconut butter softened
- 1/2 cup peanut butter softened
- 1/2 cup of granulated sugar
- 1/2 cup of brown sugar
- 2 Tbsp chia seeds soaked in 4 tablespoons water
- 1/2 tsp pure vanilla extract
- 1/2 tsp baking soda
- 1/4 tsp salt
- 1 cup of all-purpose flour

Directions:

1. Preheat oven to 360 F.

2. Add coconut butter, peanut butter, and both sugars in a mixing bowl.

3. Beat with a mixer until soft and sugar combined well.

4. Add soaked chia seeds and vanilla

extract; beat.

5. Add baking soda, salt, and flour; beat until all ingredients are combined well.

6. With your hands, shape dough into cookies.

7. Arrange your cookies onto a baking sheet, and bake for about 10 minutes.

8. Remove cookies from the oven and allow to cool completely.

9. Sprinkle with icing sugar and enjoy your cookies.

10. Place cookies in an airtight container and keep refrigerated up to 10 days.

331.Chocomint Hazelnut Bars

Preparation time: 5 minutes
Cooking time: 15 minutes
Servings: 8

Ingredients

- 1/2 cup coconut oil, melted
- 4 Tbsp cocoa powder
- 1/4 cup almond butter
- 3/4 cup brown sugar - (packed)
- 1 tsp vanilla extract
- 1 tsp pure peppermint extract
- pinch of salt
- 1 cup shredded coconut
- 1 cup hazelnuts sliced

Directions:

1. Chop the hazelnuts in a food processor; set aside.

2. Fill the bottom of a double boiler with water and place it on low heat.

3. Put the coconut oil, cacao powder, almond butter, brown sugar, vanilla, peppermint extract, and salt in the top of a double boiler over hot (not boiling) water and constantly stir for 10 minutes.

4. Add hazelnuts and shredded coconut to the melted mixture and stir together.

5. Pour the mixture in a dish lined with parchment and freeze for several hours.

6. Remove from the freezer and cut into bars.

7. Store in airtight container or freezer bag in a freezer.

8. Let the bars at room temperature for 10 to 15 minutes before eating.

332.Coco-Cinnamon Balls

Preparation time: 10 minutes
Cooking time: 5 minutes
Servings: 12

Ingredients

- 1 cup coconut butter softened
- 1 cup coconut milk canned
- 1 tsp pure vanilla extract
- 3/4 tsp cinnamon

- 1/2 tsp nutmeg

- 2 Tbsp coconut palm sugar (or granulated sugar)

- 1 cup coconut shreds

Directions:

1. Combine all ingredients (except the coconut shreds) in a heated bath - bain-marie.

2. Cook and stir until all ingredients are soft and well combined.

3. Remove bowl from heat, place into a bowl, and refrigerate until the mixture firmed up.

4. Form cold coconut mixture into balls, and roll each ball in the shredded coconut.

5. Store into a sealed container, and keep refrigerated up to one week.

333.Express Coconut Flax Pudding

Preparation time: 5 minutes
Cooking time: 15 minutes
Servings: 4

Ingredients

- 1 Tbsp coconut oil softened

- 1 Tbsp coconut cream

- 2 cups coconut milk canned

- 3/4 cup ground flax seed

- 4 Tbsp coconut palm sugar (or to taste)

Directions:

1. Press SAUTÉ button on your Instant Pot

2. Add coconut oil, coconut cream, coconut milk, and ground flaxseed.

3. Stir about 5 - 10 minutes.

4. Lock lid into place and set on the MANUAL setting for 5 minutes.

5. When the timer beeps, press "Cancel" and carefully flip the Quick Release valve to let the pressure out.

6. Add the palm sugar and stir well.

7. Taste and adjust sugar to taste.

8. Allow pudding to cool down completely.

9. Place the pudding in an airtight container and refrigerate for up to 2 weeks.

334.Full-flavored Vanilla Ice Cream

Preparation time: 5 minutes
Cooking time: 20 minutes
Servings: 8

Ingredients

- 1 1/2 cups canned coconut milk

- 1 cup coconut whipping cream

- 1 frozen banana cut into chunks

- 1 cup vanilla sugar

- 3 Tbsp apple sauce

- 2 tsp pure vanilla extract

- 1 tsp Xanthan gum or agar-agar thickening agent

Directions:

1. Add all ingredients in a food processor; process until all ingredients combined well.

2. Place the ice cream mixture in a freezer-safe container with a lid over.

3. Freeze for at least 4 hours.

4. Remove frozen mixture to a bowl and beat with a mixer to break up the ice crystals.

5. Repeat this process 3 to 4 times.

6. Let the ice cream at room temperature for 15 minutes before serving.

335.Irresistible Peanut Cookies

Preparation time: 5 minutes
Cooking time: 25 minutes
Servings: 8

Ingredients

- 4 Tbsp all-purpose flour

- 1 tsp baking soda

- pinch of salt

- 1/3 cup granulated sugar

- 1/3 cup peanut butter softened

- 3 Tbsp applesauce

- 1/2 tsp pure vanilla extract

Directions:

1. Preheat oven to 350 F.

2. Combine the flour, baking soda, salt, and sugar in a mixing bowl; stir.

3. Add all remaining ingredients and stir well to form a dough.

4. Roll dough into cookie balls/patties.

5. Arrange your cookies onto greased (with oil or cooking spray) baking sheet.

6. Bake for about 8 to 10 minutes.

7. Let cool for at least 15 minutes before removing from tray.

8. Remove cookies from the tray and let cool completely.

9. Place your peanut butter cookies in an airtight container, and keep refrigerated up to 10 days.

336.Murky Almond Cookies

Preparation time: 10 minutes
Cooking time: 15 minutes
Servings: 12

Ingredients

- 4 Tbsp cocoa powder

- 2 cups almond flour

- 1/4 tsp salt

- 1/2 tsp baking soda

- 5 Tbsp coconut oil melted

- 2 Tbsp almond milk

- 1 1/2 tsp almond extract

- 1 tsp vanilla extract
- 4 Tbsp corn syrup or honey

Directions:

1. Preheat oven to 340 F degrees.

2. Grease a large baking sheet; set aside.

3. Combine the cocoa powder, almond flour, salt, and baking soda in a bowl.

4. In a separate bowl, whisk melted coconut oil, almond milk, almond and vanilla extract, and corn syrup or honey.

5. Combine the almond flour mixture with the almond milk mixture and stir until all ingredients incorporate well.

6. Roll tablespoons of the dough into balls, and arrange onto a prepared baking sheet.

7. Bake for 12 to 15 minutes.

8. Remove from the oven and transfer onto a plate lined with a paper towel.

9. Allow cookies to cool down completely and store in an airtight container at room temperature for about four days.

337. Orange Semolina Halva

Preparation time: 15 minutes
Cooking time: 5 minutes
Servings: 12

Ingredients

- 6 cups fresh orange juice
- Zest from 3 oranges
- 3 cups brown sugar
- 1 1/4 cup semolina flour
- 1 Tbsp almond butter (plain, unsalted)
- 4 Tbsp ground almond
- 1/4 tsp cinnamon

Directions:

1. Heat the orange juice, orange zest with brown sugar in a pot.

2. Stir over medium heat until sugar is dissolved.

3. Add the semolina flour and cook over low heat for 15 minutes; stir occasionally.

4. Add almond butter, ground almonds, and cinnamon, and stir well.

5. Cook, frequently stirring, for further 5 minutes.

6. Transfer the halva mixture into a mold, let it cool and refrigerate for at least 4 hours.

7. Keep refrigerated in a sealed container for one week.

338. Seasoned Cinnamon Mango Popsicles

Preparation time: 15 minutes
Cooking time: 0 minute
Servings: 6

Ingredients

- 1 1/2 cups of mango pulp
- 1 mango cut in cubes
- 1 cup brown sugar (packed)
- 2 Tbsp lemon juice freshly squeezed
- 1 tsp cinnamon
- 1 pinch of salt

Directions:

1. Add all ingredients into your blender.
2. Blend until brown sugar dissolved.
3. Pour the mango mixture evenly in popsicle molds or cups.
4. Insert sticks into each mold.
5. Place molds in a freezer, and freeze for at least 5 to 6 hours.
6. Before serving, un-mold easy your popsicles placing molds under lukewarm water.

339.Strawberry Molasses Ice Cream

Preparation time: 20 minutes
Cooking time: 0 minute
Servings: 8

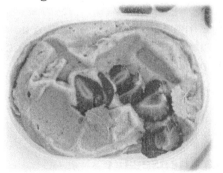

Ingredients

- 1 lb strawberries
- 3/4 cup coconut palm sugar (or granulated sugar)
- 1 cup coconut cream
- 1 Tbsp molasses

- 1 tsp balsamic vinegar
- 1/2 tsp agar-agar
- 1/2 tsp pure strawberry extract

Directions:

1. Add strawberries, date sugar, and the balsamic vinegar in a blender; blend until completely combined.
2. Place the mixture in the refrigerator for one hour.
3. In a mixing bowl, beat the coconut cream with an electric mixer to make a thick mixture.
4. Add molasses, balsamic vinegar, agar-agar, and beat for further one minute or until combined well.
5. Keep frozen in a freezer-safe container (with plastic film and lid over).

340.Strawberry-Mint Sorbet

Preparation time: 10 minutes
Cooking time: 5 minutes
Servings: 6

Ingredients

- 1 cup of granulated sugar
- 1 cup of orange juice
- 1 lb frozen strawberries
- 1 tsp pure peppermint extract

Directions:

1. Add sugar and orange juice in a

saucepan.

2. Stir over high heat and boil for 5 minutes or until sugar dissolves.

3. Remove from the heat and let it cool down.

4. Add strawberries into a blender, and blend until smooth.

5. Pour syrup into strawberries, add peppermint extract and stir until all ingredients combined well.

6. Transfer mixture to a storage container, cover tightly, and freeze until ready to serve.

341.Keto Chocolate Brownies

Preparation time: 15 minutes
Cooking time: 15 minutes

Ingredients:

1. ¼ t. of the following:
2. salt
3. baking soda
4. ½ c. of the following:
5. sweetener of your choice
6. coconut flour
7. vegetable oil
8. water
9. ¼ c. of the following:
10. cocoa powder
11. almond milk yogurt
12. 1 tbsp. ground flax
13. 1 t. vanilla extract

Directions:

1. Bring the oven to 350 heat setting.

2. Mix the ground flax, vanilla, yogurt, oil, and water; set to the side for 10 minutes.

3. Line an oven-safe 8x8 baking dish with parchment paper.

4. After 10 minutes have passed, add coconut flour, cocoa powder, sweetener, baking soda, and salt.

5. Bake for 15 minutes; make sure that you placed it in the center. When they come out, they will look underdone.

6. Place in the refrigerator and let them firm up overnight.

342.Chocolate Fat Bomb

Preparation time: 5 minutes
Cooking time: 0 minutes
Servings: 14

Ingredients:

- 1 tbsp. liquid sweetener of your choice.
- ¼ c. of the following:
- coconut oil, melted
- cocoa powder
- ½ c. almond butter

Directions:

1. Mix the ingredients in a medium bowl until smooth. Pour into the candy molds or ice cube trays.

2. Put in the freezer to set.

3. Store in freezer.

343.Vanilla Cheesecake

Preparation time: 3 hours 20 minutes
Cooking time: 0 minute
Servings: 10

Ingredients:

- 1 tbsp. vanilla extract,
- 2 ½ tbsp. lemon juice
- ½ c. coconut oil

- 1/8 t. stevia powder
- 6 tbsp. coconut milk
- 1 ½ c. blanched almonds soaked
- Crust:
- 2 tbsp. coconut oil
- 1 ½ c. almonds

Directions:

1. For the Crust:
2. In a food processor, add the almonds and coconut oil and pulse until crumbles start to form.
3. Line a 7-inch springform pan with parchment paper and firmly press the crust into the bottom.
4. For the Sauce:
5. Bring a saucepan of water to a boil and soak the almonds for 2 hours. Drain and shake to dry.
6. Next, add the almonds to the food processor and blend until completely smooth.
7. Add vanilla, lemon, coconut oil, stevia, and coconut milk and blend until smooth.
8. Pour over the crust and freeze overnight or for a minimum of 3 hours.
9. Serve and enjoy.

344.Chocolate Mousse

Preparation time: 5 minutes
Cooking time: 0 minute
Servings: 2

Ingredients:

- 6 drops liquid stevia extract
- ½ t. cinnamon
- 3 tbsp. cocoa powder, unsweetened
- 1 c. coconut milk

Directions:

1. On the day before, place the coconut milk into the refrigerator overnight.
2. Remove the coconut milk from the refrigerator; it should be very thick.
3. Whisk in cocoa powder with an electric mixer.
4. Add stevia and cinnamon and whip until combined.
5. Place in individual bowls and serve and enjoy.

345.Avocado Chocolate Mousse

Preparation time: 3 hours 20 minutes
Cooking time:
Servings: 4

Ingredients:

- 2 pinches sea salt
- 4 tbsp. sweetener of your choice
- 1 c. almond milk, unsweetened
- 2 avocados, peeled and pitted

Directions:

1. Blend everything using a machine of your choice, as long as the consistency becomes smooth for a mousse. If too thick, add some more coconut milk, ¼ teaspoon at a time.
2. Serve and enjoy.

346.Coconut Fat Bombs

Preparation time: 1 hour 5 minutes
Cooking time: 0 minute
Servings: 4

Ingredients:

- 20 drops liquid stevia
- 1 c. coconut flakes, unsweetened

- ¾ c. coconut oil
- 1 can coconut milk

Directions:

1. In a big microwave-safe mixing bowl, add coconut oil and warm on low power for 20 seconds to melt.
2. Whisk in coconut milk and stevia into the oil.
3. Add coconut flakes; combine well.
4. Pour into candy molds or ice cube trays and freeze for 1 hour.
5. Serve and enjoy.

347.Coconut Cupcakes

Preparation time: 1 hour 5 minutes
Cooking time: 20 minutes
Servings: 18

Ingredients:

- 1 tbsp. vanilla
- 1 t. baking soda
- 1 c. erythritol
- 4 t. baking powder
- 1 ¼ c. coconut milk
- ¾ c. coconut flour
- 14 tbsp. arrowroot powder
- 2 c. almond meal
- ½ c. coconut oil

Whipped Cream:

- 1 t. vanilla
- ¼ c. erythritol
- 2 13.5 oz. cans full-fat coconut milk, refrigerated overnight

Directions:

1. Prepare a muffin tin with muffin liners and bring the oven to 350 heat

setting.

2. In a big mixing bowl, add all the ingredients and beat on medium-high speed until it turns to a batter-like consistency. If too dry, add ¼ teaspoon of water at a time.
3. Fill the cupcake cups with the batter, three-quarters full.
4. Bake for 20 minutes or until the cupcakes are firm.
5. Place in the refrigerator to cool.
6. While cupcakes are cooling, make the whipped cream.
7. Remove the coconut milk from the fridge and pour the clear coconut water from the milk.
8. In a big mixing bowl, add the vanilla and erythritol; beat until fluffy.
9. Ice the cupcakes and serve.
10. Serve and enjoy.

348.Pumpkin Truffles

Preparation time: 15 minutes
Cooking time: 15 minutes
Servings: 12

Ingredients:

- 1 t. cinnamon
- 2 tbsp. coconut sugar
- 3 tbsp. coconut flour
- ½ c. almond flour
- 1 t. pumpkin pie spice
- ¼ t. salt
- ½ t. vanilla extract
- ¼ c. maple syrup
- 1 c. pumpkin puree

Directions:

1. Bring a saucepan to medium heat and add pumpkin puree, syrup, salt, and pumpkin pie spice, stirring constantly until thickened about 5 minutes.

2. Once thick, add in vanilla and continue to stir for an additional minute.

3. Remove from the heat and allow to cool.

4. Once cool, mix in the coconut and almond flour. Then put in the refrigerator to chill for 10 minutes.

5. Remove from the fridge and mix again. If the dough is too sticky, add in 1 tablespoon of almond flour until you can form a ball with the dough.

6. Form 12 balls using your hands with the dough.

7. In a little bowl, combine coconut sugar and cinnamon.

8. Roll each ball into the cinnamon-sugar mixture.

9. Serve and enjoy.

349.Simple Banana Fritters

Preparation time: 15 minutes
Cooking time: 20 minutes
Servings: 8

Ingredients

- 4 bananas
- 3 tbsps. Maple syrup
- ¼ tsp. Cinnamon powder
- ¼ tsp. Nutmeg
- 1 cup coconut flour

Directions

1. Preheat oven to 350° F.

2. Mash the bananas in a large mixing bowl along with maple syrup, cinnamon, nutmeg powder and coconut flour.

3. Mix all the ingredients well.

4. Take 2 tbsps. mixture and make small 1-inch-thick fritters from this mixture.

5. Place fritters in greased baking tray.

6. Bake fritters in preheated oven for about 10-15 minutes until golden from both sides.

7. Once done, take them out of the oven.

8. Serve with coconut cream.

9. Enjoy!

350.Coconut And Blueberries Ice Cream

Preparation time: 5 minutes
Cooking time: 0 minutes
Servings: 4

Ingredients

- 1/4 cup coconut cream
- 1 tbsp. Maple syrup
- ¼ cup coconut flour
- 1 cup blueberries
- ¼ cup blueberries for topping

Directions

1. Put ingredients into food processor and mix well on high speed.

2. Pour mixture in silicon molds and freeze in freezer for about 2-4 hours.

3. Once balls are set remove from freezer.

4. Top with berries.

5. Serve cold and enjoy!

351.Peach Crockpot Pudding

Preparation time: 15 minutes

Cooking time: 4 hours
Servings: 6

Ingredients

- 2 cups sliced peaches
- 1/4 cup maple syrup
- 1/2 tsp. Cinnamon powder
- 2 cups coconut milk
- For serving
- ½ cup coconut cream
- 1 oz. Coconut flakes

Directions

1. Lightly grease the crockpot and place peaches in the bottom.
2. Add maple syrup, cinnamon powder and milk.
3. Cover and cook on high for 4 hours.
4. Once cooked remove from crockpot.
5. For serving pour coconut cream.
6. Top with coconut flakes.
7. Serve and enjoy!

352. White Chocolate Pudding

Preparation time: 4 hours 20 minutes
Cooking time: 45 minutes
Servings: 4

Ingredients

- 3 tbsp flax seed + 9 tbsp water
- 3 tbsp cornstarch
- ¼ tbsp salt
- 1 cup cashew cream
- 2 ½ cups almond milk
- ½ pure date sugar
- 1 tbsp vanilla caviar
- 6 oz unsweetened white chocolate chips
- Whipped coconut cream for topping
- Sliced bananas and raspberries for topping

Directions

1. In a small bowl, mix the flax seed powder with water and allow thickening for 5 minutes to make the flax egg.
2. In a large bowl, whisk the cornstarch and salt, and then slowly mix in the in the cashew cream until smooth. Whisk in the flax egg until well combined.
3. Pour the almond milk into a pot and whisk in the date sugar. Cook over medium heat while frequently stirring until the sugar dissolves. Reduce the heat to low and simmer until steamy and bubbly around the edges.
4. Pour half of the almond milk mixture into the flax egg mix, whisk well and pour this mixture into the remaining milk content in the pot. Whisk continuously until well combined.
5. Bring the new mixture to a boil over medium heat while still frequently stirring and scraping all the corners of the pot, 2 minutes.
6. Turn the heat off, stir in the vanilla caviar, then the white chocolate chips until melted. Spoon the mixture into a bowl, allow cooling for 2 minutes, cover with plastic wraps making sure to press the plastic onto the surface of the pudding, and refrigerate for 4 hours.
7. Remove the pudding from the fridge, take off the plastic wrap and whip for about a minute.
8. Spoon the dessert into serving cups, swirl some coconut whipping cream

on top, and top with the bananas and raspberries. Enjoy immediately.

353.Ambrosia Salad With Pecans

Preparation time: 15 minutes
Cooking time: 10 minutes
Servings: 4

Ingredients

- 1 cup pure coconut cream
- ½ tsp vanilla extract
- 2 medium bananas, peeled and cut into chunks
- 1 ½ cups unsweetened coconut flakes
- 4 tbsp toasted pecans, chopped
- 1 cup pineapple tidbits, drained
- 1 (11 oz) can mandarin oranges, drained
- ¾ cup maraschino cherries, stems removed

Directions

1. In medium bowl, mix the coconut cream and vanilla extract until well combined.
2. In a larger bowl, combine the bananas, coconut flakes, pecans, pineapple, oranges, and cherries until evenly distributed.
3. Pour on the coconut cream mixture and fold well into the salad.
4. Chill in the refrigerator for 1 hour and serve afterwards.

354.Peanut Butter Blossom Biscuits

Preparation time: 15 minutes
Cooking time: 15 minutes
Servings: 4

Ingredients

- 1 tbsp flax seed powder + 3 tbsp water
- 1 cup pure date sugar + more for dusting
- ½ cup unsalted butter, softened
- ½ cup creamy peanut butter
- 1 large egg, at room temperature
- 1 tsp vanilla extract
- 1 ¾ cup whole-wheat flour
- 1 tsp baking soda
- ¼ tsp salt
- ¼ cup unsweetened chocolate chips

Directions

1. In a small bowl, mix the flax seed powder with water and allow thickening for 5 minutes to make the flax egg.
2. In a medium bowl using an electric mixer, whisk the date sugar, plant butter, and peanut butter until light and fluffy.
3. Mix in the flax egg and vanilla until well combined. Add the flour, baking soda, salt, and whisk well again.
4. Fold in the chocolate chips, cover the bowl with a plastic wrap, and refrigerate for 1 hour. After, preheat the oven to 375 F and line a baking sheet with parchment paper.
5. Use a cookie sheet to scoop mounds of the batter onto the sheet with 1-inch intervals. Bake in the oven for 9 to 10 minutes or until golden brown and slightly cracked on top.
6. Remove the cookies from the oven, cool for 3 minutes, roll in some date sugar, and serve.

355.Chocolate & Almond Butter

Barks

Preparation time: 35 minutes
Cooking time: 20 minutes
Servings: 4

Ingredients

- 1/3 cup coconut oil, melted
- ¼ cup almond butter, melted
- 2 tbsp unsweetened coconut flakes.
- 1 tsp pure maple syrup
- A pinch ground rock salt
- ¼ cup unsweetened cocoa nibs

Directions

1. Line a baking tray with baking paper and set aside.
2. In a medium bowl, mix the coconut oil, almond butter, coconut flakes, maple syrup, and then fold in the rock salt and cocoa nibs.
3. Pour and spread the mixture on the baking sheet, chill in the refrigerator for 20 minutes or until firm.
4. Remove the dessert, break into shards and enjoy immediately.
5. Preserve extras in the refrigerator.

356.Mini Berry Tarts

Preparation time: 35 minutes
Cooking time: 20 minutes
Servings: 4

Ingredients

- For the piecrust:
- 4 tbsp flax seed powder + 12 tbsp water
- 1/3 cup whole-wheat flour + more for dusting
- ½ tsp salt
- ¼ cup plant butter, cold and crumbled
- 3 tbsp pure malt syrup
- 1 ½ tsp vanilla extract
- For the filling:
- 6 oz cashew cream
- 6 tbsp pure date sugar
- ¾ tsp vanilla extract
- 1 cup mixed frozen berries

Directions

1. Preheat the oven to 350 F and grease a mini pie pans with cooking spray.
2. In a medium bowl, mix the flax seed powder with water and allow soaking for 5 minutes.
3. In a large bowl, combine the flour and salt. Add the butter and using an electric hand mixer, whisk until crumbly. Pour in the flax egg, malt syrup, vanilla, and mix until smooth dough forms.
4. Flatten the dough on a flat surface, cover with plastic wrap, and refrigerate for 1 hour.
5. After, lightly dust a working surface with some flour, remove the dough onto the surface, and using a rolling pin, flatten the dough into a 1-inch diameter circle,
6. Use a large cookie cutter, cut out rounds of the dough and fit into the pie pans. Use a knife to trim the edges of the pan. Lay a parchment paper on the dough cups, pour on some baking beans and bake in the oven until golden brown, 15 to 20 minutes.
7. Remove the pans from the oven, pour out the baking beans, and allow cooling.
8. In a medium bowl, mix the cashew cream, date sugar, and vanilla extract.

9. Divide the mixture into the tart cups and top with berries. Serve immediately.

357. Mixed Nut Chocolate Fudge

Preparation time: 2 hours 10 minutes
Cooking time: 0 minute
Servings: 4

Ingredients

- 3 cups unsweetened chocolate chips
- ¼ cup thick coconut milk
- 1 ½ tsp vanilla extract
- A pinch salt
- 1 cup chopped mixed nuts

Directions

1. Line a 9-inch square pan with baking paper and set aside.
2. Melt the chocolate chips, coconut milk, and vanilla in a medium pot over low heat.
3. Mix in the salt and nuts until well distributed and pour the mixture into the square pan.
4. Refrigerate for at least for at least 2 hours.
5. Remove from the fridge, cut into squares and serve.

358. Apple and Blueberries Crumble

Preparation time: 5 minutes
Cooking time: 15 minutes
Servings: 2

Ingredients:

- 1/2 cup frozen blueberries
- 1 medium apple, peeled, diced
- 2 tablespoons coconut sugar
- 1/4 cup and 1 tablespoon brown rice flour
- 1/2 teaspoon ground cinnamon
- 2 tablespoons almond butter

Directions:

1. Switch on the air fryer, insert the fryer basket, then shut it with the lid, set the frying temperature 350 degrees F, and let it preheat for 5 minutes.
2. Meanwhile, take a large ramekin, place apples and berries in it, and stir until mixed.
3. Take a small bowl, add flour and remaining ingredients in it, stir until mixed, and then spoon this mixture over fruits.
4. Open the preheated fryer, place the prepared ramekin in it in, close the lid and cook for 15 minutes until cooked and the top has turned golden brown.
5. When done, the air fryer will beep, then open the lid and remove ramekin from it.
6. Serve straight away.

359. Mug Carrot Cake

Preparation time: 5 minutes
Cooking time: 15 minutes
Servings: 1

Ingredients:

- 2 tablespoons grated carrot
- 1/4 cups whole-wheat pastry flour
- 1/8 teaspoon ground dried ginger
- 2 tablespoons chopped walnuts
- 1/4 teaspoon baking powder
- 1 tablespoon coconut sugar
- 1/8 teaspoon salt
- 1/4 teaspoon ground cinnamon

- 1 tablespoons raisin
- 1/8 teaspoon ground allspice
- 2 tablespoons and 2 teaspoons almond milk
- 2 teaspoons olive oil

Directions:

1. Switch on the air fryer, insert the fryer basket, then shut it with the lid, set the frying temperature 350 degrees F, and let it preheat for 5 minutes.

2. Meanwhile, take an ovenproof mug, place flour in it, stir in ginger, baking powder, salt, sugar, cinnamon, and allspice until mixed and then mix in carrots, raisins, nuts, oil, and milk until incorporated

3. Open the preheated fryer, place the prepared mug in it, close the lid and cook for 15 minutes until firm and a toothpick come out clean from the center of the cake.

4. When done, the air fryer will beep, then open the lid and take out the mug.

5. Serve straight away.

360.Baked Apples

Preparation time: 5 minutes
Cooking time: 11 minutes
Servings: 4

Ingredients:

- 2 medium apples, cored
- 2 tablespoons coconut sugar
- 2/3 teaspoon ground cinnamon

Directions:

1. Switch on the air fryer, insert the fryer basket, then shut it with the lid, set the frying temperature 360 degrees F, and let it preheat for 5 minutes.

2. Meanwhile, prepare the apples and for this, slice each apple lengthwise, and then remove the seeds.

3. Open the preheated fryer, place apples in it in a single layer, close the lid and cook for 10 minutes until tender.

4. Meanwhile, take a small bowl, stir together sugar and cinnamon in it, and set aside until required.

5. When done, the air fryer will beep, then open the lid, sprinkle sugar-cinnamon mixture on apples, shut with lid, and continue cooking for 1 minute.

6. When done, transfer apples to a dish and then serve.

361.Donuts

Preparation time: 5 minutes
Cooking time: 18 minutes
Servings: 2

Ingredients:

- 3 cups cherries, pitted, halved
- 1/2 teaspoon almond extract, unsweetened
- 2 tablespoons maple syrup
- 4 tablespoons granola
- 1 tablespoon almond butter melted

Directions:

1. Switch on the air fryer, insert the fryer basket, then shut it with the lid, set the frying temperature 350 degrees F, and let it preheat for 5 minutes.

2. Meanwhile, take a large ramekin, place cherries in it, and then stir in almond extract, butter and maple syrup until mixed.

3. Open the preheated fryer, place ramekin in it, close the lid and cook

for 15 minutes until cooked, stirring halfway.

4. When done, the air fryer will beep, open the lid, top cherries with granola, and then continue cooking for 3 minutes until the top has turned brown.

5. Serve straight away.

362. Peanut Butter Balls

Preparation time: 15 minutes
Cooking time: 20 minutes
Servings: 6

Ingredients:

- 1/2 cup coconut flour
- 2 tablespoons flaxseed
- 1/2 cup oats
- 1/2 teaspoon baking soda
- 1/3 cup maple syrup
- 1/2 teaspoon baking powder
- 1/2 cup peanut butter
- 5 tablespoons water, warmed

Directions:

1. Prepare the flax egg and for this, place flax seeds a small bowl, stir in water until combined and let it stand for 5 minutes.

2. Then pour flax egg in a large bowl, add butter and maple syrup, whisk until smooth and then whisk in baking powder and soda until well combined.

3. Stir in oats and flour until incorporated and dough comes together, place the dough into the refrigerator for 10 minutes until chilled, and then shape the dough into twelve balls.

4. Meanwhile, switch on the air fryer, insert the fryer basket, then shut it

with the lid, set the frying temperature 250 degrees F, and let it preheat for 5 minutes.

5. Open the preheated fryer, place balls in it in a single layer, close the lid and cook for 10 minutes until golden brown and cooked, shaking halfway.

6. When done, the air fryer will beep, then open the lid, and transfer balls to a dish.

7. Cook remaining balls in the same manner and then serve.

363. Cinnamon Churros

Preparation time: 60 minutes
Cooking time: 25 minutes
Servings: 4

Ingredients:

- For the Churros:
- 1 cup coconut flour
- 1/2 cup and 1 tablespoon coconut sugar
- 2 teaspoons cinnamon
- 1/2 teaspoon vanilla extract, unsweetened
- 1/2 cup almond butter
- 3 flax eggs
- 1 cup of water
- For the Chocolate Sauce:
- 1 teaspoon coconut oil
- 3/4 cup chocolate chips, unsweetened

Directions:

1. Prepare churros and for this, take a medium saucepan, place it over medium heat, pour in water and bring it to a boil.

2. Stir in butter and 1 tablespoon sugar, let it melts, switch heat to medium-

low level and then fold in the flour until incorporated and the dough comes together, remove the pan from heat and set aside until required.

3. Take a medium bowl, place flax eggs in it and whisk in vanilla until combined.

4. Fold the flax egg mixture into the prepared dough until well combined and then let it stand for 15 minutes until cooked.

5. Transfer cooled dough into a piping bag with a star-shaped tip, take a baking pan, line it with parchment paper and pipe churros on it, about 6-inch long, and then chill them in the refrigerator for 30 minutes.

6. Meanwhile, switch on the air fryer, insert the fryer basket, then shut it with the lid, set the frying temperature 380 degrees F, and let it preheat.

7. Then open the preheated fryer, place churros in it in a single layer, close the lid and cook for 10 minutes until golden brown and cooked, shaking halfway.

8. Meanwhile, take a small bowl, place the cinnamon and remaining sugar in it and stir until mixed, set aside until required.

9. When done, the air fryer will beep, then open the lid, dredge churros into the cinnamon-sugar mixture, place them on a wire rack and cook remaining churros in the same manner.

10. In the meantime, prepare the chocolate sauce and for this, take a heatproof bowl, place chocolate chips in it, add oil and microwave for 30 seconds until chocolate has melted, and when done, stir well.

11. Dip churros into the chocolate sauce

and serve.

364.Mango & Papaya After-Chop

Preparation time: 25 minutes
Cooking time: 0 minute
Servings: 1

Ingredients:

- ¼ of papaya, chopped
- 1 mango, chopped
- 1 Tbsp coconut milk
- ½ tsp maple syrup
- 1 Tbsp peanuts, chopped

Directions:

1. Cut open the papaya. Scoop out the seeds, chop.

2. Peel the mango. Slice the fruit from the pit, chop.

3. Put the fruit in a bowl. Add remaining ingredients. Stir to coat.

365.Sautéed Bosc Pears with Walnuts

Preparation time: 15 minutes
Cooking time: 16 minutes
Servings: 6

Ingredients:

- 2 Tbsp salted butter
- ¼ tsp cinnamon
- ¼ tsp nutmeg, ground
- 6 Bosc pears, peeled, quartered
- 1 Tbsp lemon juice
- ½ cup walnuts, chopped, toasted

Directions

1. Melt butter in a skillet, add spices and cook for 30 seconds.

2. Add pears and cook for 15 minutes. Stir in lemon juice.

3. Serve topped with walnuts.

366.Brown Rice Pudding

Preparation time: 5 minutes
Cooking time: 1 hour 30 minutes
Servings: 6

Ingredients:

- 2 cups brown rice, cooked
- 3 cups light coconut milk
- 3 eggs
- 1 cup brown sugar
- 1 tsp vanilla
- ½ tsp salt
- ½ tsp cinnamon
- ¼ tsp nutmeg

Directions:

1. Blend all ingredients well. Put mixture in a 2-quart casserole dish.

2. Bake at 300°F for 90 minutes.

3. Serve.

367.Raw Energy Squares

Preparation time: 30 minutes
Cooking time: 0 minute
Servings: 6

Ingredients:

1. 2 cups Medjool dates, chopped and pitted
2. 2 cups cashews
3. ½ cup almonds
4. ¾ cup powder, cocoa
5. Sea salt, to taste
6. 2 Tbsp vanilla extract

7. 3 Tbsp cold water

Directions:

1. Blend first five ingredients in a food processor.

2. Add the vanilla and water, give a quick pulse.

3. Put the dough into a pan, making an even layer.

4. Cut into squares and serve.

368.Date Porcupines

Preparation time: 20 minutes
Cooking time: 15 minutes
Servings: 2

Ingredients:

- 2 eggs
- 1 Tbsp extra-virgin olive oil
- 1 tsp vanilla
- 1 cup Medjool dates, pitted, chopped
- 1 cup walnuts, chopped
- ¾ cup flour
- 1 cup coconut, shredded
- ½ tsp salt

Directions:

1. Preheat oven to 350°F.

2. Beat the eggs, adding the oil and vanilla. Fold in the dates and walnuts. Add flour and salt to the mixture, mix well.

3. Form the mixture into small balls and roll in coconut. Bake for 15 minutes.

4. Serve cold.

369.Raspberry Chia Pudding Shots

Preparation time: 1 hour
Cooking time: 15 minutes

Servings: 2

Ingredients:

- ¼ cup chia seeds
- ½ cup raspberries
- ½ cup coconut milk
- ¼ cup almond milk
- 1 Tbsp cacao powder
- 1 Tbsp stevia

Directions:

1. Combine all ingredients except raspberries in a jar.
2. Let sit for 2-3 minutes and transfer to shot glasses.
3. Refrigerate 1 hour, or overnight to serve as breakfast.
4. Serve with fresh raspberries.

370.Banana Muffins

Preparation time: 15 minutes
Cooking time: 15 minutes
Servings: 10

Ingredients:

- 3 bananas
- 2 eggs
- 2 cups whole wheat pastry flour
- 1/3 cup sugar
- 1 tsp salt
- 1 tsp baking soda
- ½ cup walnuts, chopped

Directions:

1. Preheat oven to 350°F.
2. Grease and flour 10 cups of a muffin tin.
3. Mix bananas and eggs together. Add

sifted dry ingredients.

4. Add nuts. Mix well.
5. Spoon into muffin tins. Bake for 20 minutes.

371.Avocado-based Chocolate Mousse

Preparation time: 7 minutes
Cooking time: 0 minute
Servings: 3

Ingredients:

- 4 ripe avocados
- 1 cup agave syrup, divided
- 1 cup cacao, divided
- ¼ teaspoon salt
- ¼ teaspoon vanilla extract

Directions:

1. Prepare the avocados and place the meat in a food processor. Process until smooth.
2. Add half the agave syrup, half the cacao, the salt and the vanilla; process until smooth.
3. Taste to see if it needs more agave syrup or cacao and add anything that's lacking.
4. Refrigerate for at least two hours, or overnight, before serving.

372.Banana Creamy Pie

Preparation time: 10 minutes
Cooking time: 0 minute
Servings: 4

Ingredients:

- 2 large pitted dates
- 1 pre-made pie crust, cooled
- 2 very ripe bananas, peeled and sliced,

plus one a little less ripe for garnish

- 1 tablespoon coconut sugar
- 1 cup coconut milk
- ½ teaspoon vanilla
- ¼ salt

Directions:

1. Soak the dates for about an hour, then drain and dry them.

2. Place the dates and banana slices in a food processor and pulse to break them up.

3. Add the coconut sugar, coconut milk, vanilla and salt and process until smooth and creamy.

4. Pour the filling into a cooled pie crust. It must be cool, or it will make the crust soggy.

5. Cover with plastic wrap and place the pie in the freezer for at least two hours.

6. Remove from the freezer and let it thaw a bit. Slice the remaining banana and place it on top. Serve while still partially frozen.

373.Banana Mango Ice Cream

Preparation time: 30 minutes
Cooking time: 0 minute
Servings: 2

Ingredients:

- 1 banana, peeled and sliced
- 2 ripe mangos with the skin removed and the flesh cubed
- 3 tablespoons almond or cashew milk, chilled

Instructions:

1. Lay out the banana and mango slices on a baking sheet lined with parchment paper and place them in the freezer.

2. Once they are frozen solid, remove the fruit and place it in the food processor.

3. Add the cold milk and process until smooth, about three to four minutes.

4. Taste and add sweetener as needed.

5. Serve immediately.

374.Strawberry Mango Shave Ice

Preparation time: 5 hours 30 minutes
Cooking time: 0 minute
Servings: 4

Ingredients:

- ½ cup superfine sugar, divided
- 1-cup strawberries, diced
- 2 diced mangos
- 2 cups mango juice
- ½ cup coconut, toasted

Directions:

1. Add 1 cup water and ¾ cup sugar to a pot and boil over medium heat.

2. Once boiled, remove from heat and add 2 more cups of water.

3. Freeze this mixture stirring after every 45 minutes.

4. Take a blender and add all remaining ingredients and blend until smooth.

5. Strain the mixture into a container with a pour spout.

6. For serving, divide the ice into glasses and pour juice and mixture over them.

7. Serve and enjoy.

375.Avocado and 'Sausage' Sandwich

Preparation time: 5 minutes
Cooking time: 10 minutes
Servings: 1

Ingredients

- 1 vegan sausage patty
- 1 cup kale, chopped
- 2 teaspoons extra virgin olive oil
- 1 tablespoon pepitas
- Salt and pepper, to taste
- For the spicy mayo
- 1 tablespoon vegan mayo
- 1/8 teaspoon chipotle powder
- 1 teaspoon jalapeno chopped
- 1 English muffin, toasted
- ¼ avocado, sliced

Directions:

1. Place a sauté pan over a high heat and add a drop of oil.

2. Add the vegan patty and cook for 2 minutes.

3. Flip the patty then add the kale and pepitas.

4. Season well then cook for another few minutes until the patty is cooked.

5. Find a small bowl and add the mayo, chipotle powder and the jalapeno. Stir well to combine.

6. Place the muffin onto a flat surface, spread with the spicy may then top with the patty.

7. Add the sliced avocado then serve and enjoy.

376. Black Bean Burritos

Preparation time: 6 minutes
Cooking time: 24 minutes
Servings: 2

Ingredients

- For the rice
- ¾ cup white rice
- 1 ½ cups water
- ¼ tsp salt
- ½ lime, juiced
- ¼ cup chopped fresh cilantro
- For the potato and onion mixture
- 3 medium red potatoes, cut into bite-sized pieces
- ½ red onion, sliced into rings
- 1 tbsp. olive oil
- Salt & pepper, to taste
- For the beans
- 1 cup cooked black beans
- ¼ teaspoon each ground cumin garlic powder, and chili powder
- Salt & pepper, to taste
- For the slaw...
- ¼ avocado
- 2 tbsps. lime juice
- 1 cup thinly sliced purple cabbage
- 1 thinly sliced jalapeno
- ¼ tsp. salt
- ¼ tsp. black pepper
- To serve
- 2 large vegan flour tortillas
- ½ sliced avocado
- Hot sauce optional
- ¼ cup salsa

Directions:

1. Place the rice, water and salt in a pan and bring to the boil.

2. Cover and cook on low until fluffy then remove from the heat and pop to one side.

3. Place a skillet over a medium heat, add 1-2 tablespoons olive oil and add the potatoes and onion.

4. Season well then leave to cook for 10 minutes, stirring often.

5. Remove from the heat and pop to one side.

6. Take a small pan then add the beans, cumin, garlic and chili. Stir well.

7. Pop over a medium heat and bring to simmer. Reduce the heat to remain warm.

8. Take a small bowl and add the lime juice and avocado. Mash together.

9. Add the cabbage and jalapeno and stir well. Season then pop to one side.

10. Add the cilantro and lime juice to the cooked rice then toss with a fork.

11. Gently warm the tortillas in a microwave for 10-20 seconds then add the fillings.

12. Roll up, serve and enjoy.

377.Peanut Butter Ice Cream

Preparation time: 20 minutes
Cooking time: 8 hours
Servings: 3

Ingredients:

- 1 cup dark chocolate chips
- 3 cans coconut cream, divided
- ¼ cup peanut butter
- ½ cup granulated sugar
- 2 tsp vanilla extract
- ¼ tsp salt
- ¼ cup graham cracker crumbs

Directions:

1. Reserve ½ cup of the coconut cream and add the rest to the blender along with peanut butter, sugar, vanilla extract, and salt.

2. Blend until smooth and freeze the mixture for 2 hours.

3. Heat the remaining ½ cup of the coconut cream in a small pot over low heat until it starts to boil.

4. Remove the pot from the heat and add the chocolate chips to the coconut cream.

5. Let this sit for 5 minutes then stir the mixture to combine the chocolate and the cream. The chocolate chips should be completely softened by this point.

6. Let the mixture cool to room temperature.

7. Meanwhile, take out the frozen mixture and mix with the coconut cream chocolate mixture and graham cracker crumbs in a bowl.

8. Let cool for 8 hours in the refrigerator.

9. Scoop out and serve chilled.

378.Cashew Cream Cheese

Preparation time: 10 minutes
Cooking time: 0 minute
Servings: 6

Ingredients:

- 1 cup raw cashews, soaked overnight
- 2-3 tbsp water
- ¼ cup lemon juice
- ½ tsp apple cider vinegar
- 2 tbsp nutritional yeast
- Salt, to taste

Directions:

1. Wash soaked cashews in a colander then transfer them to a blender or

food processor and blend them with 2 to 3 tbsp of water until smooth.

2. Add in the rest of the ingredients and mix until combined.

3. If you'd like a vegetable cream "cheese," add chopped herbs, chives, peppers, carrots, and onions to the mixture.

379.Coconut Yogurt Chia Pudding

Preparation time: 5 minutes
Cooking time: 0 minute
Servings: 1

Ingredients:

- ½ cup vanilla coconut yogurt
- 2 tbsp chia seeds
- 3 tbsp almond milk

Directions:

1. Mix all ingredients in a bowl until well combined.

2. Place in the freezer for an hour or overnight.

3. When thickened, top with your favorite garnishes and serve.

HOME-MADE SAUCES & CONDIMENTS

380. Thai Peanut Sauce

Preparation time: 5 Minutes
Cooking time: 0 Minutes
Servings: 3

Ingredients

- Apple Cider Vinegar (2 T.)
- Thai Red Curry Paste (1/4 C.)
- Peanut Butter (1 C.)
- Coconut Milk (1 ½ C.)
- Lime Juice (1 T.)
- Brown Sugar (1/4 C.)
- Soy Sauce (2 T.)

Directions

1. For a quick and easy sauce, simply place everything into a food processor and meld until soft. Be sure you keep any sauce and dressing in the fridge to keep fresh!

381. Simple Marinara Sauce

Preparation time: 10 Minutes
Cooking time: 1 Hour
Servings: 6

Ingredients

- Crushed Tomatoes (1 Can, 56 Oz.)
- Garlic Cloves (8, Sliced)
- Olive Oil (1 T.)
- Salt (2 t.)
- Basil Leaves (4, Torn)
- Balsamic Vinegar (2 t.)

Directions

1. While you could just buy some marinara sauce from the store, the packaged stuff is typically filled with sugar! Now, with some basic ingredients, you will be able to make your own from scratch!

2. You will want to begin by heating a large saucepan over low heat. As it warms up, you can throw in the olive oil, garlic, and the basil. Go ahead and sauté until the garlic begins to turn a nice golden color.

3. Next, you will be adding in the tomatoes and gently bring everything to a stew before you add in the salt and reduce the heat.

4. For the next fifty minutes, let the sauce simmer and condense. At the end of this time, you will want to stir in your vinegar, and then your sauce will be set for serving.

382. Green Cilantro Sauce

Preparation time: 5 Minutes
Cooking time: 20 Minutes
Servings: 10

Ingredients

- Olive Oil (1 C.)
- Cilantro (1 C.)
- Water (5 T.)
- Garlic Cloves (4)
- Ground Cumin (1/4 t.)
- Sherry Vinegar (to Taste)

Directions

1. To begin this sauce, you will want to crush your garlic cloves and place it into a food processor along with the cilantro.

2. After you have processed these two ingredients together, slowly begin

adding in your olive oil and blend everything together smoothly.

3. If you would like, feel welcome to combine as much or as little water as you would like, along with the sherry vinegar for some extra flavor.

4. Finally, add in your ground cumin, stir, and the sauce will be prepared.

383.General Tso Sauce

Preparation time: 5 Minutes
Cooking time: 10 Minutes
Servings: 4

Ingredients

- Rice Vinegar (1/4 C.)
- Water (1/2 C.)
- Sriracha Sauce (1 ½ T.)
- Soy Sauce (1/4 C.)
- Corn Starch (1 ½ T.)
- Sugar (1/2 C.)

Directions

1. General Tso Sauce is a classic, and you can now make a healthier version of it! All you have to do is take out your saucepan and place all of the ingredients in.

2. Once in place, bring everything over medium heat and whisk together for ten minutes or until the sauce begins to get thick.

3. Finally, remove from the heat and enjoy!

384.Cashew Cheese Sauce

Preparation time: 5 Minutes
Cooking time: 0 Minutes
Servings: 8

Ingredients

- Olive Oil (1 T.)
- Water (1/2 C.)
- Raw Cashews (3/4 C.)
- Lemon Juice (1 T.)
- Tamari Sauce (1/2 t.)
- Salt (to Taste)

Directions

1. As you begin a plant-based diet, you may be thinking you will miss your cheese. Luckily, this cashew cheese is an excellent replacement!

2. All you will have to do is take the rest of the components, place them into a blender, and combine until completely smoothed out.

3. Once you are done, place in the fridge and enjoy!

385.Balsamic Vinaigrette Dressing

Preparation time: 5 Minutes
Cooking time: 0 Minutes
Servings: 12

Ingredients

- Garlic (1 T., Minced)
- Olive Oil (3/4 C.)
- Pepper (1/2 t.)
- Cayenne Pepper (1/4 t.)
- Salt (1 t.)
- Dijon Mustard (1 T.)
- Balsamic Vinegar (1/4 C.)

Directions

1. Looking for a light salad dressing? Take the total of the ingredients from above, place in a mixer, and mix until smoothed out.

2. Store up in the fridge and enjoy over

any salad!

386. Spicy Tahini Dressing

Preparation time: 5 Minutes
Cooking time: 0 Minutes
Servings: 3

Ingredients

- Apple Cider Vinegar (1/4 C.)
- Nutritional Yeast (1/2 C.)
- Tahini (1/4 C.)
- Lemon Juice (1/4 C.)
- Garlic (1 T., Minced)
- Tamari Sauce (1/4 C.)

Directions

1. If you like your dressing with a little kick, give this recipe a try. Simply place all into a blender, blend on high for twenty seconds, and then enjoy.

387. Ranch Dressing

Preparation time: 10 Minutes
Cooking time: 0 Minutes
Servings: 8

Ingredients

- Water (1 C.)
- Dried Dill (1/2 t.)
- Garlic Powder (1 t.)
- Chives (2 T., Chopped)
- Lemon Juice (3 T.)
- Salt (to Taste)
- Dried Parsley (1 t.)
- Raw Cashews (1 1/3 C.)
- Onion Powder (1 t.)

Directions

1. Before you begin this recipe, you will want to soak your cashews for at least one hour. This will make the next step much easier!

2. Once the cashews are done, place them into your blender along with the garlic, onion, lemon, and water. Go ahead and blend these ingredients on high until the sauce gets creamy.

3. When this is all set, you can gently stir in the chives, dill, and parsley and then enjoy your vegan dressing!

388. Fresh Raspberry Vinaigrette Dressing

Preparation time: 5 Minutes
Cooking time: 0 Minutes
Servings: 8
Calories: 190
Carbs: 1g
Fats: 15g
Proteins: 0g

Ingredients

- Apple Cider Vinegar (1/4 C.)
- Dried Basil (1 t.)
- Water (1/4 C.)
- Olive Oil (3/4 C.)
- Raspberries (1/2 C.)
- Salt (to Taste)

Directions

1. This dressing is incredible because it offers a touch of sweetness to any dish. To make the sauce, place everything into your blender and set to high for about twenty seconds.

2. Remove from blender and drizzle over anything!

389. Sweet Maple Dressing

Preparation time: 5 Minutes
Cooking time: 0 Minutes
Servings: 4

Ingredients

- Maple Syrup (1 T.)
- Olive Oil (1/2 C.)
- Salt (to Taste)
- Ground Cinnamon (1/2 t.)
- Mustard (2 t.)
- Balsamic Vinegar (1/4 C.)
- Pepper (to Taste)

Directions

1. While this recipe is a little different, you will find that maple compliments a lot of different flavors!

2. All you will need to do for this recipe is place all into the blender and blend until the ingredients are combined well. Remove, drizzle, and eat up!

390.Minty Lime Dressing

Preparation time: 10 Minutes
Cooking time: 0 Minutes
Servings: 4

Ingredients

- Olive Oil (6 T.)
- Fresh Chives (1 T.)
- Fresh Mint (1 T.)
- Lime (1)
- Salt (to Taste)
- White Wine Vinegar (2 T.)

Directions

1. For a salad dressing that is cool and refreshing, this recipe will certainly hit the spot! You will want to start out by getting a small mixing bowl out

and adding together the fresh herbs with the vinegar, salt, and the juice from your lime.

2. When these are combined well, you will slowly want to add in the olive oil while continuously whisking the ingredients together.

3. Once all of the olive oil is in, season to your liking and then enjoy over your favorite salad!

391.Keto-Vegan Ketchup

Preparation time: 5 minutes
Cooking time: 30 minutes
Servings: 12

Ingredients:

- 1/8 t of the following:
- mustard powder
- cloves, ground
- ¼ t. paprika
- ½ t. garlic powder
- ¾ t. onion powder
- 1 t. sea salt
- 3 tbsp. apple cider vinegar
- ¼ c. powdered monk fruit
- 1 c. water
- 6 oz. tomato paste

Directions:

1. In a little saucepan, whisk together all the ingredients.

2. Cover the pan and bring to low heat and simmer for 30 minutes, stirring occasionally.

3. Once reduced, add to the blender and puree until it's a smooth consistency.

4. Enjoy.

392.Avocado Hummus

Preparation time: 3 minutes
Cooking time: 2 minutes
Servings: 6

Ingredients:

- 1 tbsp. cilantro, finely chopped
- 1/8 t. cumin
- 1 clove garlic
- 3 tbsp. lime juice
- 1 ½ tbsp. of the following:
- tahini
- olive oil
- 2 avocados, medium cored & peeled
- 15 oz. chickpeas, drained
- Salt and pepper to taste

Directions:

1. In a food processor, add garlic, lime juice, tahini, olive oil, and chickpeas and pulse until combined.
2. Add cumin and avocados and blend until smooth consistency approximately 2 minutes.
3. Add salt and pepper to taste.
4. Enjoy.

393.Guacamole

Preparation time: 5 minutes
Cooking time: 5 minutes

Servings: 6

Ingredients:

- 3 tbsp. of the following:
- tomato, diced
- onion, diced
- 2 tbsp. of the following:
- cilantro, chopped
- jalapeno juice
- ¼ t. garlic powder
- ½ t. salt
- ½ lime, squeezed
- 2 big avocados
- 1 jalapeno, diced

Directions:

1. Using a molcajete, crush the diced jalapenos until soft.
2. Add the avocados to the molcajete.
3. Squeeze the lime juice from ½ of the lime on top of the avocados.
4. Add the jalapeno juice, garlic, and salt and mix until smooth.
5. Once smooth, add in the onion, cilantro, and tomato and stir to incorporate.
6. Enjoy.

394.Keto-Vegan Mayo

Preparation time: 5 minutes
Cooking time: 5 minutes
Servings: 6

Ingredients:

- ½ c. of the following:
- extra virgin olive oil
- almond milk, unsweetened

- ¼ t. xanthan gum
- Pinch of white pepper, ground
- Pinch of Himalayan salt
- 1 t. Dijon mustard
- 2 t. apple cider vinegar

Directions:

1. In a blender, place milk, pepper salt, mustard, and vinegar.
2. Turn the blender to high speed and slowly add xanthan then the olive oil.
3. Remove from the blender and allow cooling for 2 hours in the refrigerator.
4. During cooling, the mixture will thicken.

395.Peanut Sauce

Preparation time: 10 minutes
Cooking time: 5 minutes
Servings: 4

Ingredients:

- ½ t. Thai red curry paste
- 1 t. of the following:
- coconut oil
- soy Sauce
- chili garlic sauce
- 1 tbsp. sweetener of your choice
- 1/3 c. coconut milk
  - c. peanut butter, smooth

Directions:

1. Using a microwave-safe dish, add the peanut butter and heat for about 30 seconds.
2. Whisk into the peanut butter, the soy sauce, sweetener, and chili garlic then set to the side.

3. Warm a little saucepan over medium heat and add oil.
4. Cook the Thai red curry paste until fragrant then add to a microwave-safe bowl.
5. Continuously stir the peanut mixture as you add the coconut milk. Stir until well-combined.
6. Enjoy at room temperature or warmed.

396.Pistachio Dip

Preparation time: 10 minutes
Cooking time: 0 minute
Servings: 8

Ingredients:

- 2 tbsp. lemon juice
- 1 t. extra virgin olive oil
- 2 tbsp. of the following:
- tahini
- parsley, chopped
- 2 cloves of garlic
- ½ c. pistachios shelled
- 15 oz. garbanzo beans, save the liquid from the can
- Salt and pepper to taste

Directions:

1. Using a food processor, add pistachios, pepper, sea salt, lemon juice, olive oil, tahini, parsley, garlic, and garbanzo beans. Pulse until mixed.
2. Using the liquid from the garbanzo beans, add to the dip while slowly blending until it reaches your desired consistency.
3. Enjoy at room temperature or warmed.

397.Smokey Tomato Jam

Preparation time: 30 minutes
Cooking time: 15 minutes
Servings: 1 cup

Ingredients:

- ½ t. of the following:
- white wine vinegar
- salt
- 1/3 t. smoked paprika
- Pinch Black pepper
- ¼ c. coconut sugar
- 2 pounds tomatoes

Directions:

1. Over medium-high heat, bring a big pot of water to a boil.
2. Fill a big bowl with ice and water.
3. Carefully place the tomatoes into the boiling water for 1 minute and then remove, and immediately put into the ice water.
4. While tomatoes are in the ice water, peel them by hand and then transfer to a clean cutting surface.
5. Empty the pot of water.
6. Chop the tomatoes and place back into the pot; add in the coconut sugar and stir to combine.
7. Bring the pot back to medium heat and the tomatoes to a boil, cooking for 15 minutes.
8. Stir in the paprika, pepper, and salt and then bring the temperature down to the lowest setting. Let it cook until it becomes thick, which is approximately 10 minutes.
9. Remove it from the heat while continuing to stir; add in white wine vinegar.

398.Tasty Ranch Dressing/Dip

Preparation time: 45 minutes
Cooking time: 0 minute
Servings: 16

Ingredients:

- ½ c. soy milk, unsweetened
- 1 tbsp. dill, chopped
- 2 t. parsley, chopped
- ¼ t. black pepper
- ½ t. of the following:
- onion powder
- garlic powder
- 1 c. vegan mayonnaise

Directions:

1. In a medium bowl, whisk all the ingredients together until smooth. If dressing is too thick, add ¼ tablespoon of soy milk at a time until the desired consistency.
2. Transfer to an airtight container or jar and refrigerate for 1 hour.
3. Serve over leafy greens or as a dip.

399.Tofu Mayonnaise

Preparation time: 15 minutes
Cooking time: 0 minute
Servings: 6

Ingredients

- ½ pound silken tofu, pressed
- ½ of garlic clove, chopped finely
- 2 tablespoons fresh lemon juice
- 2 tablespoons Dijon mustard
- Freshly ground black pepper, to taste
- ½ cup canola oil

Directions:

1. In a blender, add tofu, garlic, lemon juice, mustard, and black pepper, and pulse until smooth.

2. While the motor is running, slowly add oil and pulse on low speed until well combined.

3. Transfer into a bowl and serve.

400.Chickpea Hummus

Preparation time: 15 minutes
Cooking time: 0 minute
Servings: 6

Ingredients

- ¼ cup tahini, well-stirred
- ¼ cup fresh lemon juice
- 1 small garlic clove, minced
- 3 tablespoons extra-virgin olive oil, divided
- ½ teaspoon ground cumin
- 1 (15-ounce) can chickpeas, rinsed and drained
- 2–3 tablespoons water
- Pinch of paprika

Directions:

1. In a food processor, add the tahini and lemon juice and pulse for about 1 minute.

2. Add the garlic, 2 tablespoons of oil, and cumin, and pulse for about 30 seconds.

3. Scrape the sides and bottom of food processor and pulse for about 30 seconds more.

4. Add half of the chickpeas and pulse for about 1 minute.

5. Scrape sides and bottom of the food processor.

6. Add remaining chickpeas and pulse

for about 1–2 minutes or, until just smooth.

7. Add water and pulse until smooth.

8. Place the hummus into a serving bowl and drizzle with the remaining oil.

9. Sprinkle with paprika and serve.

401.Peanut Butter Sauce

Preparation time: 10 minutes
Cooking time: 0 minute
Servings: 3

Ingredients

- ½ cup creamy peanut butter
- 2 tablespoons low-sodium soy sauce
- 1 tablespoon maple syrup
- 2 tablespoons fresh lime juice
- 1 teaspoon chile garlic sauce
- ¼ cup water

Directions:

1. In a bowl, place all the ingredients and beat until well combined.

2. Serve immediately.

402.Tomato Sauce

Preparation time: 20 minutes
Cooking time: 4 hours 20 minutes
Servings: 6

Ingredients

- 10 ripe tomatoes
- 3 tablespoons olive oil
- 2 carrots, peeled and chopped
- 1 green bell pepper, seeded and chopped
- 1 yellow onion, chopped
- 4 garlic cloves, minced

- 1 bay leaf
- 2 celery stalks, halved
- ¼ cup fresh basil, chopped
- 3 tablespoons homemade vegetable broth
- 2 tablespoons balsamic vinegar
- ¼ teaspoon Italian seasoning
- 2 tablespoons tomato paste

Directions:

1. In a pan of boiling water, add tomatoes and cook for about 1 minute.
2. Drain well and transfer into a bowl of ice water.
3. Let them cool. Remove the peel and seeds of the tomatoes.
4. Chop 2 tomatoes and set aside.
5. In a blender, add the remaining 8 tomatoes and pulse until a puree forms.
6. In a large pan, heat the oil over medium heat and sauté the carrots, celery, bell pepper, onion, and garlic, for about 5 minutes.
7. Add chopped tomatoes, tomato puree, and remaining all ingredients (except tomato paste) and bring to a boil.
8. Lower the heat to low and simmer for about 2 hours, stirring occasionally.
9. Stir in the tomato paste and simmer for about 2 hours more.
10. Discard the celery and bay leaf set aside to cool completely before serving.

403.Mango BBQ Sauce

Preparation time: 15 minutes
Cooking time: 25 minutes
Servings: 10

Ingredients

- ½ of Habanero pepper
- 1 cup mango, peeled, pitted, and chopped
- ½ tablespoon fresh ginger, chopped
- 2 tablespoons garlic, chopped
- ½ cup dates, pitted and chopped roughly
- 1 cup tomato sauce
- ¼ cup apple cider vinegar
- 2 teaspoons curry powder
- Salt and ground black pepper, to taste

Directions:

1. Preheat the broiler of the oven to high.
2. Arrange the Habanero pepper half onto a baking sheet, cut side down and broil for about 5–10 minutes.
3. Remove the pepper rom broiler and chop it.
4. In a pan, add pepper and remaining ingredients over medium-high heat and bring to a boil, stirring occasionally.
5. Lower the heat to medium and simmer for about 10 minutes, stirring occasionally.
6. Remove from heat and set aside to cool slightly.
7. In a food processor, add the mango mixture and pulse until smooth.
8. Set aside to cool completely before serving.

404.Runner Recovery Bites

Preparation time: 10 minutes
Cooking time: 10 minutes
Servings: 12

Ingredients:

- 1/4 cup pumpkin seeds, soaked for 1 hour
- 1/3 cup oats
- 1/4 cup sunflower seeds, soaked for 1 hour
- 5 dates
- 1 teaspoon maca powder
- 1 tablespoon goji berries
- 1 teaspoon coconut, shredded and unsweetened
- 1 tablespoon coconut water
- 1 teaspoon vanilla extract
- 1 tablespoon protein powder
- 1 tablespoon maple syrup
- 1/4 cup hemp seeds
- A pinch sea salt

Directions:

1. Drain sunflower and pumpkin seeds and add to a blender. Blend until a paste forms. Add dates and blend to mix. Add the remaining ingredients except hemp seeds and blend until a dough forms.

2. Roll 1 tablespoon dough into balls with hands. Roll the ball in hemp seeds until covered.

3. Transfer the prepared balls to a plate and freeze until firm.

4. Serve and enjoy.

405.High Protein Vegan Cheesy Sauce

Preparation time: 10 minutes
Cooking time: 10 minutes
Servings: 2 cups

Ingredients:

- 1 1/4 cups unsweetened plant-based milk
- 1 block tofu
- 1 teaspoon onion powder
- 2 teaspoon garlic powder
- 1/2 cup nutritional yeast
- 1/4 teaspoon turmeric
- 3/4 teaspoon salt

Directions:

1. Add all ingredients to a blender and blend until smooth. Combine well. Add more milk as desired.

2. Refrigerate for 24 hours.

3. Serve and enjoy.

406.Vegan High-Protein Queso

Preparation time: 5 minutes
Cooking time: 5 minutes
Servings: 2

Ingredients:

- 1/4 cup nutritional yeast
- 1/2 block tofu
- 3 tablespoon lemon juice
- 1/4 teaspoon tapioca starch
- 1/4 teaspoon garlic powder
- 1/4 teaspoon turmeric
- 1/4 teaspoon onion powder
- 1/4 cup water
- 1/2 teaspoon salt

Directions:

1. Add tofu, yeast, starch, lemon juice, salt, garlic powder, turmeric and onion powder and blend until well mixed.

2. Add water as desired. Heat in a

microwave for 30 seconds.

3. Serve and enjoy.

407.Vegan Buffalo Sauce

Preparation time: 5 minutes
Cooking time: 5 minutes
Servings: 1 cup

Ingredients:

- 1/2 cup soy milk
- 1 cup hot sauce
- 1/2 cup vinegar
- 1/2 teaspoon pepper
- 2 tablespoons sugar
- 1/2 teaspoon garlic granules
- 1 tablespoon tomato sauce

Directions:

1. Mix soy milk, hot sauce, sugar, vinegar, sugar, pepper, tomato sauce and garlic granules in a pan and cook over medium heat for 10 minutes.

2. Let cool and serve.

408.Vegan Ranch Dressing (Dipping Sauce)

Preparation time: 5 minutes
Cooking time: 5 minutes
Servings: 8

Ingredients:

- 2 tablespoons lemon juice
- 14 oz. silken tofu
- 1 tablespoon yellow mustard
- 1 tablespoon apple cider vinegar
- 1 teaspoon onion granules
- 1 tablespoon agave
- 1 teaspoon garlic granules

- 2 tablespoons parsley, minced
- 2 tablespoons dill, minced
- 1/2 teaspoon Himalayan salt

Directions:

1. Add all ingredients except parsley and dill to a blender and blend until smooth at high speed.

2. Add dill and parsley and blend until mixed.

3. Serve chilled.

409.Vegan Smokey Maple BBQ Sauce

Preparation time: 5 minutes
Cooking time: 5 minutes
Servings: 8

Ingredients:

- 1 tablespoon maple syrup
- 1/2 cup ketchup
- 1 teaspoon garlic powder
- 1 teaspoon liquid smoke

Directions:

1. Add all ingredients to a bowl. Mix them until well combined.

2. Serve and enjoy.

410.Vegan White Bean Gravy

Preparation time: 5 minutes
Cooking time: 5 minutes
Servings: 2 1/5 cups

Ingredients:

- 1 cup of soy milk
- 1 cup vegetable broth
- 1 cup white beans, rinsed and drained
- 1 tablespoon nutritional yeast

- 3 tablespoons tamari
- 1 teaspoon garlic granules, dried
- 2 teaspoons onion granules, dried
- 2 tablespoons all-purpose flour
- 1 tablespoon combination thyme, oregano, dill, minced
- 1/4 teaspoon black pepper
- 1/4 teaspoon Himalayan salt

Directions:

1. Add all ingredients except flour, herbs, and salt to a blender and blend on high speed until smooth.

2. Add this mixture to a pan placed over medium heat. Add salt, herbs, and flour, whisk all the time — Cook for 5 minutes.

3. Serve and enjoy.

411.Tahini Maple Dressing

Preparation time: 5 minutes
Cooking time: 5 minutes
Servings: 4 oz

Ingredients

- ¼ cup tahini
- 1 ½ tablespoons maple syrup
- 2 teaspoons lemon juice
- ¼ cup of water
- 1/8 teaspoon Himalayan pink salt

Directions:

1. Add all the ingredients to a bowl, Stir well to combine, until well mixed.

2. Use as a dressing for the salad or other dishes. Store in a fridge.

412.Coconut Sugar Peanut Sauce

Preparation time: 5 minutes

Cooking time: 5 minute
Servings: 1 ½ cups

Ingredients

- 4 tablespoons coconut sugar
- 6 tablespoons powdered peanut butter
- 1 tablespoon chili sauce
- 2 tablespoons liquid aminos
- ¼ cup of water
- 1 teaspoon lime juice
- ½ teaspoon ginger powder

Directions:

1. In a bowl, combine all the ingredients until properly combined. Serve as a topping for the salad or other dishes.

2. Store in a fridge.

413.Coconut Sauce

Preparation time: 15 minutes
Cooking time: 15 minutes
Servings: 3

Ingredients

- ½ cup red lentils, cooked
- 4 carrots, peeled, chopped
- 1 cup (250 ml) coconut milk, canned
- 3 tablespoons nutritional yeast
- ½ onion, diced
- 2 garlic cloves, minced
- Pepper and salt, to taste

Directions:

1. Boil the carrots for 10 minutes in a pan.

2. Blend the cooked carrots, lentils, onion, garlic, yeast and coconut milk in a blender until smooth. Stir in

pepper and salt.

3. Pour the mixture into a saucepan and cook for 2 minutes, stirring frequently.

4. Pour the sauce over the cooked pasta or salad servers.

414. Vegan Bean Pesto

Preparation time: 5 minutes
Cooking time: 5 minutes
Servings: 2

Ingredients

- 1 can (15 oz.) white beans, drained, rinsed
- 2 cups basil leaves, washed, dried
- ½ cup non-dairy milk
- 2 tablespoons olive oil
- 3 tablespoons nutritional yeast
- 1 garlic clove, peeled
- Pepper and salt to taste

Directions:

1. Blend all the ingredients (except the seasonings) in a blender until smooth.

2. Sprinkle with pepper and salt to taste, then blend for 1 extra minute. Enjoy with pasta.

415. Cheese Sauce

Preparation time: 5 minutes
Cooking time: 25 minutes
Serving: 6 servings

Ingredients:

- Pinch of salt
- Pinch of black, ground pepper
- ½ teaspoon of onion powder

- ½ teaspoon of garlic powder
- ½ cup of yeast, nutritional
- ⅓ cup of extra-virgin olive oil
- ½ cup of water
- 1 tablespoon of freshly squeezed lemon juice
- 1 cup of carrots, washed, peeled and diced
- 2 cups of potatoes, washed, peeled and diced

Directions:

1. In a medium saucepan over medium heat, boil the carrots and potatoes until they have cooked soft. Drain and add these items to the blender.

2. Add in the remainder of the ingredients to the blender and pulse until smooth.

3. Serve warm along with tortilla chips or over whole-wheat pasta.

4. Tips:

5. Seal and store in the refrigerator for up to four days, or you can freeze it too. Let thaw, add a dash of water, give it a good stir and serve.

416. Garlic Sauce

Preparation time: 5 minutes
Cooking time: 5 minutes
Serving: 1 ½ cups
Ingredients:

- Pinch of salt
- Pinch of black, ground pepper
- 1 tablespoon of rice vinegar
- 2 tablespoons of water
- 2 cloves of garlic
- 1 shallot, diced
- 1 date, pitted

- ¼ cup of mixed seeds and nuts of your choice

Directions:

1. Add all the ingredients into a blender, pulse until combined. Add more water if you feel that the sauce is too dry and until it has reached a pourable consistency.

2. Tips:

3. Add fresh herbs such as basil, cilantro, or parsley to add more flavor to the dish.

4. You may substitute the date for one tablespoon of maple syrup or honey instead.

417. Miso Sauce

Preparation time: 5 minutes
Cooking time: 8 minutes
Serving: 2 cups

Ingredients for standard miso sauce:

- Pinch of salt

- Pinch of black, ground pepper

- 2 tablespoons of extra-virgin olive oil

- 1 ½ cups of orange juice

- ½ cup of sweet white miso

- Ingredients for oriental inspired miso sauce:

- All of the above ingredients listed for the standard miso sauce along with the below-mentioned extra ingredients

- 2 cloves of garlic, minced

- 2 tablespoons of ginger, minced

- 1 teaspoon sesame oil

- 2 tablespoons of tamari

- Ingredients for Thai inspired miso sauce:

- All of the above ingredients listed for the standard miso sauce along with the below-mentioned extra ingredients

- 2 tablespoons of fresh mint

- 2 tablespoons of fresh basil

- 3 tablespoons of fresh cilantro

- ½ a chili, minced

- 1 ½ tablespoons of ginger, minced

Directions:

1. In a bowl, combine all ingredients, whisk gently for one minute and serve.

2. Tips:

3. Enhance the flavors in a salad or serve with a side or main meal.

418. Hummus

Preparation time: 5 minutes
Cooking time: 5 minutes
Serving: 8 servings

Ingredients:

- Pinch of salt

- Pinch of black, ground pepper

- ¼ cup of extra-virgin olive oil

- 2 cloves of garlic

- Juice of two lemons

- ½ cup of tahini

- 30 oz. canned chickpeas, reserve the brining liquid

- ⅓ cup of the reserved chickpea brining liquid

- 1 teaspoon of cumin

Directions:

1. Add all the ingredients to a blender, pulse until combined and smooth. If

you find that the hummus is too dry, slowly add in one to two more tablespoons of the chickpea brining liquid.

2. Drizzle a hint of extra-virgin olive oil over the hummus and serve.

3. Tips:

4. The hummus can be stored in the refrigerator and freezes well. Just thaw before use.

5. Add a pinch of paprika and a dash of parsley when serving to add more flavor to the dish.

419.Salsa

Preparation time: 5 minutes
Cooking time: 5 minutes
Serving: 1 to 1 ½ cups

Ingredients:

- Pinch of salt
- Pinch of black, ground pepper
- 1 tablespoon of extra-virgin olive oil
- ½ tablespoon of lime juice
- 1 clove of garlic, diced
- 1 shallot, diced
- 1 cup of cherry tomatoes
- 1 jalapeno pepper, seeds removed and diced
- ¼ cup of cilantro

Directions:

1. Add all ingredients into a blender, pulse until coarsely chopped or smooth depending on your preference. Serve while fresh!

2. Tips:

3. Add bell peppers or pineapple for a twist to this delicious salsa recipe.

4. For a spicier salsa, leave the jalapeno seeds intact.

420.Mayonnaise

Preparation time: 5 minutes
Cooking time: 5 minutes
Serving: 1 ½ cups

Ingredients:

- Pinch of salt
- Pinch of black, ground pepper
- 1 tablespoon of extra-virgin olive oil
- 1 cup of avocado oil
- ½ cup of soy milk, unsweetened
- 2 tablespoons of white vinegar
- 1 tablespoon maple syrup

Directions:

1. Add the ingredients into a tall jug and blend with a handheld blender until smooth and a mayonnaise consistency is reached.

2. Tips:

3. All ingredients should be at room temperature to ensure even blending and stop the mayonnaise from splitting.

4. Substitute the avocado oil with other oils of your choosing if desired.

5. Store for five days in the refrigerator.

421.Gravy

Preparation time: 5 minutes
Cooking time: 5 minutes
Serving: 8 servings

Ingredients:

- Pinch of salt
- Pinch of black, ground pepper

- ¾ teaspoon of onion powder
- ½ teaspoon dijon mustard
- 1 tablespoon of soy sauce
- ¼ cup of brown rice flour
- 2 cups of vegetable broth

Directions:

1. In a medium saucepan, over medium heat, add in all ingredients and bring to a boil. Whisk regularly until it thickens. Pour over roasted vegetables or serve with mashed potatoes.

2. Tips:

3. Keep stored in the refrigerator for a week. Add a bit of water to it when you wish to use it again.

4. You may choose to use all-purpose flour in place of the brown rice flour.

422.Enchilada Sauce

Preparation Time: 15 minutes
Cooking Time: 12 minutes
Servings: 6

Ingredients:

- 1½ cups water
- 1 can tomato sauce
- ¼ teaspoon ground cumin
- ¼ teaspoon onion salt
- ¼ teaspoon garlic powder
- ¼ cup vegetable oil
- ¼ cup red chili powder
- 2 tablespoons self-rising flour
- Salt, as required

Directions:

1. Heat the oil over pan on a medium flame and add flour and chili powder

to it, stirring well.

2. Cook for about 2 minutes and add all other ingredients.

3. Cook for about 10 minutes and remove from the flame.

4. Allow it to cool down and serve to enjoy.

423.BBQ Sauce

Preparation Time: 15 minutes
Cooking Time: 28 minutes
Servings: 20

Ingredients:

- 1¼ cups red wine vinegar
- 1¼ cups brown sugar
- ½ teaspoon celery seeds
- ½ teaspoon onion powder
- ½ teaspoon garlic powder
- 4 teaspoons hickory-flavored liquid smoke
- ½ cup molasses
- 1 teaspoon paprika
- ½ teaspoon cayenne pepper
- ¼ teaspoon chili powder
- ¼ teaspoon ground cinnamon
- 2 cups ketchup
- 2 tablespoons coconut oil
- 2 cups tomato sauce
- Salt and ground black pepper, as required

Directions:

1. Put all the ingredients to a pan and cook for about 3 minutes over medium heat, stirring occasionally.

2. Turn the heat to low and let the ingredients simmer for 25 more

minutes.

3. Remove from the heat, cool and serve.

424.Marinara Sauce

Preparation Time: 15 minutes
Cooking Time:22 minutes
Servings: 8

Ingredients:

- 1/3 cup olive oil
- 1 can tomato paste
- 2 cans stewed tomatoes
- ½ cup white wine
- ¼ cup fresh parsley, chopped
- 1 teaspoon dried oregano, crushed
- Salt and ground black pepper, as required
- 1/3 cup olive oil
- 1/3 cup onion, chopped finely
- 1 garlic clove, minced

Directions:

1. Add the tomato paste, stewed tomatoes, garlic, parsley and oregano to a blender and blend until smooth.

2. Heat oil over medium heat and sauté chopped onions for 2 minutes.

3. Add the tomato mixture and wine and cook for about 20 minutes, stirring constantly.

4. Remove from the flame and serve when cool.

425.Raspberry Sauce

Preparation Time: 15 minutes
Cooking Time: 10 minutes
Servings: 8

Ingredients:

- ¼ cup white sugar
- 2 cups fresh raspberries
- 2 tablespoons cornstarch
- 2 tablespoons fresh orange juice
- ¼ cup white sugar
- 1 cup cold water

Directions:

1. Put water and cornstarch in a bowl and beat well.

2. Add the cornstarch mixture and rest of the ingredients to a pan and cook over medium-low heat for about 5 minutes.

3. Let the ingredients simmer for about 5 more minutes to have a thick consistency.

4. Remove from the heat and cool to serve.

426.Baba Ganoush

Preparation Time: 15 minutes
Cooking Time: 20 minutes
Servings: 4

Ingredients:

- 1 garlic clove, chopped
- ¼ teaspoon salt
- 2 tablespoons tahini
- ¼ cup fresh parsley, chopped
- 1 large eggplant, pricked with a fork
- 2 tablespoons fresh lemon juice

Directions:

1. Preheat the oven to 450 degrees F and line a baking sheet with foil paper.

2. Place the eggplant on the baking sheet

and roast for about 20 minutes.

3. Remove from the oven and allow to cool.

4. Scoop out the pulp after cutting the eggplant.

5. Put this pulp to a food processor along rest of the ingredients.

6. Dish out in a bowl and serve warm.

427.Basil Pesto

Preparation Time 15 minutes
Servings: 8

Ingredients:

- 3 tablespoons nutritional yeast
- ½ cup extra-virgin olive oil
- 2 cups tightly packed fresh basil
- 1 tablespoon fresh lemon juice
- 2 garlic cloves, roughly chopped
- ½ cup walnuts
- Pinch of salt and ground black pepper

Directions:

1. Grind the basil, garlic, and walnuts in a food processor

2. Add olive oil to it while the motor is running and combine well.

3. Add the nutritional yeast, lemon juice, salt and black pepper to it.

4. Mix well and dish out to serve and enjoy.

428.Poppy Seed Dressing

Preparation Time: 15 minutes
Cooking Time: 0 minutes
Servings: 12

Ingredients:

- 2/3 cup unsweetened cashew milk
- ½ teaspoon red palm oil
- ½ cup fresh lemon juice
- ¼ cup maple syrup
- ¾ teaspoon salt
- ½ teaspoon Dijon mustard
- 1 cup raw cashews
- 1 tablespoon poppy seeds

Directions:

1. Put the cashews in a spice grinder and pulse until smooth.

2. Put the cashew milk, lemon juice, maple syrup, mustard, palm oil and salt along with ground cashews in a blender.

3. Pulse until smooth and dish out in a container.

4. Stir in the poppy seeds and refrigerate to chill for about 2 hours.

5. Drizzle over your favorite salad and serve to enjoy.

429.Cranberry Dressing

Preparation Time: 15 minutes
Cooking Time: 0 minutes
Servings: 18

Ingredients:

- ¼ cup rice vinegar
- ¼ cup Dijon mustard
- ¼ cup cranberry sauce
- ¼ cup apple cider vinegar
- ¼ cup walnut oil
- 1 cup vegetable oil
- 1 garlic clove, chopped

- Salt and ground black pepper, as required

Directions:

1. Put rice vinegar, Dijon mustard, cranberry sauce, apple cider vinegar, garlic, salt and black pepper in a blender and pulse until smooth.

2. Add walnut oil and vegetable and pulse to form a creamy mixture.

3. Dish out in a bowl and serve to enjoy.

430.French Dressing

Preparation Time: 10 minutes
Cooking Time: 0 minutes
Servings: 20

Ingredients:

- 1 cup ketchup
- ½ teaspoon salt
- ½ cup vinegar
- 1 small onion, chopped
- ¾ cup white sugar
- 1 teaspoon paprika
- 1½ cups vegetable oil
- 1 teaspoon fresh lemon juice

Directions:

1. Put all the ingredients in a blender and blend until smooth.

2. Transfer to a bowl and serve to enjoy.

431.Olive and Pumpkin Seed Tapenade

Preparation Time: 10 minutes
Cooking Time: 0 minutes
Servings: 1

Ingredients:

- ¼ cup fresh basil leaves, chopped

- ¼ teaspoon red chili flakes
- ½ teaspoon black pepper
- 2 tablespoons water
- ½ cup black and green olives, pitted
- ½ cup pumpkin seeds
- 1 tablespoon lemon juice
- 2 garlic cloves, minced
- 2 tablespoons olive oil

Directions:

1. Put all the ingredients except water to a food processor and blend until smooth.

2. Add water to the ingredients and blend again.

3. Take out the contents from the food processor and serve to enjoy.

432.Pink Peppercorn Pickled Swiss Chard Stem

Preparation Time: 15 minutes
Cooking Time: 0 minutes
Servings: 2

Ingredients:

- 2 tablespoons coconut palm sugar
- 1 tablespoon pink peppercorns
- ¼ red onion, diced
- 1 teaspoon coriander seeds
- 1 cup Swiss chard stems, sliced
- ½ teaspoon salt
- ¼ cup apple cider vinegar
- ¼ cup white vinegar

Directions:

1. Cut the Swiss chard stem into slices and season with salt.

2. Toast coriander seeds in a saucepan

and add apple cider vinegar, white vinegar, and coconut palm sugar.

3. Let the ingredients in the saucepan to boil and allow to simmer to dissolve the sugar.

4. Put onion and Swiss chard stems to a jar and pour the vinegar mixture over the contents of jar.

5. Refrigerate overnight and serve with foods you like.

433.Creamy Jalapeño Dip

Preparation Time: 50 minutes
Cooking Time: 0 minute
Servings: 4

Ingredients:

- 2 lemons, juiced
- 2/3 teaspoon garlic powder
- 2½ tablespoons apple cider vinegar
- 2 tablespoons sauerkraut
- 1 teaspoon onion powder
- 1 teaspoon salt
- 1 jalapeño, chopped
- 2 teaspoons black pepper
- 2 tablespoons chives
- 2 cups cashews, soaked in boiled water for 30 minutes and drained

Directions:

1. Put the cashews, lemon juice, water and apple cider vinegar to a high speed blender.

2. Blend for about 2 minutes and scrape off the sides of blender.

3. Add the remaining ingredients and chill to serve.

434.Easy Mayonnaise

Preparation Time: 5 minutes
Cooking Time: 5 minutes
Servings: 4

Ingredients:

- ½ teaspoon salt
- ½ teaspoon mustard powder
- 2 tablespoons olive oil
- 2 cups silken tofu
- 2 tablespoons lemon juice
- 1 teaspoon maple syrup
- 2 tablespoons apple cider vinegar

Directions:

1. Blend all ingredients in a blender except olive oil and mustard powder.

2. Add mustard powder and blend for a minute.

3. Drizzle olive oil in the mixture and blend using a food processor.

4. Put the mayonnaise in a sealed container and store.

435.Almond Dip

Preparation Time:10 minutes
Cooking Time:10 minutes
Servings: 2

Ingredients:

- ½ cup raw almonds
- ½ teaspoon cumin
- ½ teaspoon chili powder
- ¼ teaspoon ground coriander
- ¼ teaspoon paprika
- ¼ teaspoon cayenne pepper
- ½ cup water
- ¼ cup grapeseed oil
- ¼ cup lemon juice

- 2 tablespoons garlic infused oil
- ¼ teaspoon salt
- 3½ tablespoons nutritional yeast

Directions:

1. Take a blender and all the ingredients to it.
2. Blend them at a high speed for about 1 minute.
3. Take it out in a jar and cover the lid to store.
4. Enjoy whenever you like.

436.Rainbow Ketchup

Preparation Time: 5 minutes
Cooking Time: 15 minutes
Servings: 4

Ingredients:

- ¾ teaspoon salt
- 1 cup strawberries, fresh
- 1 big bay leaf
- 1 teaspoon garlic, grated
- 1 cup onion, chopped
- ¼ cup apple cider vinegar
- 1/3 cup brown sugar

Directions:

1. Take a saucepan and add all the ingredients to it.
2. Cover it and cook for 15 minutes on medium heat.
3. Uncover it and cook for another 15 minutes.
4. Remove from heat, store and enjoy.

437.Brilliant Spiced Applesauce

Preparation time: 4 hours
Cooking time: 4 hours

Yield: 24 servings

Ingredients:

- 8 apples, peeled and cored
- 1/2 teaspoon pumpkin pie spice
- 6-ounce brown sugar
- 4 fluid ounce water

Directions:

1. Slice apples and place in a 6-quarts slow cooker and add remaining ingredients.
2. Stir until just mix and cover with lid.
3. Plug in the slow cooker and let cook for 3 to 4 hours at high heat setting or until cooked through, stirring every hour.
4. Serve straight away.

438.Tangy Tomato Sauce

Preparation time: 10 minutes
Cooking time: 12 hours
Servings: 50

Ingredients:

- 10 tomatoes, peeled and seeded
- Half of a small white onion, peeled and chopped
- 1 teaspoon of minced garlic
- 1 teaspoon of salt
- 1 teaspoon of ground black pepper
- 1 teaspoon of ground cayenne pepper
- 1 teaspoon of dried oregano
- 1 teaspoon of dried basil
- 1/8 teaspoon of ground cinnamon
- 1/4 cup of olive oil

Directions:

1. Crush the tomatoes and add it to a 6-

quarts slow cooker along with the remaining ingredients.

2. Stir properly and cover it with the lid.

3. Plug in the slow cooker and let it cook for 12 hours at the low heat setting or until it is cooked thoroughly, while still stirring occasionally.

4. Let the sauce cool off completely and serve or store in sterilized jars.

439.Sweet and Spicy Marinara Sauce

Preparation time: 10 minutes
Cooking time: 3 hours
Servings: 40

Ingredients:

- 10-ounce frozen spinach, thawed and moisture squeezed out
- 1/3 cup of grated carrot
- 28 ounce of peeled and crushed tomatoes
- 4.5-ounce of sliced mushrooms
- 1 medium-sized white onion, peeled and chopped
- 3 teaspoons of minced garlic
- 2 tablespoons of salt
- 2 tablespoons of dried oregano
- 2 tablespoons of dried basil
- 2 1/2 tablespoons of crushed red pepper
- 2 bay leaves
- 1/4 cup of olive oil
- 8-ounce of tomato paste

Directions:

1. Using a 6-quarts slow cooker, place all the ingredients and stir properly.

2. Cover it with the lid, plug in the slow

cooker and let it cook for 3 hours at the low heat setting or until it is cooked thoroughly.

3. Let the sauce cool off completely and serve or store in sterilized jars.

440.Rich Spaghetti Sauce

Preparation time: 15 minutes
Cooking time: 4 hours
Servings: 60

Ingredients:

- 1 medium-sized white onion, peeled and chopped
- 1 1/2 teaspoon of minced garlic
- 3 tablespoons of dried thyme
- 3 tablespoons of dried parsley
- 1/8 teaspoon of crushed red pepper flakes
- 3 tablespoons of dried oregano
- 1 bay leaf
- 145-ounce of tomato sauce
- 18-ounce of tomato paste

Directions:

1. Using a 6-quarts slow cooker, place all the ingredients, and stir properly.

2. Cover it with the lid, plug in the slow cooker and let it cook for 4 hours at the low heat setting or until it is cooked thoroughly.

3. Let the sauce cool off completely and serve or store in sterilized jars.

441.Incredible Barbecue Sauce

Preparation time: 15 minutes
Cooking time: 6 hours
Servings: 68

Ingredients:

- 1/2 cup of chopped white onion
- 1 tablespoon of salt
- 1/4 cup of brown sugar
- 1/2 teaspoon of ground black pepper
- 4 teaspoons of paprika
- 2 tablespoons of molasses
- 1 tablespoon of apple cider vinegar
- 2 tablespoons of Worcestershire sauce
- 1 tablespoon of ground whole-grain mustard paste
- 4 cups of tomato ketchup
- 1/2 cup of water

Directions:

1. Using a 6-quarts slow cooker, place all the ingredients except for the salt, cilantro, and stir properly

2. Cover it with the lid, plug in the slow cooker and let it cook for 6 hours on the low heat setting or until it is cooked thoroughly.

3. When the cooking time is over, with an immersion blender, process the sauce.

4. Then continue cooking for 2 hours. While still stirring occasionally.

5. Let the sauce cool off completely and serve or store in sterilized jars.

442.Flavorful Roasted Red Pepper Sauce

Preparation time: 15 minutes
Cooking time: 4 hours
Servings: 6

Ingredients:

- 24 ounce of roasted red peppers drained

- 1 large white onion, peeled and sliced
- 1 1/2 teaspoons of minced garlic
- 3/4 teaspoon of salt
- 1/2 teaspoon of ground black pepper
- 1 teaspoon of dried oregano
- 2 cups of tomato passata
- 1/2 cup of cashew cream

Directions:

1. Using a 6-quarts slow cooker, place all the ingredients except for the cream, and stir properly.

2. Cover it with the lid, plug in the slow cooker and let it cook for 4 to 6 hours at the low heat setting or until it is cooked thoroughly.

3. Let the sauce cool off slightly and process it using an immersion blender.

4. Pour in the cream, stir properly and serve the sauce or store in sterilized jars.

443.Chunky Pumpkin Spinach Chili

Preparation time: 45 minutes
Cooking time: 4 hours
Servings: 6

Ingredients:

- 14-ounce of pumpkin
- 1 cup of chopped lady finger
- 1 cup of chopped broccoli
- 28 ounce of diced tomatoes
- 1 medium-sized carrot, peeled and chopped
- 1 small zucchini, stemmed and diced
- 19 ounce of cooked fava beans
- 2 cups of chopped spinach

- 1 small white onion, peeled and diced
- 1 teaspoon of minced garlic
- 1 teaspoon of salt
- 1/2 teaspoon of ground black pepper
- 1 teaspoon red of chili powder
- 2 tablespoons of coconut sugar
- 2 tablespoons of pumpkin pie spice
- 12-ounce of vegetarian ground beef crumbles
- 2 tablespoons of apple cider vinegar
- 8 fluid ounce of vegetable broth

Directions:

1. Using a 6-quarts slow cooker, place all the ingredients except for the beans, spinach, beef crumbles, and stir properly.

2. Cover it with the lid, plug in the slow cooker and let it cook for 3 to 4 hours at the high heat setting or until the vegetables get tender, while still stirring occasionally.

3. Then pour in remaining ingredients, stir properly and continue cooking for 30 minutes.

4. Serve right away.

444.Filling Three-Bean Chili

Preparation time: 15 minutes
Cooking time: 3 hours
Servings: 8

Ingredients:

- 16-ounce of kidney beans, uncooked and soaked overnight
- 16 ounce of cooked whole kernel corn
- 8-ounce of lentils, uncooked and soaked overnight
- 8-ounce of black beans, uncooked and

  soaked overnight
- 15 ounce of crushed tomatoes
- 3 medium-sized white onions, peeled and chopped
- 1 1/2 teaspoons of minced garlic
- 1 teaspoon of salt
- 1/2 cup of coconut sugar
- 2 tablespoons of red chili powder
- 1 tablespoon of ground cumin
- 1 teaspoon of paprika
- 2 tablespoons of olive oil
- 6-ounce of tomato paste
- 8 cups of water

Directions:

1. Using a 6-quarts slow cooker, place all the ingredients except for the onion, garlic, olive oil, and stir properly.

2. Cover it with the lid, plug in the slow cooker, let it cook for 6 hours at the high heat setting or until the vegetables and beans get soft, while still stirring occasionally.

3. In the meantime, place a medium-sized skillet pan over an average heat, add the oil and let it heat until it gets really hot.

4. Add the onion, garlic and let it cook for 5 minutes or until it getssoft.

5. Add this mixture to the cooked chili and continue cooking for 2 to 3 hours at the high heat setting.

6. Serve right away.

445.Comforting Quinoa Chili

Preparation time: 15 minutes
Cooking time: 4 hours
Servings: 6

Ingredients:

- 16-ounce of black beans, uncooked and rinsed
- 1 cup of quinoa, uncooked and rinsed
- 16-ounce of pinto beans, uncooked and rinsed
- 1 cup of corn kernels, uncooked
- 28 ounce of diced tomatoes
- 1 small white onion, peeled and diced
- 1 1/2 teaspoons of minced garlic
- 1 1/2 tablespoon of taco seasoning
- 1 teaspoon of dried cilantro
- 16-ounce of tomato sauce
- 2 1/2 cups of vegetable broth

Directions:

1. Using a 6-quarts slow cooker, place all the ingredients, and stir properly.
2. Cover with lid, plug in the slow cooker and let it cook for 4 hours at the high heat setting or until it is cooked thoroughly, while stirring occasionally.
3. Garnish it with the vegan Parmesan cheese and serve.

446.Sweet Potato Chili

Preparation time: 15 minutes
Cooking time: 4 hours
Servings: 4

Ingredients:

- 16 black beans, uncooked and rinsed
- 16-ounce of kidney beans, uncooked and rinsed
- 1 medium-sized green bell pepper, cored and chopped
- 8 ounces of sweet potatoes, peeled and chopped

- 28 ounce of diced fire-roasted tomatoes
- 1 medium-sized red onion, peeled and chopped
- 2 teaspoons of minced garlic
- 1 teaspoon of salt
- 1/2 teaspoon of ground black pepper
- 1 tablespoon of red chili powder
- 1 tablespoon of ground cumin
- 1/4 teaspoon of ground cinnamon
- 2 teaspoons of cocoa powder, unsweetened
- 6-ounce of tomato paste
- 8 fluid ounce of water

Directions:

1. Using a 6-quarts slow cooker, place all the ingredients, and stir properly.
2. Cover it with the lid, plug in the slow cooker and let it cook for 4 to 5 hours at the high heat setting or until the vegetables and beans are cooked thoroughly, while stirring occasionally.
3. Garnish it with the vegan Parmesan cheese and serve.
4. Drinks

447.Banana Weight Loss Juice

Preparation time: 10 Minutes
Cooking time: 0 Minutes
Servings: 1

Ingredients

- Water (1/3 C.)
- Apple (1, Sliced)
- Orange (1, Sliced)
- Banana (1, Sliced)

- Lemon Juice (1 T.)

Directions

1. Looking to boost your weight loss? The key is taking in less calories; this recipe can get you there. Simply place everything into your blender, blend on high for twenty seconds, and then pour into your glass.

448.Citrus Detox Juice

Preparation time: 10 Minutes
Cooking time: 0 Minutes
Servings: 4

Ingredients

- Water (3 C.)

- Lemon (1, Sliced)

- Grapefruit (1, Sliced)

- Orange (1, Sliced)

Directions

1. While starting your new diet, it is going to be vital to stay hydrated. This detox juice is the perfect solution and offers some extra flavor.

2. Begin by peeling and slicing up your fruit. Once this is done, place in a pitcher of water and infuse the water overnight.

449.Metabolism Water

Preparation time: 10 Minutes
Cooking time: 0 Minutes
Servings: 1

Ingredients

- Water (3 C.)

- Cucumber (1, Sliced)

- Lemon (1, Sliced)

- Mint (2 Leaves)

- Ice

Directions

1. At some point, we probably all wish for a quicker metabolism! With the lemon acting as an energizer, cucumber for a refreshing taste, and mint to help your stomach digest, this water is perfect!

2. All you will have to do is get out a pitcher, place all of the ingredients in, and allow the ingredients to soak overnight for maximum benefits!

450.Stress Relief Detox Drink

Preparation time: 5 Minutes
Cooking time: 0 Minutes
Servings: 1

Ingredients

- Water (1 Pitcher)

- Mint

- Lemon (1, Sliced)

- Basil

- Strawberries (1 C., Sliced)

- Ice

Directions

1. Life can be a pretty stressful event. Luckily, there is water to help keep you cool, calm, and collected! The lemon works like an energizer, the basil is a natural antidepressant, and mint can help your stomach do its job better. As for the strawberries, those are just for some sweetness!

2. When you are ready, take all of the ingredients and place into a pitcher of water overnight and enjoy the next day.

451.Strawberry Pink Drink

Preparation time: 10 Minutes
Cooking time: 5 Minutes
Servings: 4

Ingredients

- Water (1 C., Boiling)
- Sugar (2 T.)
- Acai Tea Bag (1)
- Coconut Milk (1 C.)
- Frozen Strawberries (1/2 C.)

Directions

1. If you are looking for a little treat, this is going to be the recipe for you! You will begin by boiling your cup of water and seep the tea bag in for at least five minutes.

2. When the tea is set, add in the sugar and coconut milk. Be sure to stir well to spread the sweetness throughout the tea.

3. Finally, add in your strawberries, and you can enjoy your freshly made pink drink!

452.Avocado Pudding

Preparation time: 10 minutes
Cooking time: 0 minute
Servings: 8

Ingredients:

- 2 ripe avocados, peeled, pitted and cut into pieces
- 1 tbsp fresh lime juice
- 14 oz can coconut milk
- 80 drops of liquid stevia
- 2 tsp vanilla extract

Directions:

1. Add all ingredients into the blender and blend until smooth.

2. Serve and enjoy.

453.Almond Butter Brownies

Preparation time: 10 minutes
Cooking time: 20 minutes
Servings: 4

Ingredients:

- 1 scoop protein powder
- 2 tbsp cocoa powder
- 1/2 cup almond butter, melted
- 1 cup bananas, overripe

Directions:

1. Preheat the oven to 350 F/ 176 C.

2. Spray brownie tray with cooking spray.

3. Add all ingredients into the blender and blend until smooth.

4. Pour batter into the prepared dish and bake in preheated oven for 20 minutes.

5. Serve and enjoy.

454.Raspberry Chia Pudding

Preparation time: 3 hours 10 minutes
Cooking time: 0 minute
Servings: 2

Ingredients:

- 4 tbsp chia seeds
- 1 cup coconut milk
- 1/2 cup raspberries

Directions:

1. Add raspberry and coconut milk in a blender and blend until smooth.

2. Pour mixture into the Mason jar.

3. Add chia seeds in a jar and stir well.

4. Close jar tightly with lid and shake well.

5. Place in refrigerator for 3 hours.

6. Serve chilled and enjoy.

455.Chocolate Fudge

Preparation time: 10 minutes
Cooking time: 0 minute
Servings: 12

Ingredients:

- 4 oz unsweetened dark chocolate
- 3/4 cup coconut butter
- 15 drops liquid stevia
- 1 tsp vanilla extract

Directions:

1. Melt coconut butter and dark chocolate.

2. Add ingredients to the large bowl and combine well.

3. Pour mixture into a silicone loaf pan and place in refrigerator until set.

4. Cut into pieces and serve.

456.Quick Chocó Brownie

Preparation time: 10 minutes
Cooking time: 2 minutes
Servings: 1

Ingredients:

- 1/4 cup almond milk
- 1 tbsp cocoa powder
- 1 scoop chocolate protein powder
- 1/2 tsp baking powder

Directions:

1. In a microwave-safe mug blend together baking powder, protein powder, and cocoa.

2. Add almond milk in a mug and stir well.

3. Place mug in microwave and microwave for 30 seconds.

4. Serve and enjoy.

457.Simple Almond Butter Fudge

Preparation time: 15 minutes
Cooking time: 0 minutes
Servings: 8

Ingredients:

- 1/2 cup almond butter
- 15 drops liquid stevia
- 2 1/2 tbsp coconut oil

Directions:

1. Combine together almond butter and coconut oil in a saucepan. Gently warm until melted.

2. Add stevia and stir well.

3. Pour mixture into the candy container and place in refrigerator until set.

4. Serve and enjoy.

458.Coconut Peanut Butter Fudge

Preparation time: 1 hour 15 minutes
Cooking time: 0 minute
Servings: 20

Ingredients:

- 12 oz smooth peanut butter
- 3 tbsp coconut oil
- 4 tbsp coconut cream
- 15 drops liquid stevia
- Pinch of salt

Directions:

1. Line baking tray with parchment paper.

2. Melt coconut oil in a saucepan over low heat.

3. Add peanut butter, coconut cream, stevia, and salt in a saucepan. Stir well.

4. Pour fudge mixture into the prepared baking tray and place in refrigerator for 1 hour.

5. Cut into pieces and serve.

459.Lemon Mousse

Preparation time: 10 minutes
Cooking time: 0 minute
Servings: 2

Ingredients:

- 14 oz coconut milk
- 12 drops liquid stevia
- 1/2 tsp lemon extract
- 1/4 tsp turmeric

Directions:

1. Place coconut milk can in the refrigerator for overnight. Scoop out thick cream into a mixing bowl.

2. Add remaining ingredients to the bowl and whip using a hand mixer until smooth.

3. Transfer mousse mixture to a zip-lock bag and pipe into small serving glasses. Place in refrigerator.

4. Serve chilled and enjoy.

460.Chocó Chia Pudding

Preparation time: 10 minutes
Cooking time: 0 minutes
Servings: 6

Ingredients:

- 2 1/2 cups coconut milk
- 2 scoops stevia extract powder
- 6 tbsp cocoa powder
- 1/2 cup chia seeds
- 1/2 tsp vanilla extract
- 1/8 cup xylitol
- 1/8 tsp salt

Directions:

1. Add all ingredients into the blender and blend until smooth.

2. Pour mixture into the glass container and place in refrigerator.

3. Serve chilled and enjoy.

461.Spiced Buttermilk

Preparation time: 5 minutes
Cooking time: 0 minute
Servings: 2

Ingredients:

- 3/4 teaspoon ground cumin
- 1/4 teaspoon sea salt
- 1/8 teaspoon ground black pepper

- 2 mint leaves
- 1/8 teaspoon lemon juice
- ¼ cup cilantro leaves
- 1 cup of chilled water
- 1 cup vegan yogurt, unsweetened
- Ice as needed

Directions:

1. Place all the ingredients in the order in a food processor or blender, except for cilantro and ¼ teaspoon cumin, and then pulse for 2 to 3 minutes at high speed until smooth.

2. Pour the milk into glasses, top with cilantro and cumin, and then serve.

462.Turmeric Lassi

Preparation time: 5 minutes
Cooking time: 0 minute
Servings: 2

Ingredients:

- 1 teaspoon grated ginger
- 1/8 teaspoon ground black pepper
- 1 teaspoon turmeric powder
- 1/8 teaspoon cayenne
- 1 tablespoon coconut sugar
- 1/8 teaspoon salt
- 1 cup vegan yogurt
- 1 cup almond milk

Directions:

1. Place all the ingredients in the order in a food processor or blender and then pulse for 2 to 3 minutes at high speed until smooth.

2. Pour the lassi into two glasses and then serve.

463.Brownie Batter Orange Chia Shake

Preparation time: 5 minutes
Cooking time: 0 minute
Servings: 2

Ingredients:

- 2 tablespoons cocoa powder
- 3 tablespoons chia seeds
- ¼ teaspoon salt
- 4 tablespoons chocolate chips
- 4 teaspoons coconut sugar
- ½ teaspoon orange zest
- ½ teaspoon vanilla extract, unsweetened
- 2 cup almond milk

Directions:

1. Place all the ingredients in the order in a food processor or blender and then pulse for 2 to 3 minutes at high speed until smooth.

2. Pour the smoothie into two glasses and then serve.

464.Saffron Pistachio Beverage

Preparation time: 5 minutes
Cooking time: 0 minute
Servings: 2

Ingredients:

- 8 strands of saffron
- 1 tablespoon cashews
- 1/4 teaspoon ground ginger
- 2 tablespoons pistachio
- 1/8 teaspoon cloves
- 1/4 teaspoon ground black pepper
- 1/4 teaspoon cardamom powder

- 3 tablespoons coconut sugar
- 1/4 teaspoon cinnamon
- 1/8 teaspoon fennel seeds
- 1/4 teaspoon poppy seeds

Directions:

1. Place all the ingredients in the order in a food processor or blender and then pulse for 2 to 3 minutes at high speed until smooth.

2. Pour the smoothie into two glasses and then serve.

465.Mexican Hot Chocolate Mix

Preparation time: 5 minutes
Cooking time: 0 minute
Servings: 2

Ingredients:

- For the Hot Chocolate Mix:
- 1/3 cup chopped dark chocolate
- 1/8 teaspoon cayenne
- 1/8 teaspoon salt
- 1/2 teaspoon cinnamon
- 1/4 cup coconut sugar
- 1 teaspoon cornstarch
- 3 tablespoons cocoa powder
- 1/2 teaspoon vanilla extract, unsweetened
- For Serving:
- 2 cups milk, warmed

Directions:

1. Place all the ingredients of hot chocolate mix in the order in a food processor or blender and then pulse for 2 to 3 minutes at high speed until ground.

2. Stir 2 tablespoons of the chocolate

mix into a glass of milk until combined and then serve.

466.Pumpkin Spice Frappuccino

Preparation time: 5 minutes
Cooking time: 0 minute
Servings: 2

Ingredients:

- ½ teaspoon ground ginger
- 1/8 teaspoon allspice
- ½ teaspoon ground cinnamon
- 2 tablespoons coconut sugar
- 1/8 teaspoon nutmeg
- ¼ teaspoon ground cloves
- 1 teaspoon vanilla extract, unsweetened
- 2 teaspoons instant coffee
- 2 cups almond milk, unsweetened
- 1 cup of ice cubes

Directions:

1. Place all the ingredients in the order in a food processor or blender and then pulse for 2 to 3 minutes at high speed until smooth.

2. Pour the Frappuccino into two glasses and then serve.

467.Cookie Dough Milkshake

Preparation time: 5 minutes
Cooking time: 0 minute
Servings: 2

Ingredients:

- 2 tablespoons cookie dough
- 5 dates, pitted
- 2 teaspoons chocolate chips
- 1/2 teaspoon vanilla extract,

unsweetened

- 1/2 cup almond milk, unsweetened
- 1 ½ cup almond milk ice cubes

Directions:

1. Place all the ingredients in the order in a food processor or blender and then pulse for 2 to 3 minutes at high speed until smooth.

2. Pour the milkshake into two glasses and then serve with some cookie dough balls.

468.Strawberry and Hemp Smoothie

Preparation time: 5 minutes
Cooking time: 0 minute
Servings: 2

Ingredients:

- 3 cups fresh strawberries
- 2 tablespoons hemp seeds
- 1/2 teaspoon vanilla extract, unsweetened
- 1/8 teaspoon sea salt
- 2 tablespoons maple syrup
- 1 cup vegan yogurt
- 1 cup almond milk, unsweetened
- 1 cup of ice cubes
- 2 tablespoons hemp protein

Directions:

1. Place all the ingredients in the order in a food processor or blender, except for protein powder, and then pulse for 2 to 3 minutes at high speed until smooth.

2. Pour the smoothie into two glasses and then serve.

469.Blueberry, Hazelnut and Hemp Smoothie

Preparation time: 5 minutes
Cooking time: 0 minute
Servings: 2

Ingredients:

- 2 tablespoons hemp seeds
- 1 ½ cups frozen blueberries
- 2 tablespoons chocolate protein powder
- 1/2 teaspoon vanilla extract, unsweetened
- 2 tablespoons chocolate hazelnut butter
- 1 small frozen banana
- 3/4 cup almond milk

Directions:

1. Place all the ingredients in the order in a food processor or blender and then pulse for 2 to 3 minutes at high speed until smooth.

2. Pour the smoothie into two glasses and then serve.

470.Mango Lassi

Preparation time: 5 minutes
Cooking time: 0 minute
Servings: 2

Ingredients:

- 1 ¼ cup mango pulp
- 1 tablespoon coconut sugar
- 1/8 teaspoon salt
- 1/2 teaspoon lemon juice
- 1/4 cup almond milk, unsweetened
- 1/4 cup chilled water
- 1 cup cashew yogurt

Directions:

1. Place all the ingredients in the order in a food processor or blender and then pulse for 2 to 3 minutes at high speed until smooth.

2. Pour the lassi into two glasses and then serve.

471. Mocha Chocolate Shake

Preparation time: 5 minutes
Cooking time: 0 minute
Servings: 2

Ingredients:

- 1/4 cup hemp seeds
- 2 teaspoons cocoa powder, unsweetened
- 1/2 cup dates, pitted
- 1 tablespoon instant coffee powder
- 2 tablespoons flax seeds
- 2 1/2 cups almond milk, unsweetened
- 1/2 cup crushed ice

Directions:

1. Place all the ingredients in the order in a food processor or blender and then pulse for 2 to 3 minutes at high speed until smooth.

2. Pour the smoothie into two glasses and then serve.

472. Chard, Lettuce and Ginger Smoothie

Preparation time: 5 minutes
Cooking time: 0 minute
Servings: 2

Ingredients:

- 10 Chard leaves, chopped
- 1-inch piece of ginger, chopped
- 10 lettuce leaves, chopped
- ½ teaspoon black salt
- 2 pear, chopped
- 2 teaspoons coconut sugar
- ¼ teaspoon ground black pepper
- ¼ teaspoon salt
- 2 tablespoons lemon juice
- 2 cups of water

Directions:

1. Place all the ingredients in the order in a food processor or blender and then pulse for 2 to 3 minutes at high speed until smooth.

2. Pour the smoothie into two glasses and then serve.

473. Red Beet, Pear and Apple Smoothie

Preparation time: 5 minutes
Cooking time: 0 minute
Servings: 2

Ingredients:

- 1/2 of medium beet, peeled, chopped
- 1 tablespoon chopped cilantro
- 1 orange, juiced
- 1 medium pear, chopped
- 1 medium apple, cored, chopped
- 1/4 teaspoon ground black pepper
- 1/8 teaspoon rock salt
- 1 teaspoon coconut sugar
- 1/4 teaspoons salt
- 1 cup of water

Directions:

1. Place all the ingredients in the order in a food processor or blender and

then pulse for 2 to 3 minutes at high speed until smooth.

2. Pour the smoothie into two glasses and then serve.

474.Berry and Yogurt Smoothie

Preparation time: 5 minutes
Cooking time: 0 minute
Servings: 2

Ingredients:

- 2 small bananas
- 3 cups frozen mixed berries
- 1 ½ cup cashew yogurt
- 1/2 teaspoon vanilla extract, unsweetened
- 1/2 cup almond milk, unsweetened

Directions:

1. Place all the ingredients in the order in a food processor or blender and then pulse for 2 to 3 minutes at high speed until smooth.

2. Pour the smoothie into two glasses and then serve.

475.Chocolate and Cherry Smoothie

Preparation time: 5 minutes
Cooking time: 0 minute
Servings: 2

Ingredients:

- 4 cups frozen cherries
- 2 tablespoons cocoa powder
- 1 scoop of protein powder
- 1 teaspoon maple syrup
- 2 cups almond milk, unsweetened

Directions:

1. Place all the ingredients in the order

in a food processor or blender and then pulse for 2 to 3 minutes at high speed until smooth.

2. Pour the smoothie into two glasses and then serve.

476.Strawberry Shake

Preparation time: 10 minutes
Cooking time: 10 minutes
Servings: 2

Ingredients

- 1½ cups fresh strawberries, hulled
- 1 large frozen banana, peeled
- 2 scoops unsweetened vegan vanilla protein powder
- 2 tablespoons hemp seeds
- 2 cups unsweetened hemp milk

Directions:

1. In a high-speed blender, place all the ingredients and pulse until creamy.

2. Pour into two glasses and serve immediately.

477.Chocolatey Banana Shake

Preparation time: 10 minutes
Cooking time: 10 minutes
Servings: 2

Ingredients

- 2 medium frozen bananas, peeled
- 4 dates, pitted
- 4 tablespoons peanut butter
- 4 tablespoons rolled oats
- 2 tablespoons cacao powder
- 2 tablespoons chia seeds
- 2 cups unsweetened soymilk

Directions:

1. Place all the ingredients in a high-speed blender and pulse until creamy.

2. Pour into two glasses and serve immediately.

478.Fruity Tofu Smoothie

Preparation time: 10 minutes
Cooking time: 10 minutes
Servings: 2

Ingredients

- 12 ounces silken tofu, pressed and drained
- 2 medium bananas, peeled
- 1½ cups fresh blueberries
- 1 tablespoon maple syrup
- 1½ cups unsweetened soymilk
- ¼ cup ice cubes

Directions:

1. Place all the ingredients in a high-speed blender and pulse until creamy.

2. Pour into two glasses and serve immediately.

479.Green Fruity Smoothie

Preparation time: 10 minutes
Cooking time: 10 minutes
Servings: 2

Ingredients

- 1 cup frozen mango, peeled, pitted, and chopped
- 1 large frozen banana, peeled
- 2 cups fresh baby spinach
- 1 scoop unsweetened vegan vanilla protein powder
- ¼ cup pumpkin seeds

- 2 tablespoons hemp hearts
- 1½ cups unsweetened almond milk

Directions:

1. In a high-speed blender, place all the ingredients and pulse until creamy.

2. Pour into two glasses and serve immediately.

480.Protein Latte

Preparation time: 10 minutes
Cooking time: 10 minutes
Servings: 2

Ingredients

- 2 cups hot brewed coffee
- 1¼ cups coconut milk
- 2 teaspoons coconut oil
- 2 scoops unsweetened vegan vanilla protein powder

Directions:

1. Place all the ingredients in a high-speed blender and pulse until creamy.

2. Pour into two serving mugs and serve immediately.

481.Health Boosting Juices

Preparation time: 10 minutes
Cooking time: 15 minutes
Serving: 2

Ingredients for a red juice:

- 4 beetroots, quartered
- 2 cups of strawberries
- 2 cups of blueberries
- Ingredients for an orange juice:
- 4 green or red apples, halved
- 10 carrots

- ½ lemon, peeled
- 1" of ginger
- Ingredients for a yellow juice:
- 2 green or red apples, quartered
- 4 oranges, peeled and halved
- ½ lemon, peeled
- 1" of ginger
- Ingredients for a lime juice:
- 6 stalks of celery
- 1 cucumber
- 2 green apples, quartered
- 2 pears, quartered
- Ingredients for a green juice:
- ½ a pineapple, peeled and sliced
- 8 leaves of kale
- 2 fresh bananas, peeled

Directions:

1. Juice all ingredients in a juicer, chill and serve.

482.Thai Iced Tea

Preparation time: 5 minutes
Cooking time: 10 minutes
Serving: 4

Ingredients:

- 4 cups of water
- 1 can of light coconut milk (14 oz.)
- ¼ cup of maple syrup
- ¼ cup of muscovado sugar
- 1 teaspoon of vanilla extract
- 2 tablespoons of loose-leaf black tea

Directions:

1. In a large saucepan, over medium heat bring the water to a boil.

2. Turn off the heat and add in the tea, cover and let steep for five minutes.

3. Strain the tea into a bowl or jug. Add the maple syrup, muscovado sugar, and vanilla extract. Give it a good whisk to blend all the ingredients together.

4. Set in the refrigerator to chill. Upon serving, pour ¾ of the tea into each glass, top with coconut milk and stir.

5. Tips:

6. Add a shot of dark rum to turn this iced tea into a cocktail.

7. You could substitute the coconut milk for almond or rice milk too.

483.Hot Chocolate

Preparation time: 5 minutes
Cooking time: 15 minutes
Serving: 2

Ingredients:

- Pinch of brown sugar
- 2 cups of milk, soy or almond, unsweetened
- 2 tablespoons of cocoa powder
- ½ cup of vegan chocolate

Directions:

1. In a medium saucepan, over medium heat gently bring the milk to a boil. Whisk in the cocoa powder.

2. Remove from the heat, add a pinch of sugar and chocolate. Give it a good stir until smooth, serve and enjoy.

3. Tips:

4. You may substitute the almond or soy milk for coconut milk too.

484.Chai and Chocolate Milkshake

Preparation time: 5 minutes
Cooking time: 15 minutes
Serving: 2 servings

Ingredients:

- 1 and ½ cups of almond milk, sweetened or unsweetened
- 3 bananas, peeled and frozen 12 hours before use
- 4 dates, pitted
- 1 and ½ teaspoons of chocolate powder, sweetened or unsweetened
- ½ teaspoon of vanilla extract
- ½ teaspoon of cinnamon
- ¼ teaspoon of ground ginger
- Pinch of ground cardamom
- Pinch of ground cloves
- Pinch of ground nutmeg
- ½ cup of ice cubes

Directions:

1. Add all the ingredients to a blender except for the ice-cubes. Pulse until smooth and creamy, add the ice-cubes, pulse a few more times and serve.
2. Tips:
3. The dates provide enough sweetness to the recipe, however, you are welcome to add maple syrup or honey for a sweeter drink.

485.Colorful Infused Water

Preparation time: 5 minutes
Cooking time: 1 hour
Serving: 8 servings

Ingredients:

- 1 cup of strawberries, fresh or frozen
- 1 cup of blueberries, fresh or frozen
- 1 tablespoon of baobab powder
- 1 cup of ice cubes
- 4 cups of sparkling water

Directions:

1. In a large water jug, add in the sparkling water, ice cubes, and baobab powder. Give it a good stir.
2. Add in the strawberries and blueberries and cover the infused water, store in the refrigerator for one hour before serving.
3. Tips:
4. Store for 12 hours for optimum taste and nutritional benefits.
5. Instead of using strawberries and blueberries, add slices of lemon and six mint leaves, one cup of mangoes or cherries, or half a cup of leafy greens such as kale and/or spinach.

486.Hibiscus Tea

Preparation time: 1 Minute
Cooking time: 5 minutes
Serving: 2 servings

Ingredients:

- 1 tablespoon of raisins, diced
- 6 Almonds, raw and unsalted
- ½ teaspoon of hibiscus powder
- 2 cups of water

Directions:

1. Bring the water to a boil in a small saucepan, add in the hibiscus powder and raisins. Give it a good stir, cover and let simmer for a further two minutes.
2. Strain into a teapot and serve with a side helping of almonds.

3. Tips:

4. As an alternative to this tea, do not strain it and serve with the raisin pieces still swirling around in the teacup.

5. You could also serve this tea chilled for those hotter days.

6. Double or triple the recipe to provide you with iced-tea to enjoy during the week without having to make a fresh pot each time.

487.Lemon and Rosemary Iced Tea

Preparation time: 5 minutes
Cooking time: 10 minutes
Serving: 4 servings

Ingredients:

- 4 cups of water
- 4 earl grey tea bags
- ¼ cup of sugar
- 2 lemons
- 1 sprig of rosemary

Directions:

1. Peel the two lemons and set the fruit aside.

2. In a medium saucepan, over medium heat combine the water, sugar, and lemon peels. Bring this to a boil.

3. Remove from the heat and place the rosemary and tea into the mixture. Cover the saucepan and steep for five minutes.

4. Add the juice of the two peeled lemons to the mixture, strain, chill, and serve.

5. Tips:Skip the sugar and use honey to taste.

6. Do not squeeze the tea bags as they can cause the tea to become bitter.

488.Lavender and Mint Iced Tea

Preparation time: 5 minutes
Cooking time: 10 minutes
Serving: 8 servings

Ingredients:

- 8 cups of water
- ⅓ cup of dried lavender buds
- ¼ cup of mint

Directions:

1. Add the mint and lavender to a pot and set this aside.

2. Add in eight cups of boiling water to the pot. Sweeten to taste, cover and let steep for ten minutes. Strain, chill, and serve.

3. Tips:

4. Use a sweetener of your choice when making this iced tea.

5. Add spirits to turn this iced tea into a summer cocktail.

489.Pear Lemonade

Preparation time: 5 minutes
Cooking time: 30 minutes
Serving: 2 servings

Ingredients:

- ½ cup of pear, peeled and diced
- 1 cup of freshly squeezed lemon juice
- ½ cup of chilled water

Directions:

1. Add all the ingredients into a blender and pulse until it has all been combined. The pear does make the lemonade frothy, but this will settle.

2. Place in the refrigerator to cool and then serve.

3. Tips:

4. Keep stored in a sealed container in the refrigerator for up to four days.

5. Pop the fresh lemon in the microwave for ten minutes before juicing, you can extract more juice if you do this.

490.Energizing Ginger Detox Tonic

Preparation time: 15 minutes
Cooking time: 10 minutes
Servings:

Ingredients:

- 1/2 teaspoon of grated ginger, fresh
- 1 small lemon slice
- 1/8 teaspoon of cayenne pepper
- 1/8 teaspoon of ground turmeric
- 1/8 teaspoon of ground cinnamon
- 1 teaspoon of maple syrup
- 1 teaspoon of apple cider vinegar
- 2 cups of boiling water

Directions:

1. Pour the boiling water into a small saucepan, add and stir the ginger, then let it rest for 8 to 10 minutes, before covering the pan.

2. Pass the mixture through a strainer and into the liquid, add the cayenne pepper, turmeric, cinnamon and stir properly.

3. Add the maple syrup, vinegar, and lemon slice.

4. Add and stir an infused lemon and serve immediately.

491.Warm Spiced Lemon Drink

Preparation time: 10 minutes
Cooking time: 2 hours
Servings: 12

Ingredients:

- 1 cinnamon stick, about 3 inches long
- 1/2 teaspoon of whole cloves
- 2 cups of coconut sugar
- 4 fluid of ounce pineapple juice
- 1/2 cup and 2 tablespoons of lemon juice
- 12 fluid ounce of orange juice
- 2 1/2 quarts of water

Directions:

1. Pour water into a 6-quarts slow cooker and stir the sugar and lemon juice properly.

2. Wrap the cinnamon, the whole cloves in cheesecloth and tie its corners with string.

3. Immerse this cheesecloth bag in the liquid present in the slow cooker and cover it with the lid.

4. Then plug in the slow cooker and let it cook on high heat setting for 2 hours or until it is heated thoroughly.

5. When done, discard the cheesecloth bag and serve the drink hot or cold.

492.Soothing Ginger Tea Drink

Preparation time: 5 minutes
Cooking time: 2 hours 20 minutes
Servings: 8

Ingredients:

- 1 tablespoon of minced gingerroot
- 2 tablespoons of honey
- 15 green tea bags
- 32 fluid ounce of white grape juice
- 2 quarts of boiling water

Directions:

1. Pour water into a 4-quarts slow cooker, immerse tea bags, cover the cooker and let stand for 10 minutes.

2. After 10 minutes, remove and discard tea bags and stir in remaining ingredients.

3. Return cover to slow cooker, then plug in and let cook at high heat setting for 2 hours or until heated through.

4. When done, strain the liquid and serve hot or cold.

493.Nice Spiced Cherry Cider

Preparation time: 1 hour 5 minutes
Cooking time: 3 hours
Servings: 16

Ingredients:

- 2 cinnamon sticks, each about 3 inches long

- 6-ounce of cherry gelatin

- 4 quarts of apple cider

Directions:

1. Using a 6-quarts slow cooker, pour the apple cider and add the cinnamon stick.

2. Stir, then cover the slow cooker with its lid. Plug in the cooker and let it cook for 3 hours at the high heat setting or until it is heated thoroughly.

3. Then add and stir the gelatin properly, then continue cooking for another hour.

4. When done, remove the cinnamon sticks and serve the drink hot or cold.

494.Fragrant Spiced Coffee

Preparation time: 10 minutes
Cooking time: 3 hours
Servings: 8

Ingredients:

- 4 cinnamon sticks, each about 3 inches long

- 1 1/2 teaspoons of whole cloves

- 1/3 cup of honey

- 2-ounce of chocolate syrup

- 1/2 teaspoon of anise extract

- 8 cups of brewed coffee

Directions:

1. Pour the coffee in a 4-quarts slow cooker and pour in the remaining ingredients except for cinnamon and stir properly.

2. Wrap the whole cloves in cheesecloth and tie its corners with strings.

3. Immerse this cheesecloth bag in the liquid present in the slow cooker and cover it with the lid.

4. Then plug in the slow cooker and let it cook on the low heat setting for 3 hours or until heated thoroughly.

5. When done, discard the cheesecloth bag and serve.

495.Bracing Coffee Smoothie

Preparation time: 5 minutes
Cooking time: 5 minutes

Servings: 1

Ingredients:

- 1 banana, sliced and frozen
- ½ cup strong brewed coffee
- ½ cup milk
- ¼ cup rolled oats
- 1 tsp nut butter

Directions:

1. Mix all the ingredients until smooth.
2. Enjoy your morning drink!

496.Vitamin Green Smoothie

Preparation time: 5 minutes
Cooking time: 5 minutes
Servings: 2

Ingredients:

- 1 cup milk or juice
- 1 cup spinach or kale
- ½ cup plain yoghurt
- 1 kiwi

- 1 Tbsp chia or flax
- 1 tsp vanilla

Directions:

1. Mix the milk or juice and greens until smooth. Add the remaining ingredients and continue blending until smooth again.
2. Enjoy your delicious drink!

497.Strawberry Grapefruit Smoothie

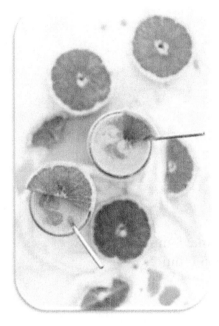

Preparation time: 5 minutes
Cooking time: 5 minutes
Servings: 2

Ingredients:

- 1 banana
- ½ cup strawberries, frozen
- 1 grapefruit
- ¼ cup milk
- ¼ cup plain yoghurt
- 2 Tbsp honey
- ½ tsp ginger, chopped

Directions:

1. Using a mixer, blend all the ingredients.

2. When smooth, top your drink with a slice of grapefruit and enjoy it!

498.Inspirational Orange Smoothie

Preparation time: 5 minutes
Cooking time: 5 minutes
Servings: 1

Ingredients:

- 4 mandarin oranges, peeled
- 1 banana, sliced and frozen
- ½ cup non-fat Greek yoghurt
- ¼ cup coconut water
- 1 tsp vanilla extract
- 5 ice cubes

Instructions:

1. Using a mixer, whisk all the ingredients.

2. Enjoy your drink!

499.Simple Avocado Smoothie

Preparation time: 5 minutes
Cooking time: 3 minutes
Servings: 4

Ingredients:

- ½ cup full-fat coconut milk
- ½ cup coconut water
- ½ avocado
- ¼ cup baby spinach
- 1 handful fresh parsley
- 1 drop stevia extract

Directions:

1. Combine all the ingredients in a blender and mix until smooth.

2. Enjoy your tasty smoothie!

500.High Protein Blueberry Banana Smoothie

Preparation time: 5 minutes
Cooking time: 5 minutes
Servings: 2

Ingredients:

- 1 cup blueberries, frozen
- 2 ripe bananas
- 1 cup water
- 1 tsp vanilla extract
- 2 Tbsp chia seeds
- ½ cup cottage cheese
- 1 tsp lemon zest

Directions:

1. Put all the smoothie ingredients into the blender and whisk until smooth.

2. Enjoy your wonderful smoothie!

501.Ginger Smoothie with Citrus and Mint

Preparation time: 5 minutes
Cooking time: 3 minutes
Servings: 3

Ingredients:

- 1 head Romaine lettuce, chopped into 4 chunks
- 2 Tbsp hemp seeds
- 5 mandarin oranges, peeled
- 1 banana, frozen
- 1 carrot
- 2-3 mint leaves

- ½ piece ginger root, peeled
- 1 cup water
- ¼ lemon, peeled
- ½ cup ice

Directions:

1. Put all the smoothie ingredients in a blender and blend until smooth.

2. Enjoy!

502.Strawberry Beet Smoothie

Preparation time: 5 minutes
Cooking time: 50 minutes
Servings: 2

Ingredients:

- 1 red beet, trimmed, peeled and chopped into cubes
- 1 cup strawberries, quartered
- 1 ripe banana
- ½ cup strawberry yoghurt
- 1 Tbsp honey
- 1 Tbsp water

- Milk, to taste

Directions:

1. Sprinkle the beet cubes with water, place on aluminum foil and put in the oven (preheated to 204°C). Bake for 40 minutes.

2. Let the baked beet cool.

3. Combine all the smoothie ingredients.

4. Enjoy your fantastic drink.

503.Peanut Butter Shake

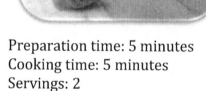

Preparation time: 5 minutes
Cooking time: 5 minutes
Servings: 2

Ingredients:

- 1 cup plant-based milk

- 1 handful kale

- 2 bananas, frozen

- 2 Tbsp peanut butter

- ½ tsp ground cinnamon

- ¼ tsp vanilla powder

Directions:

1. Use a blender to combine all the ingredients for your shake.

Enjoy it!

CONCLUSION

Individuals are, for the most part, veggie lovers, and we dismiss, at our hazard, our vegan primate family line. Vegetarian nourishment is, just, a guilty pleasure. At the point when you humor, you grant yourself to appreciate the absolute best. Vegetarian eating is a genuinely liberal lifestyle, as veggie lovers normally participate in the absolute best nourishments—the most nutritious, engaging, and scrumptious—that nature brings to the table. As you'll discover, when you investigate the plans in this book, vegetarian nourishment is tempting and energizing. A well-made veggie-lover plate offers a celebration of flavors, surfaces, and hues that makes each dinner a stylish festival. You might be astounded to find out about extravagance in a veggie-lover cookbook. You may even think about a vegetarian diet as Spartan or odd. Without a doubt, the veggie lover slims down are as yet remarkable in numerous circles. In any case, veggie lover/vegan eating is no longer on the social periphery. Today we have more data on the fundamental connection between diet and wellbeing. Our contracting world welcomes us to hobnob with more societies and experience their cooking styles. Our anxiety about the state of our condition develops, and our distraught ways of life send us looking for straightforwardness. Today, eating a vegetarian diet bodes well for the individuals who look to settle on close to home decisions that positively affect their very own lives and the world on the loose. Great wellbeing and liking our decisions empower us to be increasingly powerful in our connections and our work. At the point when we treat ourselves to a sound and astute way of life, we have the vitality to handle errands enormous and little with reestablished force. Once in awhile, a little guilty pleasure goes a long, long way. For those perusers for whom veggie lover eating is another thought, this book will give an assortment of motivations to checking out it.

The sooner we dump the 'meat makes man' legend, the better for our prosperity. We were never proposed to eat meat, our bodies are not intended to eat a delicate living animal, and our success is bearing an immediate consequence of it. At the point when we dismiss animal things from our eating regimens, our own special prosperity, our planet's welfare, and the lives of billions of animals will be better for it. At precisely that point, can we sincerely maintain to be a sharp chimp.

For all perusers, including experienced veggie lovers and vegetarians, this book offers energizing plans to spark your interest for nourishment and life much further. Most importantly, veggie lover eating is tied in with living great in wellbeing, agreement, and euphoria.

Made in the USA
Monee, IL
16 August 2020